The building of Queen Elizabeth 2

the world's most famous ship

Acknowledgements

No book is the work solely of the author. All of them depend to varying degrees on the effort of others. Those others deserve to be thanked.

My thanks go firstly to a variety of authors - the authors of shelves of files in the Cunard archives at Liverpool University, and also some still retained by Cunard, and the authors of many books either about various aspects of QE2 or touching on the subject.

I would like to thank my publisher, Miles Cowsill, without whom this book would have remained on a computer hard drive. And Captain Ian McNaught for kindly writing the foreword and for all the assistance he has given me over the years.

The following should also be mentioned for their support either with advice or images: Lynda Bradford, Jane Cross, Richard Faber, Henry Grossman, Hank Grossman, Anders Johannessen, Richard P De Kerbrech, Rob Lightbody, Stephen Payne, Peter Quartermaine, Peter Wiffen, Sian Wilks and David Williams.

To Bob
When you're cold, I'll be there. By your side.

Smoke emanating from the funnel for the first time as the three boilers were sequentially lit for testing and the start of dock trial, Thursday 19 September 1968. *(Author's collection)*

Ferry
Publications

Published by:
Ferry Publications, PO Box 33, Ramsey, Isle of Man IM99 4LP
Tel: +44 (0) 1624 898445   Fax: +44 (0) 1624 898449
E-mail: ferrypubs@manx.net   Website: www.ferrypubs.co.uk

The building of Queen Elizabeth 2

Contents

Introduction

When asked why and what was so special about *Queen Elizabeth 2* I would often answer that she just was. This was a convenient response to a question I have still not been able to fully answer myself. As with many things in life, a favourite this or a favourite that establishes itself within and once there it is difficult for anything else to take its place.

She was special. And will always be to me.

Certain ships have always captured minds and hearts in a way like no other. Cunard Chairman Sir Basil Smallpeice wrote of *Queen Mary* just before her retirement:

"Very few ships…if any… have won the particular affection and esteem she has enjoyed. Her claim to precedence has been more than a royal name painted on her bow. It is impossible to define the certain quality which causes one ship to proceed at full steam to capture and hold the public's love, leaving all others in her wake."

The first *Mauretania* was also held in deep affection and the American President Franklyn D. Roosevelt is said to have wept when he heard she was being withdrawn from service, writing:

"Neither size nor speed alone could have given Mauretania her fame. That rested on something more secure and intangible – on her personality; for Mauretania was a ship with a fighting heart.

"If ever there was a ship which possessed a thing called a 'soul', the Mauretania did… very few ships have earned the right, and the Mauretania has earned it, to be remembered 100 years hence."

The same can be said of *QE2* and whether a fan of the ship or not, and I accept there are as many fans as those who think she does not deserve the revered attention given to her, but it cannot be denied that the story of *QE2* is a great one and one that has been told countless times in countless books over the years. To commemorate the 50th anniversary of her launch on 20 September 2017 I wanted to tell the story of her conception and construction in detail and I hope I have done so.

After a shaky conception, *QE2's*

QE2 on sea trials, November 1968. *(Author's collection)*

gestation and birth were bedeviled by one potentially fatal drama after another. Building *QE2* was "hell", said Cunard's company secretary at the time. Strikes, management incompetence, restrictive practices, vandalism, financial crises, business reorganisation and larceny on a grand scale all conspired to make the process of *QE2's* construction one of conflict and recrimination.

It is incredible to think that a long-established, poorly-managed and financially-weak company such as Cunard and a long-established, poorly-managed and financially-weak shipyard such as John Brown & Co. could produce one of the greatest, if not the greatest, ship ever to sail. A bold claim indeed but *QE2's* subsequent record in service stands today as a testament to her achievements.

And all of this from a ship the sceptics said would have to be mothballed, laid up or even sold by Cunard before her first year of service was complete.

Other Cunarders can also lay claim to being the greatest ever but there was always something about *QE2*. She was a ship that defied the odds. She was a ship that attracted admirers. She was a ship that divided opinion. And she was a ship that often did things her way and was never far from the headlines making good or bad news.

I have had the honour of meeting two men who played an instrumental role in the construction of *QE2*. From the shipyard, I had the privilege of showing John Brown (later Sir John) around *QE2* when she visited Greenock in 1994. His final task as Deputy Chairman had been to gain the order for *QE2* and thus complete the trio of great Queens built on the Clyde. From Cunard, I chatted with Tom Kameen when he attended a commemorative concert for *QE2* at Liverpool's Anglican Cathedral in 2008. I told him he had given Cunard a great ship and, without pause, he replied *"I know!"*

It was the perfect response.

Sadly, I never got to meet the two men who played such an instrumental role: Sir John Brocklebank and Sir Basil Smallpeice – the Cunard Chairmen who made the right decisions at the right time. Sir John cancelled the potentially disastrous *Q3* project and embarked on one of Cunard's biggest-ever gambles with *Q4* while Sir Basil accepted the challenge of building and delivering one of Cunard's greatest ships.

Work taking place to apply the name on the portside bow. The name would be unusual not only for its use of an Arabic '2' but for the font and use of upper and lower case lettering. While unusual it was in keeping with the modern styling of the new ship. *(Author's collection)*

The returning 'guinea-pig' passengers watch proceedings as QE2 berths alongside the Ocean Terminal, Thursday 2 January 1969. *(Author's collection)*

Foreword

Tel: 020 - 7481 6902
Fax: 020 - 7480 7662
email: deputy.master@thls.org
www.trinityhouse.co.uk

Trinity House

TRINITY HOUSE,
TOWER HILL,
LONDON, EC3N 4DH

Michael Gallagher DEPUTY MASTER
CAPTAIN IAN McNAUGHT MNM
May 2017

"Ships have been boring too long" was the marketing slogan used by Cunard to launch QE2 into the cruising world in 1969, and they were right. Along with P&O's Canberra and the Oriana of Orient Line, these three ships were a radical departure from all those liners built after the war, and indeed, so different from Queen Mary and Queen Elizabeth.

The design had to allow for her to be a trans-Atlantic liner but also fit into the locks of the Panama Canal so that she could go cruising as well. Her interiors were to be modern and her exterior design had to be sleek and purposeful.

Her design went through stages of rigorous change. The archives at John Brown's Shipyard in Glasgow reveal frustration at seemingly ever-changing interior designs but, despite the clashes, the interior design became a harmonised British band of modernism with acknowledgement of the pop colours and materials of the swinging sixties.

Cunard were keen to publicise the new ship and in 1968 there was an exhibition at the Council of Industrial Design in London entitled "QE2 – a first look inside the new Cunarder". Princess Margaret opened the exhibition and enthused "this new Cunarder will show that design in Britain is not only exciting and full of vigorous common sense, but it is always out in front, leading the field. A great ship like Queen Elizabeth 2 must inevitably be looked upon as a sort of flagship for the nation".

It might just have been a grandmotherly chintzy hotel, but she was not and the Daily Telegraph commented "there is nothing of the old lady about the new Queen Elizabeth 2, she is smart, crisp and modern".

This book tells the story of how Cunard Line moved from ageing Queen Mary and Queen Elizabeth, through the Q3 and Q4 projects to job number 736 and how they, along with some of Britain's greatest designers, naval architects and with the skills of John Brown's Shipyard, created the last British built trans-Atlantic liner, the Queen Elizabeth 2, a true Queen of the seas and a ship that became very dear to me in the years I had the pleasure and privilege of serving her.

Ian McNaught

May 2017

The people who designed and built the QE2

Sir Basil Smallpiece

Tom Kameen

Dan Wallace

Jo Pattrick

Gaby Schreiber

Lord Aberconwy

Cunard MD John Whitworth, Cunard Chairman Sir Basil Smallpeice, Master of the QE2 Captain William 'Bill' Warwick and Cunard Deputy Chairman Lord Mancroft

September 1967

Tony Benn inspecting the damaged turbines in 1969

Sir Basil Smallpeice (centre)

Naval Architects Office, Cunard Building Liverpool

A pre-fabricated section of the aluminium superstructure

he new ship dominated the skyline of Clydebank

A launching to remember, Wednesday 20 September 1967

Wednesday 21 June 1967

June 1967

CHAPTER ONE

Q3: Cunard's replacement dilemma

The most successful double act ever seen on the Atlantic was getting on in years and, as the 1950s progressed, the mighty Cunard Line was faced with the dilemma of replacing its iconic *Queen Mary* and *Queen Elizabeth*. In the years after the Second World War the Queens had plied the North Atlantic between Europe and North America with a dominance, regularity and luxury that had brought full passenger lists and huge profits to Cunard. These were the glory days for the company which provided a glamorous, fast and luxurious weekly shuttle across the Atlantic where standards were exemplary and have become legendary and the ships were home from home for royalty, moguls, film stars and statesmen.

That was until 1957 when, in that year, the numbers of passengers travelling by sea began to decline as the new jet airliners took to the air. And the grand old Queens were becoming just that: too grand and too old.

This problem was also hindered by the likely impact of new competition. The *United States* literally swept across the Atlantic in 1952 and now Cunard's main rival, French Line, ordered its new flagship, the *France*, in 1957. She was to be a traditional express liner of around 66,000 tons but one with an overall length of 1,035-feet which surpassed the record held by the *Queen Elizabeth* since 1940.

Simultaneously it became apparent that the United States Lines was actively considering a sister ship for *United States*. Congress had already passed a Bill for the second ship's construction, making provision for the US Government to fund $70 million of he estimated build cost of $120 million. Added to this were plans by the Norwegians, the Dutch, the Germans and the Italians for new ships.

Notice was taken of the fact the US Government built the liner *United States* at a cost more than $75 million (£27 million) and then made the vessel available to the United States Lines, Cunard's competitor, for less than $34 million (£12 million). Similarly, the French Government would heavily

The Cunard flagship **Queen Elizabeth**, the biggest passenger ship ever built from 1946 to 1996, entering New York. While one-half of the most successful double act in Atlantic history even **Queen Elizabeth** seemed overshadowed by her slightly-elder sister but would be the first to have the most revered ship name used by Cunard. *(Author's collection)*

The **Queen Mary** today remains one of the most beloved liners ever built, her legendary status established when introduced in 1936 with the hopes and aspirations for a brighter future of a nation emerging from the despair of the Great Depression. *(Author's collection)*

support construction costs of France (and provide a subsidy once the ship had entered service).

Suddenly for Cunard, the pressure was on. The company had anticipated that they would eventually have to replace their two beloved Queens and replacement plans were begun that were intended to enable Cunard to retain the position of pre-eminence that it had enjoyed over the previous 12 or so years.

Cunard Chairman Sir Percy Bates was largely responsible for the creation of *Queen Mary* and *Queen Elizabeth* in a project dating from the mid-1920s. Now his brother, Colonel Denis Bates, was at Cunard's helm and he favoured a continuation of the 'Big Ship' policy.

A trifle optimistically, perhaps, Cunard said there would be no question this time of a Government subsidy being required when they were ready to order replacement liners, for though they had been forced to obtain loans to build the Queens, with adequate compensation for war service between 1939 and 1945, and excellent business in the post-war years, these loans had long since been repaid.

In 1957, the company reserved a berth with John Browns of Clydeside for a 20,000-ton passenger ship replacement for Britannic. This vessel would cost around £10 million for the Liverpool to New York service, but the keel laying had to be postponed indefinitely because of financial setbacks.

In fact, though Cunard had contemplated the construction of two large Queen-replacement liners, there were now not the reserves to embark on such a project, at the current costs (which were bound to be in the region of £40 million) and that expenditure was quite out of the question without a loan.

Profits of the company and its subsidiaries had decreased by £2 million in 1957, through a combination of industrial troubles and the Cold War; incidents in Hungary and Egypt

had deterred tourists, so that the anticipated normal passenger services were down by 11,000 bookings, with a subsequent million-pound drop in Cunard earnings; the equivalent of having three ships laid up for the whole year, doing nothing to earn their keep, let alone produce profits. These facts were reflected in balance sheets, which showed that the operating surplus of the Cunard Group had fallen in 1957 by £6,230,030.

The new two-ship plan involved vessels on a 'like-for-like' basis to the Queens with updated technology. Within the company's Board of Directors there was a hard-core of traditionalists who believed that the aircraft presented no more than a temporary setback to the institution that was Cunard and passengers would always prefer to travel by sea!

The number of available aircraft seats was still relatively low, and consequently fares were comparatively expensive, realistically affordable by only the wealthier class of traveller

No consideration was entertained that the ships might go cruising during the unprofitable winter months when the prospect of a rough crossing on the notoriously wintery North Atlantic, the roughest ocean in the world at that time of year, deterred many a prospective traveller. The proposed ships would continue the usual North Atlantic trade and be designed purely for that route.

Cunard did, however, have to decide whether they should consider new ships of the Queen Class, or whether to build an entirely new type of liner with much greater use of light alloys, and a much shallower draft as, in the past, to the company's loss, both Queens had to be forced to lie at anchor outside Southampton awaiting the tide while the *United States*, with a much shallower draft, could enter Southampton Water at will at almost any time and tide.

By now some quite radical deviations from established

The magnificent *France* probably entered service too late to have the career she should have. Interestingly, *QE2* became the largest passenger ship in the world when the *France* was withdrawn from service in 1974 but relinquished the position when France returned to service as *Norway* in 1980. *(FotoFlite)*

North Atlantic shipping practice were being enthusiastically expounded as alternative options for the ocean crossing. Several shipping enterprises suggested the introduction of vast, one-class, no-frills / no-extras passenger liners dedicated exclusively to a Tourist-Class clientele.

Such novel schemes had been promoted earlier, in the 1940s, but without result. For certain, the idea did not appeal to Cunard, whose traditions lay with a more conventional style of operation serving a range of classes based on all-in fares. Besides, conventional wisdom held that, despite the encroachment of aircraft, there would be a continuing demand for luxury-class travel by sea, and Cunard remained committed to capturing the bulk of it. The way forward, therefore, appeared to dictate the construction of two traditional, three-class ships as straight replacements for *Queen Mary* and *Queen Elizabeth*.

Interestingly, Cunard's view of 'no frills' would change and the concept would appear decades later in its Q5 plans which, again, never came to fruition. This revolutionary ship would have offered four classes of accommodation: two Super Deluxe, a First and a Tourist Class with the latter initially having to enjoy buffet food - for which they would pay extra. Again, this concept was way ahead of cruise lines such as Aida and Ocean Village which would appear several years after Q5.

Cooper Bros issued a memorandum on 21 January 1959 which stated:

"If Government aid is not obtained Q3 and Q4 cannot be built. If this were to happen the Company would continue to run the Queens until their normal economic lives expire in five to ten years' time and with the major portion of the Company's world-wide organization closed Britain would thereafter cease to participate in the fast North Atlantic passenger services."

On 2 February 1959 Colonel Bates wrote in a letter:

"We cannot justify to our shareholders a larger expenditure on Q3 than £12 million nor can we afford anything more than that figure."

In March 1959, Colonel Bates told the Annual Meeting of Cunard that the entire future of its North Atlantic service, and therefore perhaps the future of Cunard itself, had been placed before the Government.

Bates commented:

"Faced with the overwhelming odds of ever increasing governmental subsidies to our competitors on the score of national prestige, your Board have decided it is impossible to continue with such unequal and unfair competition to free enterprise."

The Queens were described as "full of life", but they could not be run forever, and the *Queen Mary* probably would be well over thirty before her replacement would take to the sea. Competitively this was not advantageous to Cunard. Bates continued:

"With the concurrence of the Minister of Transport the technical teams of Cunard and Messrs. John Brown of Clydebank who built the two Queens are now working on the specification of their replacements."

In April, as discussions concerning the financing of replacement vessels continued between Cunard and the Government, John Brown and Co was engaged to draw up preliminary plans and outline specifications for ships of the 'express' type.

Forming the basis of construction tenders to be invited subsequently, these called for two quadruple-screw vessels of circa 80,000 gross tons with an overall length of 990-feet (301.7 metres) and a service speed of 29 - 30 knots. The estimated cost of each ship would be in the order of £30 million.

Between then and September 1959, the yard of John Brown worked with Cunard exclusively on the Q3 design. (After failing to secure the contract, the yard reminded Cunard of the work it had undertaken for them during this period and asked for consultancy fees of £100,000 – both companies later agreed on £75,000).

Several issues needed to be considered when planning vessels to replace the Queens:

- The distance between Southampton and New York which would require, on a two-ship basis, a minimum sea speed of 28.5 knots.

- The carrying capacity must be as big as possible but the space available per passenger had to be attractive and if overall dimensions to achieve this became excessive, the added displacement would increase the engine power and fuel required for the same speed, which would add to the displacement and a stage would be reached where unacceptable limitations in the freedom of operation at terminal ports would pose a problem.

- Most European and Scandinavian liner companies had already dispensed with the old cabin-class in favour of accommodation for a minimum first-class and a maximum tourist-class passenger. This new class of ocean traveller regarded air transport as quite beyond the reach of their smaller finances yet, obviously, if surface transport was to hold its own it had to do something practical, probably revolutionary, and soon.

- For a given speed a certain minimum length of 900-feet would be required, in addition to the force of engine power, to secure an average speed of 30 knots.

- The use of new materials and knowledge gained from use of materials would have to be considered. In the four ships built for the Canadian trade in the mid-fifties (*Saxonia, Ivernia,* Carinthia and *Sylvania*), experiments of many kinds were carried out mainly toward the goal of saving weight in the construction and accommodation areas. Much was done in the engineering aspects to save weight as well as to improve efficiency. The results of these experiments would be used in any future replacements for the Queens.

Colonel Denis Bates:

"The Atlantic Ferry makes the ultimate demands on reliability in any ship. Day after day, year in and year out, she must continue for 25 years or more."

Official public notice of plans to replace the Queens was given on 8 April 1959, when Harold Watkinson, of the Ministry

The 'Speed Queen' **United States** snatched the Blue Riband from **Queen Mary** in July 1952 before being laid-up in 1969. In the 1990s Cunard considered taking part in the proposed reactivation of **United States** to run alongside **QE2**. *(FotoFlite)*

Sir John Brocklebank, Cunard Chairman 1959 – 1965, was faced with the dilemma of replacing **Queen Mary** and **Queen Elizabeth** and took the ultimate decision to cancel **Q3** and embark on Q4 which would become perhaps the greatest passenger liner ever built. *(Author's collection)*

of Transport, announced to the House of Commons that negotiations were underway with Cunard to try to maintain the First-Class North Atlantic service.

Cunard still insisted on 'big ships' being the solution to their replacement problems and they concluded that two ships of 75,000-tons would be the only answer; being the slowest and smallest vessels capable of meeting the company's Atlantic requirements throughout the whole year; and if Cunard was to maintain the high standard of luxury and service to passengers which it had, quite rightly, been famous all over the world and on which much of its reputation had been built. However, despite insisting on the 'big ship' principle, the company had no money to build such a vessel.

The normal method of financing a replacement was to pay for it out of money set aside each year against depreciation, by borrowing in the finance market, and by the liner's earnings in the first five years of her life. However, heavy taxation and high building costs made this impossible for Cunard.

At the Annual General Meeting in the Cunard Building Liverpool on 28 May 1959, Colonel Bates advised that negotiations were progressing with the British Government for the building of two new superliners which would eventually replace the popular Queens and explained that it would take a minimum of five years before the first of the new ships would be ready for service. He added:

"The situation today is that there is no financial commitment on either side [from Cunard or the Government], though naturally I have intimated the available limits to which our own resources can go, and having accorded a very understanding reception of our case the Government called for an independent report on our financial position. This has been duly carried out covering the whole Cunard Group and the result confirmed the figures and limits which I had originally intimated to HM Government.

"The Minister of Transport then asked for more information as to the broad lines of the specification which we would contemplate for the replacement of the elder ship Queen Mary together with as close as estimate of the cost as is possible: he has also asked for a survey on travel across the North Atlantic, including supersonic air, over the next 25 years.

"All this I hope will be completed and forwarded by the end of this month.

"It is of course impossible to produce detailed plans for a ship of this class in a matter of weeks and there will necessarily be another 12 / 18 months of work on the drawing and planning board before actual construction is commenced and then, say a further some four years to completion. The two Queens therefore will not be retired for some years to come and there should be as long a gap as possible between the replacement of the two ships. All this is normal practice and is quite practicable because these two grand Queen ships are still full of life and will continue to give their well-known and proven service to all our many patrons. I want to emphasize this because the idea seems to have gained currency, especially in America, that the two Queens are on the point of being withdrawn from service, which as I have just indicated, is fare from the case.

"In my statement, I gave a brief background of the many factors which led up to the construction of the Queen Mary and how technical know-how never stayed idle. Even ion the few years' gap between the two present ships there are significant differences as for instance in the boiler rooms where the Queen Mary has 24 boilers whilst the Queen Elizabeth has only 12. So today a wealth of improved knowledge is open to us though of course the main factors such as the distance from Southampton to New York, the working speed over that distance necessary on a two-ship weekly service, and the nature of the Atlantic waves and weather remain immutable.

"In very broad terms the comparable figures for the Queen Mary and her replacement are at present stage of our investigation as follows:

	Queen Mary	*Replacement*
Length	*1,019 feet*	*990 feet*
Breadth	*118 feet*	*116 feet*
Draught	*39 feet*	*30 feet*
Working Speed	*28.5 knots*	*30 knots*
Gross Tonnage	*81,237*	*80,000*

"In the important sphere of the engine room machinery and remembering the Atlantic Ferry makes the ultimate demands on reliability in any ship I think today it must be a matter of turbines.

"For ships of this size and power it is natural to be attracted by nuclear propulsion and eventually I believe the technicians will achieve e its success but up to the present date I feel it would be premature to use this commercially untried method of propulsion for a replacement Queen Mary though it may well be a practical possibility for the later replacement Queen Elizabeth and we are watching its development very closely and intimately."

When the designs were advanced far enough, Cunard approached the Government for financial assistance, in the form of a loan not a subsidy, to enable the company to proceed with the new project. Assistance from the British Government was not new to Cunard - the company had received a loan of £2.6 million toward the building of Lusitania and *Mauretania* in the 1900s and for *Queen Mary* (£4.5 million) and *Queen Elizabeth* (£5 million) in the 1930s. These loans had been repaid on time which made Cunard unique among its rivals in operating self-sufficient rather than subsidised ships.

Now Cunard was seeking up to £40 million.

Minister of Transport and Civil Aviation, Harold Watkinson, responded to a questioner in the House of Commons:

"…as the Government was already a shareholder in the Cunard Company, it was therefore natural that it should be interested in plans for replacing the two transatlantic liners."

Naturally enough, Members of Parliament were extremely nervous about the Government arbitrarily granting loans of this magnitude to Cunard, especially as prospects seemed less assured, but the Macmillan administration was swift to quell the concerns. Cunard would receive no offer of financial

A model of how **Q3** would have looked while building on the Tyne if the contract had actually been placed with Vickers and Swan Hunter Limited. *(Author's collection)*

assistance from the public purse, it declared, until after a committee had fully investigated all the options and reported back to Parliament with its findings and recommendations.

So in September 1959, the Conservative Government, committed by a vague election promise, acted when the Minister of Transport, Ernest Marples, set up the three-man Chandos Committee consisting of Lord Chandos, John Hobhouse and Thomas Robson. J N Wood acted as Secretary and he had the responsibility to evaluate the situation and report back by June 1960.

Colonel Bates wrote his appraisal of the situation on behalf of the company in his own hand writing. He pleaded for help on the grounds of prestige, stressing that it was important for Britain that big ships should maintain the Atlantic express service. He stressed that Cunard was convinced of the necessity to maintain this service if the company was to survive in its present and traditional form.

Bates believed that if Cunard did not maintain that service the company would fade away and he also pointed out that the company had paid so much in taxation over the years that it deserved a loan. In fact his thinking was based on the Weir Report which had done so much to get work restarted on the *Queen Mary* when building was halted due to the world economic crisis in the 1930s.

The Committee began with the assumption that two liners would ultimately be built to replace the Queens and maintain the existing service. After initial investigations, two 30-knot, 75,000-ton ships were considered with passenger capacities of 2,270.

A letter from Cunard to the Committee on 14 December 1959 stated:

"…the bigger the ship, the newer the ship and the faster the ship, the higher the rates (passage rates) that will be established. Because of this Q3 would have to charge higher rates for all classes that the Queen Elizabeth, and, in fact, would command higher rates from the traveling public. This largely account for the estimated increase in passenger receipts.

"It can be taken that a new Q3 and Q4 could each be expected to earn the revenue indicated without damaging each other. In fact, experience shows that from an earning point of view, with a weekly service of the type contemplated, far from one ship damaging the other, each ship is in fact complementary to each other. Conversely, history shows that in the North Atlantic a one ship service is almost always a failure.

"We have no hesitation in saying that the specified power if Q3 are necessary the whole year round. The delays die to rough weather, fog, breakdowns etc. can occur at any time during the year…It is really not an exaggeration to say that the 'winter' season in the North Atlantic can be for one reason or another regarded as from January 1 to December 31, and in view of this we could not contemplate altering the specifications of the ship even if she only sailed in the so-called summer months.

"In any new ship of ours we contemplate, In First Class the present Queen Elizabeth standard of area must be maintained. The Cabin and Tourist Class standard must show a marked improvement over both the United States and Queen Elizabeth."

"…there is no doubt that the standards being built into the France will be not less than what we have proposed for Q3 and thus the France would be the Q3's competitor in respect if quality of accommodation. The difference in tonnage between France and Q3 represents, in our opinion, indispensable earning capacity."

To paraphrase the above:

Translating these standards (above) from *Q3* to a 55,000-ton design of comparable speed to *Q3* the following points are important:

1. The speed schedule requires four screws, so that the power reduction leads only to a small reduction in machinery spaces.

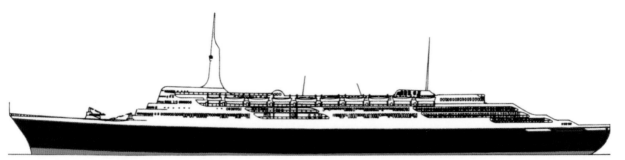

Q3 as proposed in a drawing issued on Friday 31 March 1961. *(Author's collection)*

2. Deck, Engine and Catering crew show little change despite the tonnage reduction.

3. Many spaces essential to north Atlantic express ships do not reduce effectively as tonnage decreases. Committed to four screws and all the amenities associated with the North Atlantic service, it pays to go to the largest ship which meets terminal port limitations of draft and maneuvering. The tonnage reduction only has the effect, broadly speaking, of reducing passenger accommodation, i.e. earning capacity.

"…our policy would be to maintain our existing organization and run two ships each earning a gross revenue of £7,600,000, rather than cut back on our gross revenue by using two smaller ships only earning £5,450,000 each, without any assurance that we could achieve this hypothetical saving in organization expenses.

"…our estimate is that there may be a saving of £5,000,000 in building the smaller ship. This reduction in cost is, I think, more than Offset by the proportionately much greater reduction in earning capacity."

Days after the formation of the Chandos Committee, Colonel Bates died and on 16 September 1959 Sir John Brocklebank was appointed his successor. Sir John, an expert in cargo ship operations, had joined the board of Cunard in 1951 and was elected Deputy Chairman and Managing Director in 1953.

Minutes from the seventh meeting of the Chandos Committee held on 31 December 1959 state:

"The Chairman (Lord Chandos) said that there was no possibility of the Committee's recommending replacement of the Queens by two ships of similar size. Lord Wehir had recommended Government help for the building of the present Queens on the assumption that they would be profitable when in service. Replacement Queens could not be economic without a subsidy. The initial cost of each ship would be £29 million, not allowing for possible increases in building costs, while the earnings of each ship were estimated at £1.74 million before depreciation.

"…the return on the total investment would be under 2%, while if Cunard were to be assured of a reasonable return on their own capital of £12 million it would be impossible to repay fully any loan of the remaining £17 million. On these grounds alone it would be difficult for the Committee to recommend to the Government the building of two ships of the size envisaged by Cunard.

"There were, however, other reasons why the Committee would not recommend a scheme which involved such a large measure of subsidy. The guaranteeing of any level of

The model put together by Cunard's naval architects to make *Q3* look like a ship and described by James Gardner as "clumsy". *(Author's collection)*

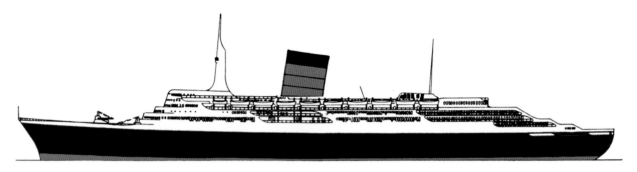

How a Caronia-type funnel, which was one of the largest funnels to go to sea, would look if built on **Q3**. *(Author's collection)*

return to the Cunard shareholders and the limitation of their risk to the two replacement ships would give them an unfair advantage over the shareholders in other companies. Also, a large measure of Government help for their Atlantic service would give Cunard an unfair advantage over their competitors in other trades.

"The chief arguments for the granting of a large measure of Government help for the replacement of the Queens were on grounds of defence and prestige. The Committee had not yet received formal advice on the strategic value of the new Queens but it seemed that it would be small. The view had been expressed that the true prestige of the UK shipping industry lay in its ability to stand on its own two feet and therefore any form of subsidy would in fact be a blow to its prestige. The Committee did not consider that Cunard in the North Atlantic passenger trade were faced with competition of such a unique nature that a unique form and degree if Government help could be justified. If therefore substantial help were given to Cunard it seemed almost certain that it would be followed by similar requests from other sections of the industry and that other countries will be encouraged in their policies of subsidy and flag discrimination.

"The Committee had therefore been forced to consider alternative schemes which might be economically viable with the aid of a Government guarantee or loan at a 'humane' rate of interest. The main weakness in the Cunard scheme was the heavy loss incurred on the North Atlantic in winter and therefore one possible alternative was the use of the ships elsewhere in winter. Another alternative was that the two ships should continue of the North Atlantic but at a slower speed either throughout the year, or in the winter; the standard if service, etc., would remain high.

"Sir John Brocklebank and Mr Donald said that a 7-day crossing would not attract passengers who were used to a 4½ day crossing and a regular weekly schedule. United States Lines had in fact conceded that a weekly two ship service was best for the Atlantic and would soon be operating on this basis Competitors were introducing fast luxury ships such as France and to retain their business Cunard had to follow suit.

"It was difficult to design a multi-purpose ship which could be successful on the Atlantic. Passengers were attracted to the Queens by the high standard of comfort and service and it would be difficult to get them to accept anything less. The building of smaller ships would mean a reduction either in the numbers carried or in passenger support.

"If the alternative employment were to be cruising, luxurious standards would still be necessary but with a different emphasis on, for example, open air swimming pools. Cunard would not consider joining a consortium to charter the ships for cruising. If the Australian or Pacific liner trades were envisaged there would be considerable difficulties in design since for these trades more open deck space but a lower standard of accommodation was necessary.

"The Committee felt, however, that with ingenious design, the use of modern materials and flexibility between classes, much could be done to overcome these problems. If there was to be any hope of evolving a scheme based on a level of Government help which the Committee would feel able to recommend, the whole matter would have to be considered in relation not so much to what was desirable but to the necessity of avoiding the heavy losses involved in operating large liners on the Atlantic in winter."

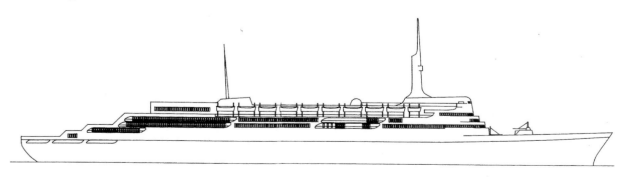

The March 1961 **Q3** profile is probably the first sight of the proposed new liner by James Gardner. *(Author's collection)*

On 8 January 1960 Sir John Brocklebank wrote:

"The whole weakness in their argument (the Committee's) lies in paragraph 4 where they say that the main weakness in our scheme is the heavy loss incurred on the North Atlantic in winter. On their scheme one would reduce this loss by a small amount in winter but decrease the profit by Heaven knows how many times more in the much longer summer."

An extract from Sir John's notes of a meeting in the Cunard Building with Mr Norton and Mr Wood on 11 January 1960 stated:

"…we finally got Wood to agree that if four screws were to be used, reducing the size below our proposition will only result in reducing the profit; similarly, if two screws are used we are them limited to 110,000 h.p maximum, and with that amount and a speed of say 29½knots, we are not left with much of a hull."

In the Annual Report and Accounts of 1959, Sir John reported:

"…as far as has been shown by their contacts with this company the Chandos Committee have carried out their investigation with patience and in the most thorough manner. Needless to say, we have co-operated with the Committee to the very best of our ability.

"…our design team have put in a great deal of excellent work in examining a wide variety of ships which might suit our requirements but although their studies have produced a few minor adjustments in design which collectively would reduce cost and improve the profit we, that is your Board and Management, are still firmly convinced that two ships of about 75,000 gross registered tons with a service speed of 30 knots would be the best and most profitable units with which to maintain our Weekly Express Service which has shown itself to be the most efficient method of carrying passengers across the North Atlantic by sea."

Reports indicated that the new liners would feature three classes and that studies by the company's design team had produced "a few minor improvements" that would cut costs. Presumably these would cover the considerable use of light alloys, shallower draughts, fewer boilers, and an improved engine design.

During the early years of his chairmanship, Sir John resurrected an idea that had originally been formulated in the early 'thirties by Sir Percy Bates, to put Cunard in the air business. Sir John spent £8.5 million on various deals for the new air enterprise. Subsequently, in March 1960, Cunard bought Eagle Airways.

Cunard-Eagle applied for a license to fly the Atlantic to New York and at the same time purchased two Boeing aircraft to show their determination. The license was granted and then revoked after an appeal by BOAC. Cunard carried on its air operations from the UK to Bermuda (and from there to New York etc.) and the company finally came to an agreement with BOAC in June 1962 when BOAC-Cunard

was formed. Cunard held a 30 per cent interest.

This complicated matters regarding *Q3* as far as the Government was concerned and, perhaps seeing Cunard invest £8.5 million in this enterprise resulted in second thoughts by the Chandos Committee about the number of ships that should be built. Cunard had been hedging its bets in the changing travel climate, but it's pre-emptive moved served to fire a cautionary shot across the bows of the Chandos Committee.

Cunard had previously informed its shareholders at its 1960 Annual General Meeting that each of its two new ships would take four years to build, with the first order anticipated at the end of 1961 after some further 18 months of detail design work and procurement planning. Sir John Brocklebank indicated his support for the project by announcing that Cunard was "still convinced that two ships of 75,000 gross tons and a service speed of 30 knots would be the best and most profitable units to maintain our weekly express service."

Newspaper reports in May 1960 confirmed that Cunard was still "firmly convinced" that two ships of about 75,000 tons with a service speed of 30 knots *"would be the best to replace the Queens."* In his statement with the annual accounts Sir John described the 1960 outlook as *"decidedly more promising."* He confirmed that studies by the company's design team had produced *"a few minor improvements"* that would cut costs – these areas included considerable use of light alloys, shallower draughts, fewer boilers and improved engine design. Sir John advised that the Chandos Committee had carried out its investigations with patience and thoroughness and that the report was *"likely to be in the hands of the Minister shortly"* but he could say no more until the Minister had studied it.

Before a final decision could be made by the Chandos Committee, a great deal of work was undertaken and many meetings were held over the months involving Cunard, the Government, the Economist Intelligence Unit and Research Services Ltd.

Many options were considered including reducing the speed of any replacement liner and offering a seven-day crossing but this was dismissed by Cunard.

The recommendation of the Chandos Committee was made on 1 June 1960 with the publication of a report summary (the full report would never be published publicly).

The Committee stated:

"…after long discussions with our professional advisers and with the Cunard company we have come to the conclusion – and the Cunard Company agree – that a ship having the following characteristics would best and most economically replace the 'Queen Mary' and maintain the British express passenger service across the North Atlantic:

Gross Tonnage	*75,000*
Service Speed	*29.5 knots*
Length Overall	*990 feet*
Beam	*114 feet*
Draught	*30 feet 3 inches*
Passenger Capacity	*2,270*

The Committee estimated the cost at between £25 – £28 million but Cunard insisted the cost would be higher. Cunard

One of two profile proposals developed by Vickers and Swan Hunter Limited. *(Author's collection)*

only had £12 million available from its own resources to invest in the project, the Government would have to provide the remainder of the capital cost (up to £18 million being provided by a low-interest Government loan).

The Committee did stipulate certain conditions and insisted that:

- The ship be a three-class vessel – a condition resulting from interviewing many leading industrialists and insurance chiefs while making their assessment.

- The liner must be kept on the North Atlantic and Cunard were forbidden to cruise her. (Maintaining a year-round Atlantic service with no off-season cruising was in complete agreement with Cunard's thinking).

- The total construction cost of the vessel should not exceed £30 million.

- The two Queens had now been written-off and their scrap value was put around £800,000 each.

- The construction of the ship to be put out to open competitive tender with all appropriate shipyards.

- The ship to be owned and operated by the Cunard Company through a separate company to which the Cunard Company would subscribe £12 million as equity capital. The remainder of the cost, not exceeding £18 million, would be provided by the Government as loan capital. Alternatively, the ship could be owned and/or operated by the Cunard Company so long as the Government were left in the same position as regards security and redemption as if the ship were owned by a separate Company.

The loan would bear interest at 4½ per cent per annum from the date on which the ship entered service and would be redeemed by the operation of a 4½ per cent sinking fund over 25 years.

The summary continued:

"We have not attempted to make any recommendations about the replacement of the Queen Elizabeth or the use of nuclear propulsion because such a recommendation would be premature. If, by the time when replacement of the Queen Elizabeth becomes necessary, no major change has occurred in the need for the maintenance of a British express sea service across the North Atlantic and in its

prospects as a commercial service, we assume that HMG would be prepared to assist in a manner appropriate in the circumstances. At that times experience, will have been gained from the operation of the first ship, further knowledge of the effect of competition from the air will be available, and it will be possible to assess whether nuclear propulsion can be applied to passenger liners."

This effectively put off a full decision on the future of the Queens to a later date and bought time to see what else would transpire.

On 10 October 1960, Ernest Marples announced the Governments acceptance of the recommendations of the Chandos Committee and approval of an £18 million loan at 4½ per cent interest over 25 years:

"The Government has been considering the report of the Committee presided over by Lord Chandos on the replacement of the Cunard liners Queen Mary and Queen Elizabeth. A summary of the report was circulated to Parliament on June 1. The Government has decided to give assistance towards the replacement of Queen Mary by a new ship such as the Committee re commended of some 75,000 tons gross. Discussions have taken place with the Cunard Company and provisional agreement has now been reached on the extent and terms of assistance which the Government will give. The extent of Government assistance will be similar to that suggested by the Chandos Committee but its form and conditions will be different in certain respects. Parliament will be informed of the detailed arrangements when it reassembles. Meanwhile, the Cunard Company is drawing up an invitation to tender so that it may be sent out to all appropriate shipyards in the country as soon as practicable."

British taxpayers, whether they liked it or not, were being asked to contribute to the costs of a new ship of state when the whole future of large luxury liners was somewhat vague and uncertain and many probably believed that there were many other uses to which £18 million could be more profitably employed. But many also believed that a new Cunard express liner would yield a reasonably handsome return over its expected 25-year life.

Construction of such a replacement vessel would not, of course, necessarily mean that Britain would come anywhere near domination of the North Atlantic passenger trade, but it would mean that at least Britain could enjoy equality with all competitor nations, and that was what really mattered. To dominate the luxury trade, it would be necessary to build a replacement vessel that was completely revolutionary in design, size, speed, and luxury, far surpassing anything which existed or was contemplated by any other nation; in any event, purely luxury traffic was decreasing, some said almost to vanishing point, and might well disappear entirely within a decade from 1960.

Vociferous opposition occurred almost immediately from some members of Parliament who regarded the loan as an unprecedented subsidy, and from a vocal group of Cunard stockholders who regarded the building of another giant Atlantic liner in the face of competition from the jet airplane as insane.

The critics contended that to build another traditional liner in the face of the changing nature of the transatlantic and travel industries was to fly in the face of common sense and reality.

Undeterred, Cunard continued with their plans. The timetable now being worked on considered the months required to prepare the invitation to tender, three months to consider received tenders resulting in a keel laying taking place in the spring of 1962.

In response to the call for smaller ships, Cunard stated:

"During the currency of the Chandos Committee the Cunard Company considered itself bound to silence and issued no statement about its proposals for continuance of the British weekly express liner service across the North Atlantic. With the publication in June of the summary of the Chandos Committee's report it was revealed that several different types and sizes of ships and various types and patterns of service had been examined before the conclusion was reached that a ship of 75,000 tons gross "…would best and most economically replace the Queen Mary and maintain the British express passenger service across the North Atlantic." Nonetheless, doubt has been expressed in some quarters that this was the right ship to build and an alternative which has had some advocacy is a series of smaller ships of dual purpose design.

"The essence of a liner service is its regularity. Regularity entails the creation of a pattern of service using a carefully determined number of ships. Examination of the history of almost every deep-sea passenger trade reveals a progressive trend – especially over the last 30 years – towards larger and fewer ships taking the places of several smaller ships, with the advantage of lower overheads in manning, in operation and in maintenance, pus the very real advantage of greater areas for passenger accommodation. Partly because of the fiercely nationalistic character of its competition and partly because the geographical distance separating Britain and America favoured it, the North Atlantic trade was the first trade to carry this process to its logical conclusion by putting into service two ships offering the same regularity and frequency of service hitherto needing several ships. It was not so much a question of creating a weekly service for its own sake as of offering regular sailings with the smallest possible number of ships. The sales value of constant departure times every week is very great as operators in other trades have found to their profit, but geographical

distances have compelled the to employ several ships to achieve this regularity.

"On the North Atlantic, to work a weekly schedule a sea speed of 29.5 knots is the ideal. Speed costs money; therefore, to pay for the speed the ship must be able to carry enough passengers in accommodation equaling the quality of her most formidable competitor. For maximum earning potential at 29.5 knots, four screws and a 1,000-foot hull are required, which automatically raises the North Atlantic weekly service ship into the superliner class. It has been said that 29.5 knots could be achieved in a hull much smaller than the 75,000 / 80,000 tons of the projected Q3 and Q4. This is true; but the only positive advantage – a reduction in first cost – is more than offset by a loss in earning power which would extend over the ship's life. Take, for example, a 55,000-ton ship. Four screws are still necessary for 29.5 knots, and the power reduction leads only to a small reduction in machinery spaces.

"The number of crew shows little change despite the tonnage reduction. Many spaces essential to North Atlantic express service ships, e.g. offices, hospitals, gymnasia, travel bureau, do not reduce effectively as tonnage decreases and it is passenger cabins which are sacrificed. The difference in tonnage between the 55,000-ton ship and the 75,000-ton ship therefore represents indispensable earning capacity. Committed to four screws and all the passenger amenities essential for success in the North Atlantic service it is best to build the largest ship which meets terminal port limitations of draft and maneuvering.

"There is the question of the dual-purpose ship. We in Cunard have not only theoretically re-examined the potentialities of such a ship but have had practical experience. Our 34,000-ton Caronia, a post-war ship, was built with cruising primarily in mind but with the intention that she could take her place in the North Atlantic trade. In actual fact, she has proved far more profitable as a cruise unit that in the North Atlantic trade and this primarily because she could not compete effectively with the type of service provided by ships of the class of the Queen Liners. This practical experience has underlined the fallacy of any attempt to produce a design of ship which would both fulfill the highest North Atlantic requirements and prove profitable as a cruise ship. The design of a dual purpose North Atlantic/Cruise Ship must be a compromise. It necessitates a reduction in North Atlantic capacity to compensate for the introduction of 'cruise features'. For example, high quality interchangeable cabins, a high standard of space and decoration in public rooms throughout the ship (to achieve uniformity when the ship is cruising, with one class) open-air swimming pools and lido decks, and the provision of greater areas of living space capable of being thrown open to the sky.

"Still considering the smaller ship, it has been said that several very fast small ships could operate just such a weekly service as provided by the Queens, but the plain fact is that the speed and power requirements could not be achieved economically or with any commercial attraction in a 20,000 or 30,000-tin hull because so much of the ship would be taken up with machinery and her operating costs would make economic nonsense of her earning capacity.

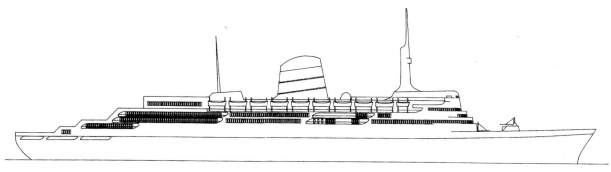

Q3 with the large Strombos funnel Cunard favoured. *(Author's collection)*

"The Queen Mary's successor will be an outstanding ship; she could not otherwise live in the fiercely competitive trade for which she is destined. The French Line examined several different types of ship to maintain their own North Atlantic services, including a proposal for several smaller ships which, after investigation, they rejected in favour of the 70,000-ton France now fitting out. They would not have begun this ship if they had had any doubt about the future of the North Atlantic sea travel. The building of any ship is an act of faith. We share the beliefs of foreign operators that there will be a continuing and developing demand for sea travel, especially amongst the tourist conscious Americans who are the main source of traffic.

"In fact, close on 70 per cent of our business originates in North America, which underlines the very great contribution which the British North Atlantic sea services makes to the economy. The dollar earnings of the two Queens up to the end of 1959 total no less than $ [not revealed] and it must be remembered that it was not until 1947 that these two ships began the weekly service for which they had been designed.

"The Queens are in excellent shape and they will continue to maintain the express service between Southampton and New York via Cherbourg. Work on the specification for the Queen Mary's replacement is well advanced but there is much to be done on the drawing board before an artist's impression of the ship can be published. It is expected that tenders will be invited in about six months time and after the placing of the building contract there will be approximately twelve months preparatory work before the keel is laid so that the new ship may incorporate the very latest and best features of design. The actual construction period will be 3½ to 4 years.

"In any comparison between size of ship and passenger capacity the yardstick is the amount of space allocated to each passenger and this must be related to the requirements of the trade and the quality of competitive tonnage. In the Atlantic trade, to increase passenger capacity by reducing the amount of space per passenger would destroy the ship's competitive power."

Interestingly it has been claimed that P&O approached Cunard with the notion of sharing the ship. In the summer months the new ship would undertake Atlantic service before switching to the Australian run in the winter when that route experienced high demand. Cunard rebuffed the audacious approach stating that express liners designed for the Atlantic route were unsuitable for any other form of deployment. This is reflected in the comment that the ship "would be of a size and speed which would make it unsuitable for any other service."

A preliminary meeting between Cunard and six contending shipyards was held in the Cunard Building in Liverpool on 15 December 1960 to discuss the preparation of the specification for the new ship. It was expected that the tender specification would be complete by the end of March 1961.

Only a few British yards were capable of handling a contract of this size and six firms were expected to tender: John Brown and Company, Clydebank; Fairfield Shipbuilding and Engineering Ltd, Glasgow; Vickers-Armstrong's (Shipbuilders), Tyne; Swan, Hunter and Wigham Richardson Ltd, Wallsend; Harland and Wolff Ltd, Belfast and Cammell Laird & Company (Shipbuilders and Engineers) Ltd, Merseyside.

The general assumption that the replacements for the Queens would be built at Clydebank touched a nerve with Dr Dennis Rebbeck, Deputy Managing Director of Harland &

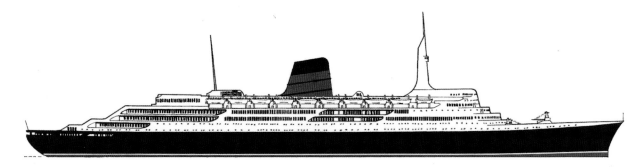

James Gardner described the initial profiles of **Q3**: "The ship will have no sweeping curves; she is a block of utility flats dumped in the sea, and must ride uncomfortably high to pack in the essential accommodations - a piece of floating real estate". *(Author's collection)*

Wolff. He said that it had become a source of irritation to him and his colleagues on the board and referred to White Star's aborted Oceanic project:

"Public memory is notoriously short. It has apparently been forgotten that in 1927 we laid the keel of a 1,000-foot passenger liner for the White Star Line. Though it was started it was never finished, due to the economic blizzard in the late 1920s."

In January 1961, it was announced by the north-eastern yards that for this venture, Messrs. Vickers and Messrs. Swan Hunter proposed to join forces to win. The plan was to construct the hull at the Wallsend yard, birthplace of the Carpathia and the *Mauretania*, and to fit it out 1.5 miles upstream at Vickers' Walkers Naval Yard. It was a powerful combination. Both firms were at the forefront of ship construction and were arguably the most technically advanced shipbuilders in Britain. Additionally, Vickers's Barrow-in-Furness yard had produced the 45,000-ton *Oriana* for P&O in 1960, a revolutionary ship embodying many new design concepts valuable to the builders of *Q3* and to the eventual owners.

Early in 1961, the investments from Cunard White Star were transferred to the Cunard Company. For administrative convenience and in agreement with Her Majesty's Government it was decided that the new ship would be operated by a one-ship company and for various reasons the Cunard White Star Company lent itself readily for this purpose. As the financing of the venture was to be undertaken by The Cunard Steamship Company, it was felt that the investments should be transferred to that company.

By 22 March 1961, the 'Memorandum of Points of Agreement between the Cunard Steamship Company Limited and Her Majesty's Government' was printed as a white paper together with the explanatory and financial memorandum on the North Atlantic Shipping Bill.

The agreement was the subject of debate for several months.

On 30 March 1961, invitations to tender for the new ship together with the detailed specifications were sent to the yards.

"The directors will be glad to learn if you are prepared to submit a tender in accordance with the following requirements…

Length between perpendiculars	*942 feet*
Breadth moulded	*115 feet*
Depth moulded to Upper Deck	*48 feet 9 inches*
Mean Draft for scantlings and subdivision	*32 feet 6 inches*
Total deadweight at a maximum draft in S.W. and not less than	*12,650 tons*
Departure draft with single voyage oil fuel	*30 feet maximum*
Service Spee	*30 knots*

Service Power 30% in excess of power for 30 knots on trial at mean ocean draft from 31 feet six inches departure draft

The make-up of deadweight is:

Fresh Water	*1,300 tons*
Reserve Feed Water	*550 tons*
Passengers and Bagga	*400 tons*
Stores – Consumable	*450 tons*
Engineers' Stores – Consumable	*100 tons*
Crew and Effect	*150 tons*
Mails	*200 tons*
Cargo and Cars	*250 tons*
Swimming Pools	*250 tons*
Oil Fuel: Round Voyage	*9,000 tons*
Single Voyage	*4,700 tons"*

Cunard encouraged the yards to put forward their own ideas on her overall design concept too and tenders were to be received by the end of July 1961.

The next day, 31 March, artist's renderings of the *Q3* were released and these depicted a rather conventional, traditional profile with an enormous single ovoid funnel, in traditional Cunard red, amidships. Fully forward there was a second exhaust uptake incorporated into the mast. The double-deck promenades were glass enclosed amidships but open fore and aft.

At the same time plans revealed the following:

Wheelhouse Top

Navigating Bridge

Sun Deck (First and Tourist)
Tourist Sun Deck Lounge
Tourist Deck Space
Dog Kennels
First and Tourist Deck Space

Boat Deck (First and Tourist)
Tourist Deck Space and Promenades
Tourist Lounge (with dome)
First Deck Space and Promenades
Verandah Grill (180 seats)

Verandah Deck (First, Cabin and Tourist)
Tourist Open Deck
Tourist Cocktail Lounge
Tourist Synagogue
Tourist Shops (x 2)
Tourist Barber Shop
Tourist Beauty Parlour
Tourist Club Room
Tourist Promenades
Tourist Nursery and Crèche
Tourist Library
Cabin and Tourist Lecture Room
Tourist Teenage Club
Cabin Cocktail Lounge
First Balcony Theatre
Cabin and Tourist Theatre Entrance
Cabin Hall Lounge
Cabin Library
Cabin Teenage Club
Cabin Lounge
Cabin Promenades and Deck Space

Promenade Deck (First, Cabin and Tourist)

First Promenades and Deck Space
First Nursery
First Shops (x 5)
First News Room
First Lounge (with dome)
First Lounge Bar
Cabin and Tourist Theatre
First Private Function Room
First Library
First Writing Room
First Smoking Room
First Cocktail Lounge / Nightclub

Upper Deck (First, Cabin and Tourist)

First Travel Bureau
First Pursers Office
First Barbers Shop
First Beauty Parlour
First Bank
Cabin Shops (x 2)
Cabin Nursery and Crèche
Cabin Pursers Office
Cabin Travel Bureau
Cabin Bank
Cabin Barbers Shop
Cabin Beauty Parlour
Cabin Lido Lounge
Cabin Deck Space

Main Deck (First, Cabin and Tourist)

First (indoor) Swimming Pool
First Gymnasium and Female and Male
Changing Rooms
Cabin (indoor) Swimming Pool
Cabin Gymnasium and Changing Rooms
Cabin Launderette
Cabin Deck Space

Foyer Deck (First, Cabin and Tourist)

Tourist Entrance
Tourist Pursers Office
Tourist Travel Bureau
Tourist Bank
First Class Entrance
First Dining Room Entrance
First Health Facilities
Cabin Entrance

A Deck (First, Cabin and Tourist)

First Restaurant

B Deck (Cabin and Tourist)

Tourist Entrance
Tourist Restaurant

C Deck (Cabin and Tourist)

Hospital
Cabin Restaurant

D Deck

E Deck (Tourist)
Tourist Gymnasium
Tourist Swimming Pool
Tourist Launderette

F Deck

G Deck and Tank Top

Double Bottom

Initially the restaurants would not have windows as they were placed in the centre of the ship with either passenger cabins (First and Tourist Classes) along each side or passenger cabins and crew areas (Cabin Class) along the sides. However as designs for *Q3* progressed the restaurants were – for the first time on an Atlantic liner – placed high in the ship and the First Class dining room had an entrance on the deck above (Foyer) with a grand horseshow style staircase leading down into the room. Cabin and Tourist Restaurants would share a galley which would be located aft of the Tourist Restaurant and above the Cabin Restaurant – escalators between the two being provided.

The Tourist Lounge was connected on the port side by a spiral staircase with the Tourist Club Room on the Verandah Deck below and, in keeping with the traditional North Atlantic design, no outdoor swimming pool was provided.

Passenger accommodation would be provided for 2,298 passengers in 1,147 cabins in three-classes:

First Class	750 passengers	393 cabins
Cabin Class	644 passengers	333 cabins
Tourist Class	904 passengers	421 cabins

The cabin breakdown:

652 outside cabins (around 56%)
495 inside cabins (around 43%)
158 single cabins (158 passengers)
249 cabins with upper and lower berths (498 passengers)
611 two-bedded cabins (1222 passengers)
71 two bedded with Pullman berth cabins (213 passengers)
58 two bedded with 'ex' cabins (207 passengers)

First Class

DECK	OUTSIDE CABINS	INSIDE CABINS	TOTAL
Upper	99	14	113
Main	105	13	118
Foyer	72	7	79
A	64	19	83
	340	**53**	**393**

• Deluxe Suite and Semi-Suite Rooms on Upper Deck.

• Suite Rooms on Main Deck.

• 85 single cabins (85 passengers)

• 1 cabin with upper and lower berth (2 passengers)

• 258 two bedded cabins (516 passengers)

• 24 two bedded with Pullman berth cabins (72 passengers)

- 25 two bedded with 'ex' cabins (75 passengers)

Cabin Class

DECK	OUTSIDE CABINS	INSIDE CABINS	TOTAL
Main	19	18	37
Foyer	25	44	69
A	26	43	69
B	91	34	125
C	21	12	33
	182	151	333

- 50 single cabins (50 passengers)

- 57 cabins with upper and lower berth (114 passengers)

- 205 two bedded cabins (410 passengers)

- 14 two bedded with Pullman berth cabins (42 passengers)

- 7 two bedded with 'ex' cabins (28 passengers)

Tourist Class

DECK	OUTSIDE CABINS	INSIDE CABINS	TOTAL
Upper	14	52	66
Main	20	78	98
Foyer	27	63	90
A	16	25	41
B	38	50	88
C	15	23	38
	130	291	421

- Tourist cabins on C Deck without private toilet and shower.

- 23 single cabins (23 passengers)

- 191 cabins with upper and lower berth (382 passengers)

- 148 two bedded cabins (296 passengers)

- 33 two bedded with Pullman berth cabins (99 passengers)

- 26 two bedded with 'ex' cabins (104 passengers)

- 81 cabins (175 passengers) were interchangeable between First and Cabin on Upper, Main, Foyer and A Decks and 103 cabins (205 passengers) were interchangeable between Cabin and Tourist on B and C Decks.

There would be 1298 crew divided as follows:

Deck Dept.	111
Engine	191
Pursers	66
Medical	13
Catering	917

The Captain's and Staff Captain's cabins were located directly below the Wheelhouse on Sun Deck with Officer's and Engineering Officer's cabins located in blocks forward on Boat, Verandah and Promenade Decks and an Officer's Lounge forward on Sun Deck. Crew accommodation and facilities were located on Foyer, A, B, C and D Decks.

Cars would be loaded onto A Deck forward and stowed on E Deck also forward.

On the question of a three-class vessel, Sir John responded:

"There is a continuing demand for cabin class among people

who will not travel tourist, and for whom first class is too expensive.

"We have canvassed our American organisation, and sounded the views of American travel agents, and they are quite firm in their view that a three-class ship is right in one of this size and capacity. Their views are important, because it has been said so often that close on 70 per cent of Cunard passenger business originates in North America."

Sir John added that *Q3* would have a *"first-class design team"* to make sure the décor fitted the requirements of the cosmopolitan trade.

It is interesting to speculate what name would have been given to *Q3* with reports that Cunard may have finally gotten a Queen Victoria or Victoria. *Q3* would have entered service before *Queen Mary* or *Queen Elizabeth* had retired so she could not have taken either of their names.

At the Cunard Annual General Meeting in May 1961 desperate shareholders urged the immediate cancellation of the *Q3* Project because of worsening trading results. Ironically, the Annual Report revealed that the airline acquisition, Cunard Eagle Airways, was also losing money, unable to compete with the non-stop direct services of PanAm and BOAC.

It is a fact that the early 1960s was not a particularly good time for Cunard or its ageing Queens, whose passenger numbers and revenues were declining drastically. The company was fighting a losing battle against air travel and subsidized competition from foreign liners, and there were times when the *Queen Mary* and *Queen Elizabeth* sailed across the Atlantic with fewer passengers than their crew complements.

In a bid to revive their flagging fortunes both Queens were diverted to off-peak cruising, and for the first time, from February 1963, Cunard's all year-round weekly express service from either side of the Atlantic was interrupted. To increase her appeal as a cruise vessel, a lido area was created on the aft decks of *Queen Elizabeth* complete with outdoor swimming pool. Also, because their interiors could be like furnaces in the tropics, as many Second World War servicemen would attest, partial air-conditioning was extended throughout both ships to provide a measure of relief from the heat. In reality. The Queens were not suited to cruise work as they were inherently North Atlantic vessels built for speed in more demanding conditions, with palatial interiors designed to offer sanctuary from cold rather than warm weather. What is more, their deep draught precluded entry to many of the ports on the traditional cruise circuit. The experiment was relatively short-lived, and premature retirement threatened, for the *Queen Mary* at least.

James Gardner was one of the first shoreside professional designers to be involved in the external styling of *Q3*. Following the war, the Council of Industrial Design had commissioned him to oversee various exhibition projects, the most significant of these was the 'Britain Can Make It' exhibition of industrial and product design in 1946. Gardner had also been involved in the Festival of Britain in 1951 and he was also Chief Designer at Battersea Park Pleasure Gardens. His earliest exposure with *Q3* came as soon as he could possibly have been hoped for - the building contract had not even been signed.

He met with Sir John Brocklebank at the Cunard Building in Liverpool and in his autobiography, The ARTful Designer, would later write:

"Brocklebank's purpose in meeting me was to make it clear that, whatever I did with the rest of her, the ship must have the traditional Cunard funnel. 'It is the insignia of the line you know, Cunard red'."

After meeting with the Cunard Chairman, Gardner ventured into the drawing department to become acquainted with the 'happening' he was being asked to shape. There he met with a frustrated team trying desperately to make the vessel look like a ship.

Gardner's initial impression of the vessel:

"The ship will have no sweeping curves; she is a block of utility flats dumped in the sea, and must ride uncomfortably high to pack in the essential accommodations – a piece of floating real estate."

Gardner recalled how the drawing office had put together a 'clumsy' model to make Q3 look like a ship:

"One vent has been shaped like an obese 'streamlined' funnel, and the other which comes up at an unfortunate place, is disguised as mast. For the rest, it is an assembly of bits borrowed from the old Queen Mary."

Later in 1961, a builder's model of the Q3 was unveiled. It was a design approved by Cunard and Gardner's influence

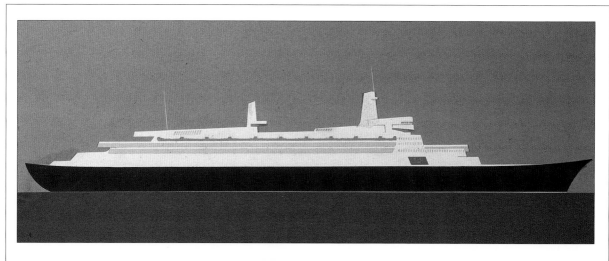

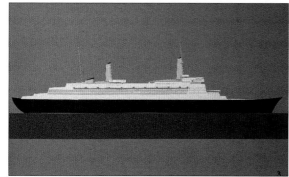 

James Gardner described the initial profiles of **Q3**: "The ship will have no sweeping curves; she is a block of utility flats dumped in the sea, and must ride uncomfortably high to pack in the essential accommodations - a piece of floating real estate". *(Author's collection)*

Gardner's final design for **Q3** was certainly distinctive – note the Cunard houseflag on the forward superstructure. *(Author's collection)*

and ideas had now created a radically different profile to the initial renderings – the primary aim of this new design and look was to impress the press.

Gardner's design displayed a radical exterior profile which was enclosed for full air-conditioning but despite the modern profile, she remained essentially a traditional ocean liner. The ship had clean crisp lines which bore little resemblance to her predecessors and which conveyed a modern impression of timeless elegance. The overall contour of the superstructure was refined and the double-deck promenades were fully enclosed. The navigating bridge had been given a modern cantilevered form, which appeared to float above the forward superstructure. Below, the foredeck featured a whaleback like that favoured by the French on *Normandie* and *France*. The most striking feature was that the great red funnel was gone! A second slender white mast-like exhaust had replaced it. The forward mast-stack, was now visually balanced by the aft uptake, slightly abaft the midships line. This was probably the most striking element in conveying the new ship's new image. After all, within the preceding two years *Rotterdam* and *Canberra* had emerged without conventional funnels as the world's two most admired ships.

This was the last ever seen externally of *Q3*.

Q3 would host several new ideas that were incorporated into her internal layout and design:

- the dining rooms were relocated to the upper decks. This was done so that these spaces would be on the same decks as the other principle public rooms whose size demanded some additional deckhead or ceiling height.

- the lower headroom acceptable for cabins could therefore be maintained universally below, throughout the 'tween decks. The passenger public area and sleeping accommodations were thus divided virtually horizontally, which simplified things considerably. Each deck would be for either one purpose of the other, and a constant height would be maintained throughout its entire length.

- apart from locating the passenger restaurants at the top of the ship, crew messing facilities were to be located nearby

with the crew cafeterias forward and below in the upper 'tween deck and the officers' mess higher up, beneath the bridge.

- together all these facilities were to form an integrated catering complex, organised around the central nucleus of a single galley and its related pantries, bars, services, bakery, larders and so on. This was planned to be as far forward as possible so that the mast above the bridge housing could also double as an exhaust stack and to provide direct access to the stores and cold rooms below from the forward hatches.

It has been said that in terms of interior styling *Q3* perhaps would have been similarly appointed as the *France* which could have resulted in disappointment as the interior design and furnishings of the *France* attracted much criticism from the travel trade for being bland, dull and lacking style. The *France* was all about service and French joie de vivre.

While *Q3* may have been the wrong size and wrong-type of ship there is no doubt she would have embodied advances in design and technology and introduced features never seen before at sea or on the Atlantic. The quest to reduce weight produced a liner with a draft two metres less than that of the old Queens which was remarkable considering her principal statistics were similar to *Queen Mary* and *Queen Elizabeth*.

Q3 would have employed the best of the best which was appropriate given her role and status carrying British pride and international passengers on her Atlantic routes for at least 20 years and probably more.

Despite the bad omens the *Q3* Project was gathering an unstoppable momentum. On 29 June 1961, the North Atlantic Shipping Bill became an Act if Parliament, paving the way for Cunard to place the construction order. It seems that there was little to prevent what was looking increasingly like a fatally flawed concept from proceeding.

Such was the prestige of the contract – considered the most exciting and important of the decade – John Brown was so keen to win that they claimed the price they quoted would not result in a profit. The other shipyards were suspected of employing the same tactics. One tender suggested the use of

An artists' impression of **Q3**, using the final Gardner model as inspiration, produced many years after the project itself was shelved. *(Author's collection)*

American turbines while another suggested an unusual hull.

Cunard insisted it would not proceed with construction if the price exceeded £30 million. That would result in Cunard making a complete reappraisal of their passenger trade, both sea and air. An actual final price was difficult to establish as all the shipyards had different ideas on how to achieve the speed, performance and capacity Cunard demanded.

Thanks to the lowest cost and earliest delivery date, by several months, the joint bid from Vickers Armstrong and Swan Hunter & Wigham Richardson became the favourite. Cunard could take advantage of the 1965 summer season meaning an additional year's earnings on the transatlantic trade and 1965 would see Queen Mary celebrate her 30th Birthday. It was this group which also offered the most progressive ideas on the ship's construction.

In fact, the consortium had submitted two designs to Cunard: one was the all-steel four-shaft ship Cunard had asked for; the other was a smaller two-shaft alloy / steel design.

The disturbing news for the John Brown yard was that the consortium's four shaft all-steel design was preferred on cost and design to their own. It was later found that Clydebank's price was £1.8 million higher than the consortium's. John Brown's hull would have cost £2.15 million more to build although its machinery was £0.35 million lower, and its hull was a much heavier and stiffer structure than the consortium's and required more power and therefore more expense to propel it.

However, it was the consortium's smaller two-shaft design which caused Cunard to pause. Many of the features it embraced were based on the *Oriana* – a fact that placed an

entirely different perspective on *Q3*.

Compared with John brown's specification for *Q3*, the Swan Hunter / Vickers design variant had a shorter hull by 70-feet (21.3 metres), at 920-feet (280.4 metres) overall. The accommodation, for 2,270 passengers, was spread over 12 decks. Four Pametrada steam turbines would have given her the required service speed if 30 knots when rated at 112,500-shp, but it was calculated that the powerplant had sufficient reserve for her to challenge the *United States'* grasp on the Atlantic Blue Riband, if so desired, for she had the potential for an astonishing 40 knots at the maximum output of 140,000-shp! Doubtless the performance of the John Brown design would have been comparable, but it must be remembered that this is pure conjecture.

Assuming the order had been received before the end of 1961, the keel would have been laid in May 1962, the launch would have taken place in December 1963, and the new 'Queen' would have been delivered to Cunard in April 1965 – during the company's 165th Anniversary year.

Many of the young Directors were still unhappy about the type of ship that was being selected and found an ally in Sir John Brocklebank who was also concluding that *Q3* was the wrong ship.

Two senior executives who felt that the whole *Q3* concept was *"crazy"* drew up proposals for a twin-screw liner which could go cruising in the winter and operate on the North Atlantic in the profitable summer months. They believed *Q3* would be a *"write-off"* if she did not go cruising. The management rejected this paper. The executives persisted and, eventually, met Sir John who explained that no such paper had ever been submitted to him by the management

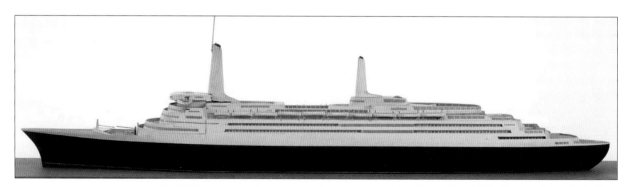

On Thursday 30 October 2013 this waterline concept model of **Q3** by John Brown was auctioned by Charles Miller Ltd. The model, 29 x 110.5 x 26 cm, was built by Charles N Longbotom in London and included carved lifeboats in davits and applied paper windows. *(Author's collection)*

A glum Sir John Brocklebank announces the cancellation of **Q3**, Thursday 19 October 1961. *(Author's collection)*

'The Queen That Never Was', a painting of **Q3** by Mervyn Pearson *(courtesy of David Williams)*

and he was in full sympathy with their views. Eventually the paper went to the Board but it was put on ice – tradition had triumphed again.

One shareholder, Raymond Gregory, mounted a six-month struggle to persuade Cunard to scrap plans to replace *Queen Mary*, claiming that Q3 would be a *"gigantic waste and ruin Cunard."* After a motion of his to scrap the project was dismissed in June, he wrote to 20,000 shareholders in July 1961 telling them what was at stake and asking them to vote against Q3. More than 16% replied to the letter – 4,227 in support of Gregory and 297 wanting Q3. In total, the value of shares of those against represented £1.5 million.

Sir John Brocklebank met with Ernest Marples on 17 October to discuss the future of Q3.

The following day the Cunard Board met to discuss the situation. Sir John reappraised the whole situation - dwindling passenger numbers, increasing losses and the potential actual cost of Q3 by the time of build. It was essentially his prudent reappraisal of the objectives that led to a fundamental redirection of thinking.

On 19 October 1961, Sir John reluctantly announced that Cunard could not see its way clear to order the Q3 - rising labour and material costs had increased the price of the ship by several million pounds and the Government loan was not sufficient to cover the escalator clauses in the shipbuilding tenders. The plans were therefore postponed indefinitely as trading conditions could not justify replacing the Queens by similar tonnage and it was back to the drawing board.

In the Annual Report, Sir John commented:

"You will expect me to say something about the postponement of the placing of an order for a new Express ship. In this connection, I am glad to say that the two 'Queens' have several working years ahead of them and an immediate decision is not, therefore, necessary."

Simultaneously it was revealed that the company was studying an alternative design concept presented by John Brown and Co for a smaller, two-class, dual-role, twin-screw liner.

It was all very disappointing for those who were not intimately involved in the know, the national press resurrecting memories of the 1930s, when the *Queen Mary* had been suspended on the slipway at Clydebank.

Nevertheless, the company was left facing difficult operational problems. It had planned to introduce Q3 into service before *Queen Mary* was retired, but these intentions were overtaken by events, compounded in June 1963 when the company confirmed that it would be proceeding with the dual-role option – Q4 as it was called. The earliest date that the revised replacement ship could be completed was 1968, and, given the imminent retirement of *Queen Mary*, Cunard faced the prospect of having, albeit briefly, only one large express ship in service, *Queen Elizabeth*.

So, what Was Wrong with Q3? The design was based on a long-standing premise that a Cunard express Atlantic liner could not be made suitable for use in other trades. This supported the belief that a much higher standard of First-Class accommodation was essential in North Atlantic service

To some **Q3** was the way forward for Cunard but to others she was considered "a gigantic waste and ruin Cunard". *(Author's collection)*

A working sketch by James Gardner of **Q3**'s bridge front. *(Author's collection)*

than in markets elsewhere. Together with the conventional approach to powering this ship with quadruple screws, the resulting 75,000-ton size emerged at only slightly less her predecessors. As a virtual replacement of *Queen Mary*, she would have been too big and too conventional in concept.

If built, she would probably have turned out rather like a larger version of the liner *France*, which was under construction at the time. The *France* saw 12 years of service before being laid up in 1974 when subsidies were withdrawn.

Q3's time had passed before she even left the drawing board. In addition to ferocious competition from the air there was deep underlying uncertainty about the future of passenger shipping and she was being conceived for a trade that was fast disappearing.

The abandonment of Q3 would ultimately prove to be the correct one. Sir John Brocklebank would later claim building her would have been *"a disaster"* and history would prove him right - Cunard had narrowly averted creating perhaps the greatest floating white elephant since Brunel's Great Eastern. Interestingly, Sir John would later claim it would have been *"a disaster not to build the Q4."*

But his decision and the triumph for Cunard's younger Directors still didn't solve Cunard's *Queen Mary* and *Queen Elizabeth* replacement dilemma. And while Q3 herself would not leave the drawing board many aspects of her design certainly would as Cunard embarked on its most ambitious ship ever.

TENDER COMPARISONS

YARD	TENDER DATED	COST	PASSENGERS	DELIVERY DATE
Harland & Wolff	28 July 1961	£24,650,000	1037 feet overall 942 feet bp 12,650 tons dw 200,000 shp 2298	December 1965
Cammell Laird and Company	29 July 1961	£27,980,000	1041 feet overall 942 feet bp 2298	End 1965
Fairfield Shipbuilding and Engineering Co	28 July 1961	£27,177,800	1040 feet overall 942 feet bp 12,650 tons 150,000 shp 2298	March / April 1966
John Brown & Co	29 July 1961	£24,051,880		End May 1965
Vickers and Swan Hunter Limited	31 July 1961	£21,944,600	180,000	April 1965

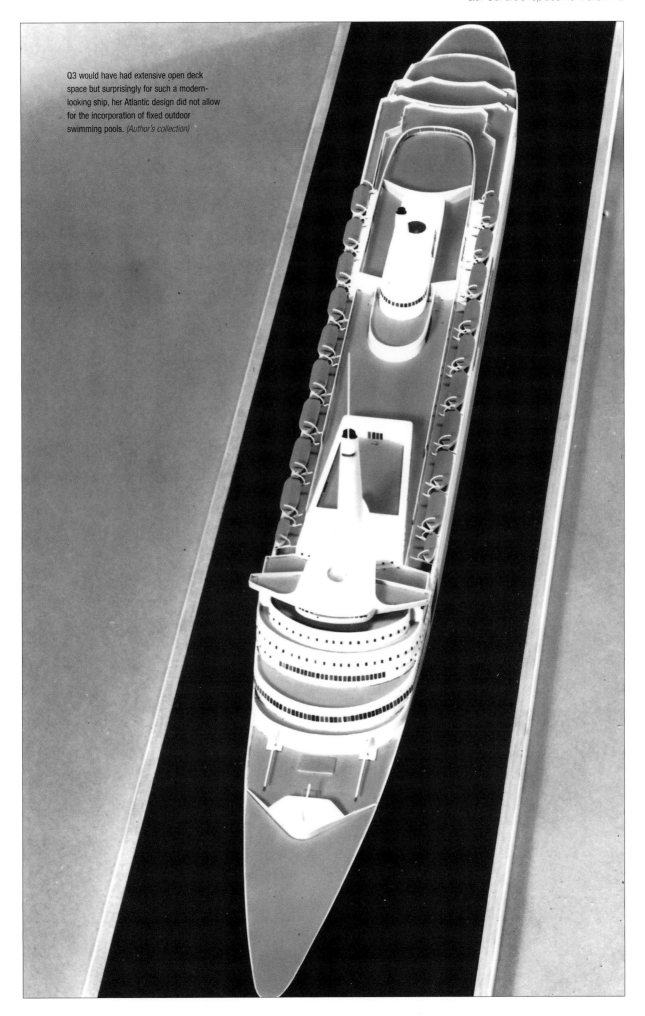

Q3 would have had extensive open deck space but surprisingly for such a modern-looking ship, her Atlantic design did not allow for the incorporation of fixed outdoor swimming pools. *(Author's collection)*

CHAPTER TWO

Q4: conception to contracts

For over a year things looked grim, until it was announced in December 1962 that Cunard was involved in plans for a smaller and more versatile liner: Q4

Now Cunard would take a fresh approach to its requirements and learn from the advances that had been made in design, technologies in shipbuilding, in propulsion and in materials available to the shipbuilder. The new ship, or the "New Cunarder" as Sir John Brocklebank liked to refer to her, would be a re-working of the Q3 rather than an updated version of the beloved Queen Mary and Queen Elizabeth.

Cunard's design team was headed by Chief Naval Architect Robert Wood, Assistant Naval Architect Dan Wallace and Technical Director Tom Kameen. Since Robert Wood was due for retirement Dan Wallace would take the lead on the project before becoming Chief Naval Architect in 1964. Wallace was responsible for the overall design and construction of the Q4 and had begun his career as an apprentice draughtsman at John Brown's shipyard in 1931 (the first ship on which he worked there was the Queen Mary) before joining Cunard in 1951.

Tom Kameen was responsible for the mechanical operations – everything from the engine room to the galley, the plumbing and the air conditioning. He had started his apprenticeship at Cammell Laird's yard in Birkenhead in 1932, joining Cunard four years later as an engineer officer serving on Aquitania, Berengaria and Queen Mary. During the latter stages of the Second World War, he was stationed in New York, serving the Ministry of War Transport there, before returning to Cunard in 1945 as the line's Assistant Superintendent Engineer in Southampton. He became the Technical Director in 1963.

Wallace and Kameen were both highly experienced and affable gentlemen, whose accumulated knowledge and unflappable determination steered the Q4 project through to a successful conclusion. Working with Cunard's directorate, their job was to establish the optimum size, capacity and speed of the new liner and Dan Wallace drafted the very first specifications for Q4 at home in the evening while seated at his dining room table on 21 and 25 October 1961.

The new proposal initially evolved with Vickers in October 1961 and was for a ship strikingly similar to Oriana which they had launched for P&O in 1960. Oriana was a dual-purpose cruise or passage vessel, not a giant at 42,000 tons, but carrying 2,000 passengers on five decks in stabilised and fully air-conditioned comfort. She was novel in several ways: the first British ship to have an all aluminium superstructure, and the first to have a bulb bow. She was a twin-screw steamer, and she had lateral propulsion units for independent docking. The new vessel proposed for Cunard could be described almost identically, except for its size – about 60,000 tons.

The novel **Oriana**. (Author's collection)

Extensive design work on the hull was carried out by the Cunard architects at the Cunard Building Liverpool and the National Physical Laboratory, the national measurement standards laboratory for the United Kingdom, at Teddington in Middlesex. The staff at John Brown's also put the hull form through test after test in the yard's experimental tank in order to perfect the final design and fed the results into the new IBM computer which analyzed the statistics and fed back evaluations within the hour – a process that used to take weeks.

One of the earliest Q4 documents circulated privately to Cunard Directors laid out the initial concepts and thinking behind the ship which would have its foundations in the lessons learned from Q3. Cunard was satisfied that a ship of some 58,000 tons, with two screws, could do the job of Q3 – a ship of 75,000 tons gross with four screws.

- Q4 would have an estimated first cost of £23 million, a length of 960 feet and a beam of 104 feet. She was to have a shaft horsepower of about 105,000 on two screws, giving a service speed of about 29½ knots. Q4 would be able to pass through the Panama Canal, with just 18 inches clearance on either side, if required and her deployment would consist of roughly eight months on the Atlantic, three months cruising and one month in overhaul. The 29½ knot weekly Atlantic service would be achieved with less power margins than Q3.

- The three-class vessel would be very flexible when it came to class allocation. First Class would range from 300 to

Dan Wallace, Cunard's Chief Naval Architect. *(Author's collection)*

Tom Kameen, Cunard Technical Director. *(Author's collection)*

500; Cabin Class from 526 to 600 and Tourist Class from 770 to 954.

- Cunard planned to engage to best outside designers, not only for the passenger accommodation, but also for the exterior profile, to ensure the ship was attractive and forward looking in every way.

- It would take about four years to build *Q4* which would give an approximate delivery date towards the end of 1966, allowing for the development of the design. Delivery in the spring of the year was no longer important as *Q4* was designed for cruising as much as for the North Atlantic service. Cruising was becoming increasingly attractive to Cunard.

Most importantly the concept of *Q4* had three radical departures from that of the Queens Mary and Elizabeth and *Q3*: the ability to cruise successfully; increased flexibility between the classes and greatly reduced operating costs.

The evolution of *Q4*

The design for *Q4* would rise phoenix-like from the ashes of *Q3* with the earlier ship forever influencing the final design of what would become *Queen Elizabeth 2*.

Although *Q3* was rejected overall for being the wrong ship for the jet age, her design embodied several progressive elements which survived. On *Q3* Cunard had already decided to abandon the conventional arrangement of public rooms on the promenade deck, dining rooms as low down as possible to minimise the effects of motion at sea, and cabins located on the decks in between, favouring an absolute linear split between the ship's cabin and

communal areas. The new *Q4* layout was also to take up this approach, with all passenger cabins located exclusively on the uppermost five hull decks and the public spaces, including the dining rooms and galleys, arranged throughout the three principal superstructure decks, above.

Indeed, the *Q4* design would develop further the most progressive ideas of *Q3*'s layout albeit in the reduced overall

Cunard Building Liverpool, 'birthplace' of the designs for many Cunarders, including Q3 and Q4, seen in the mid-1960s. *(Author's collection)*

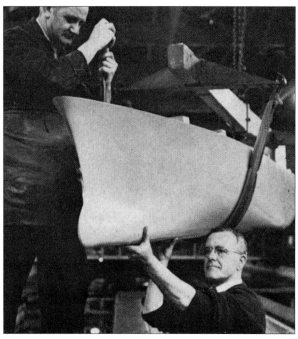

Adjustments being made to a hull model of the new Cunarder during tank tests at Clydebank. *(Author's collection)*

The Naval Architects Office on the fifth floor of the Cunard Building Liverpool. The initial designs for **Queen Mary**, **Queen Elizabeth**, **Q3**, **Q4**, the second **Mauretania**, **Caronia** and the 1950s Canadian quarter, among others, originated here. *(Author's collection)*

dimensions of Q4:

- Much of the work done by Cunard's design department in reducing structural complexity and weight in Q3 would ultimately prove vital in Q4.

- Since structurally Q4 would be no less a "block of flats dumped in the sea" (as James Gardner described his first view of Q3), then so too would James Gardner's ideas be kept.

- The final funnel shape of Q4 was based on initial work undertaken on that for Q3 which is somewhat resembled.

- Several new ideas which appeared on Q4 had originally been developed for Q3: the relocation of dining rooms and crew messing facilities etc.

- A great deal of work in terms of Q3 cabin planning and

layouts would be used for Q4

Q3 propulsion machinery designs were resurrected and modified until the machinery for Q4 was finally chosen. Reliability, simplicity and efficiency were the watchwords and because of the experience gained in planning the machinery for Q3, it was decided to specify turbines of Pametrada design, driving two propellers and maintain an average speed of 28.5 knots.

The placement of the engines just aft of amidships (for stability and strength) dictated the funnel location which would affect the layout and expanse of open deck space necessary for warm weather cruising.

The New Cunarder's initial concept was for the 27 boilers on Queen Mary and the 12 on Queen Elizabeth to be reduced to four and the four propellers on each of the old Queens to be reduced to two. Modern engines now enabled an almost

One of several different models of **Q4**'s hull is shown being put through its paces in simulated rough weather conditions. *(Author's collection)*

An April 1967 artists' impression of **QE2** in the Panama Canal. *(Author's collection)*

equal amount of power to be obtained from a smaller installation. Enough fuel would be carried to last a complete round North Atlantic voyage at an average speed of 28.5 knots. The new ships would accommodate 2,000 passengers in three classes but the rooms would be flexible in as much as they could be changed from one class to another. In terms of propulsion machinery – boilers, turbines, gearboxes, condensers and propeller shafts – the *Q3* designs would be resurrected and modified until the machinery for *Q4* was chosen.

In October 1961 Dan Wallace paid a visit to the Panama Canal and reported back to the Cunard Board on 1 December. The Canal authorities had indicated that a ship of 960-feet overall and 104-feet beam would be allowed to pass through providing it was not too often (say once a year) and were well planned in advance. By the end of 1964 the authorities indicated that they would now accept vessels up to 106-feet beam and because the Builder's estimate for the centre of gravity for *Q4* was slightly higher it was decided to

increase the beam at the waterline by one foot to 105 feet. During her career, what would become *QE2* would transit the Panama Canal a total of 39 times (26 times from the Caribbean to the Pacific) and pass through the Suez Canal 11 times – all but one of those transits being to the Mediterranean with the only transit to the Middle East through the Canal being during her final voyage.

Q4 would be a dual-purpose liner battling across the Atlantic in summer and taking it easy in the sun in the winter. This is a summary of the main items added to the vessel as a North Atlantic ship for cruising:

- Several lifeboats adapted so that they may be used as cruise launches.

- Certain cargo spaces insulated and refrigerated to provide additional storage space when cruising.

- Increase in certain storerooms.

- Passenger embarkation gangway facilities.

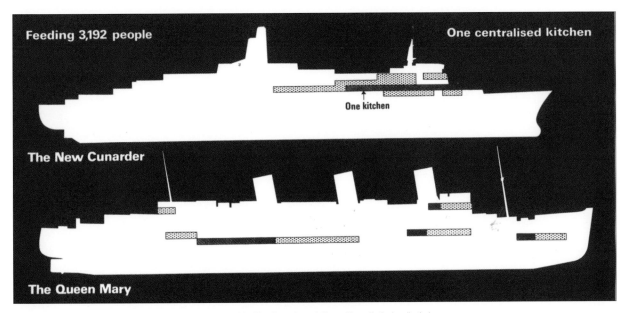

An interesting comparison of the kitchen-restaurant relationship of the New Cunarder and **Queen Mary**. *(Author's collection)*

An April 1967 artists' impression of QE2 in one of the locks of the Panama Canal. *(Author's collection)*

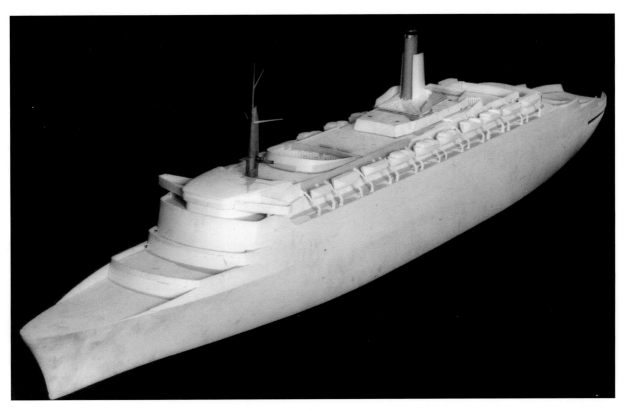

The final waterline model for aerodynamic evaluation at the National Physical Laboratory. *(Author's collection)*

- Outdoor pools.

- Library convertible to Cruise Office.

- Additional cruise entrance.

- Additional mooring equipment for Panama Canal.

- Tendency for cabins to have larger wardrobes etc.

- Deck buffet and pantries.

- Larger laundry with consequent additional fresh water storage capacity.

- Cruise Director's accommodation and office.

- Increase in kitchen facilities and bedroom service.

In addition to the above, there were many other minor items.

The experience in building *Sylvania* in 1955 would not be

forgotten. Plastic piping, plastic baths, lightweight furniture and specially-developed, deeper than usual, girders (which had holes cut into them to enable easy passage of piping and electrical cables) had been used to facilitate the saving of weight and these ideas were to be used to advantage now in *Q4*.

Cunard studied other Atlantic liners, such as the *France* and the *United States*, that had been sent cruising in the winter months. The lessons learned from the conversions of its *Saxonia* and *Ivernia* to *Carmania* and *Franconia* in 1962 were of great practical benefit when facilities and materials to be incorporated into *Q4* were being considered.

It was planned that the *Q4* would have a greatly reduced beam and draught in comparison to her predecessors and this was made possible by stringent weight saving through the careful use of lighter materials in her construction. The new ship would be able to enter ports that were inaccessible

A model of *QE2* with test funnel number 8 in the National Physical Laboratory wind tunnel with a relative wind speed of 28 knots from dead ahead. *(Author's collection)*

A stern view of the final waterline model for aerodynamic evaluation at the National Physical Laboratory. *(Author's collection)*

to previous Cunarders and moor alongside jetties in sheltered waters allowing her passengers to embark and disembark directly from ship to shore in comfort.

On the forefoot of the ship, a 'bulb' would be fitted for the first time on a Cunard ship and this bulbous bow would punch a hole in the water ahead thereby cutting down water resistance on the hull.

1,100 tons of aluminium alloy, supplied by Alcan, was to be used for the superstructure which was the largest amount and would see some of the biggest plates ever used on a British liner. Alcan would organise a special training centre within the yard and the trained welders would be periodically checked for standards. The use of aluminium helped the design team to reduce the new ship's draft by several feet than if steel had been used in the superstructure and enabled the number of decks to be increased from 12 on the old Queens to 13 on Q4.

This extra passenger deck more than compensated for the limits on length and beam that had been imposed by the planned usage of the Panama and Suez Canals and had also been made possible by the reduction of six to nine inches in the heights of the other decks by running electrical cables, piping and ventilation trunking over main passageways and bathrooms where a lower headroom was acceptable. Cunard's engineering staff also managed to save three feet in height off the machinery spaces.

The aluminium superstructure was part of the ship's strength structure so expansion joints were omitted.

To prevent any corrosive electrolytic interaction between the steel hull and the aluminium superstructure a careful bonding method had to be utilised. A special epoxy compound was spread along the joints between the two metals and then steel rivets were used for the final connection.

The various weight saving initiatives would prove their worth in practical and profitable ways but they affected the centre of gravity which had to be lowered. Instead of applying the usual remedy – adding useless ballast to the bottom of a ship (in Q4's case a total of 750 tons would have had to have been added) the designers instead did away with this deadweight and turned it to advantage by increasing certain plate thicknesses in areas where greater than usual wear of corrosion could be expected to occur during the vessel's

service. These areas included the lower most structure in way of machinery and the fore part of the hull which was also strengthened against ice. The double bottom cells were constructed more closely and with thicker steel which also added to the strength of the hull.

The use of aluminium and the inclusion of stabilisers enabled Cunard to place the restaurants and main galley in the superstructure

Q4 would be designed and constructed to comply with both the American and British regulations in relation to fireproofing. This meant using as little inflammable material as possible (US) and supplying adequate water sprinklers and an inert gas smothering system where electrical and other water sensitive equipment was in use (UK). This foresight would keep the vessel in date with regard to fireproofing regulations for decades.

Uncluttered upper decks with two large swimming pools, lido areas which were to be the largest afloat, a hitherto unexcelled use of large glass windows in promenade decks, side screens, passenger cabins and in the restaurants (themselves located above the main deck) would contribute to the ship's modern appearance; and the extensive use if glass itself would mean a maximum amount of natural daylight. For instance, 1,400 passengers would be accommodated in cabins with portholes. Again, recognizing that passengers expected continuing improvement in the standards of cabin comfort, Cunard gave a lot of thought to fitting the greatest possible number of actual beds rather than upper berths. Of a total passenger capacity of 2,050, all accommodated in rooms matching the highest standards of competitive ships, only 10% would occupy upper berths.

It was these features which were essential to North Atlantic service as well as cruising and the ship would be able to hold her own on the Atlantic while also being one of the most fabulous resorts in the world.

While Cunard deliberated upon the type of vessel the new Q4 should be, the prediction that Lord Aberconway made about John Brown's Clydebank shipyard not being able to maintain its skilled workforce together if it didn't win the Q3 contract began to become fact especially after completing Union Castle's Transvaal Castle in December 1961.

If the yard was to secure the contract for Q4 it would have to retain a large complement of finishing trades so, during

Sir John Brocklebank (far left) discusses plans with colleagues including Dan Wallace (third from left) in the Naval Architects Office, Tuesday 21 January 1964. *(Author's collection)*

Dan Wallace discusses Q4, Tuesday 21 January 1964. *(Author's collection)*

1962, the company tendered for the Norwegian America Line's *Sagafjord* contract. This would have maintained John Brown's traditional business and kept key trades together. However, the order went instead to the Société. des Forges de la Méditerranée (La Seyne sur Mer) as John Brown's price was £160,000 higher than the best British price, which was that of Swan Hunter at £5,630,000.

In February 1962 Cunard announced that a decision on a replacement for *Queen Mary* would be made by the end of April that year. Immediate speculation focused on a conventionally powered ship of between 50,000 and 60,000 tons costing up to £25 million and that Swan Hunters on the Tyne would build the new ship. Sir John Brocklebank would not be drawn but confirmed that she would be in service by 1966 and that she would be "quite a bombshell."

Sir John:

"We are firmly convinced that there is a great future for a new express ship of a very different type from the present Queens. She must be a top flight cruise ship and a revolutionary North Atlantic unit. We are not yet ready to announce our plans for this ship but design work is well advanced and we are in close consultation with our American organization."

The next tendering opportunity for John Brown in Clydebank lay with the Swedish American Line, which was considering the construction of a new intermediate liner to replace the existing *Kungsholm* of 1953. Almost certainly, concerns over John Brown's growing uncompetitiveness conditioned the board's attitude towards this contract.

The process started on 17 December 1962, when the Managing Director wrote to the Swedish American Line, asking that they be permitted to tender for the new ship, initially to be named the Salholm. The Swedish American Line was known throughout the shipbuilding industry for commercial astuteness. Following intensive negotiations in Gothenburg between John Brown and the Swedish American Line, it was agreed that John Brown would tender for this ship by the deadline of 4 June 1963.

John Brown's tender was successful at £6,780,000, carrying with it a stipulated delivery date of October 1965. To ensure every chance of winning the contract, a price had been quoted, based on charges only with no profit and with no escalator clauses to protect costs against inflationary rises in labour and material. In other words, provided nothing went wrong, the yard would break even. The ship, later named the *Kungsholm*, was laid down on 1 January 1964. By the end of that year, it was clear, for a number of reasons, that the delivery date could not be met, forcing the yard to re-negotiate a delivery date of 19 December 1965. The new contract specified that delivery beyond then would incur penalties of £3,000 per day.

As the *Kungsholm* began to take shape on the building berth at Clydebank, Cunard was well into the process of determining the specifications for their new *Q4* – a project being undertaken by its unusually strong technical department. Dan Wallace and Tom Kameen were supported by a small technical staff who maintained an exceptionally close involvement with the design and development of the company's ships.

Vickers Armstrong's imaginative *Q3* and initial *Q4* design earned them a development contract from Cunard, signed in May 1963, to work out a concept proposal to build *Q4* at Barrow. They were to work in close collaboration with Cunard and carry out calculations for the proposed new vessel. Although Cunard maintained a dialogue with John Brown's throughout the development period of the new ship, technically important work had been lost to Vickers Armstrong. The combination of Cunard and Vickers brought together three things: Vicker's ideas for improvements in the ratio between size, power and speed; Cunard's requirement to reach beyond the stringent American safety standards and the many lessons learned from *Q3*.

Q4's design developed into a ship of 57,000 tons with two shafts which, unlike *Q3*, was capable of negotiating the Panama Canal and, therefore, able to cruise from ports on either coast of the United States.

Cunard first approached the Government in July 1963 for a loan of £18 million over 25 years but this was initially rejected.

The Ministry of Transport wrote to Cunard on 17 October 1963 advising them that the Minister Ernest Marples had agreed that a loan should be offered. The Government decided to grant Cunard's application for a loan after considering advice tended to it by the Shipbuilding Credit

Dennis Lennon *(Author's collection)*

James Gardner *(Author's collection)*

Stefan Buzas *(Author's collection)*

Theo Crosby *(Author's collection)*

Advisory under the chairmanship of Lord Piercy and the money was to be advanced through the Government's shipbuilding credit scheme.

The loan was offered for the vessel of £17.6 million, or alternatively of 80% of the final building cost of the new liner including all extras, whichever should be the less. The final building cost for this purpose would be the sum agreed by Cunard and the Minister on the basis of certificates issued by the Builder's auditors as to the final price charged.

The terms included 4½ per cent interest - the then present Government lending rate – over 10 years by twenty equal half-yearly installments with the first payment to be made at the expiration date of six months from the date of the loan being made. Cunard had the right to repay the whole of the outstanding balance of the loan at any time on six months' prior written notice.

It was stipulated that the Building Contract for the construction of the new liner was to be made with a shipbuilder in the UK who had submitted the best tender following invitations to tender. The Minister would also have to give prior approval to the choice of shipbuilders invited to tender; the terms of the invitations to tender and associated documents;

the final choice of the shipbuilder and the final specification of the new liner as agreed by Cunard and the shipbuilder.

Cunard also had to ensure that the new liner would be registered in the UK, that it would be classed +100 A1 by Lloyds and that all monies due to the Builders under the Building Contract on the delivery of the new liner had been paid.

Cunard had to place the statutory mortgages for *Carmania*, *Franconia* and *Media* with the Ministry as well as pay engagement and commitment fees – the former being £66,000 which would not be returnable in any event and the latter of £176,000 but this amount would be refunded when the first half-yearly payment on the loan was made. The company was also responsible for all investigation and legal expense, stamp duties, registration fees and any other charges incurred by the Minister in connection with the preparation of the loan and security documents and otherwise in connection with the loan.

Ernest Marples:

"The offer is made in accordance with normal procedures under the scheme. Because, however, of the considerable

The builder's model before the final funnel design had been selected. *(Author's collection)*

preparatory work needed with a ship of this kind, construction work will not start until later than with other ships being financed under the scheme."

Sir John Brocklebank signed and accepted the offer and its terms and conditions and the offer was made public on 21 October 1963 when Cunard announced it was to go ahead with the building of the new liner.

Sir John:

"We are satisfied not only that the ship we are proposing to build is the right one but also that we are embarking on a commercially profitable project."

The Government would advance £17.6 million over ten years to be paid when the liner was delivered. The balance would be raised through the Finance Corporation for Industry, and a consortium of 11 clearing banks and five Scottish banks.

Tenders called for a new 58,000-ton express liner expected to cost in the region of £22 million with the outstanding amount to be provided by Cunard itself. Sir John said it was the company's intention that the new liner should be so advanced that she would provide the travelling public standard of comfort and relaxation hitherto unsurpassed. She

would carry about 2,000 passengers and 1,000 crew and was expected to be delivered at the end of 1967. There was still doubt as to the number of classes the ship would feature.

One of the terms of the loan was that the new liner would have to be built in Britain and Sir John confirmed that shipyards would be invited to tender in the late summer of 1964 with work starting before the end of that year.

Cunard issued an interim report on the general plans in May 1964 and that disclosed two important decisions the company had taken: the ship would carry three classes of passenger and have three restaurants located above the main passenger deck – a total break with tradition. All cabins would be fitted baths or showers and toilets. The estimated cost of the ship was £22 million and the general plans were scheduled for completion in August 1964.

At the same time it was announced that tenders for building the new ship would be sought that summer which resulted in the usual feverish speculation of who would win the order.

At the same time secret tests were being carried out at the Ship research Laboratory on a 22-foot long wax model of the hull of the proposed new ship. The most significant development from the tests was the provision of a slightly bulbous bow to reduce pitching in rough seas. The model had already been tried in the 1,300-fot long tank at Feltham, the longest of its kind in the world.

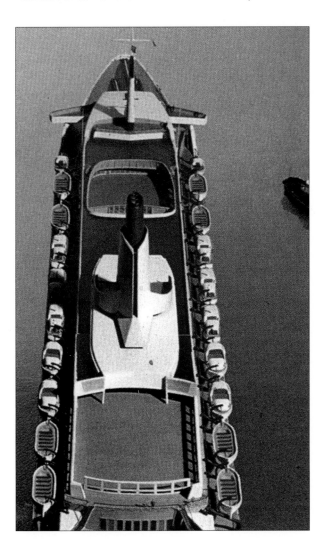

The clean uncluttered top decks. *(Author's collection)*

The cascading aft decks. *(Author's collection)*

The new Cunarder would be 960 feet in length and have a draught of 31 feet and a gross tonnage about 58,000. Her twin-screw turbine machinery would be capable of developing a maximum of 110,000 horse power and give a service speed of 28½ knots on less than half the fuel consumption of a 'Queen'. Again, the machinery weight would only be one third that of a 'Queen' liner and the engine room complement considerably less than half. And, the ship would carry as many passengers as a 'Queen'.

The Design Team(s)

As early as March 1962, Cunard's chairman, Sir John Brocklebank, gave some indication of how the new flagship would appear and, with an emphasis on design, how this would be achieved:

"The decision to build 'Q4' is a major turning point in Cunard history, and the design concept of the ship is a complete break with tradition. The Company has no intention of abandoning its hard-won position as the leading North Atlantic shipping line. Cunard policy is changing as the trade is changing, and the Company is beginning 1962 with positive evidence that it is applying its know-how and resources to producing a ship which will be the pacemaker on the North Atlantic, and will be equally successful as a cruise ship.

Regarding the liner's external appearance, he announced that James Gardner had been re-appointed to style the Q4's superstructure and to design the livery. Brocklebank was confident *"that the exterior profile of 'Q4' will be both attractive and forward looking, and, when the time comes to tackle the interior decoration, the same progressive policy will be pursued and a team of the very best designers will be engaged."*

Quoted in the September 1961 edition of The Architectural Review as suggesting a Georgian-style interior for Q3, Sir John Brocklebank announced in October 1963 that the revised Q4 ship would rather be closer to *"the spirit of Jacqueline Kennedy than to Queen Victoria."* In one sentence Sir John had confirmed that the new ship would take Cunard in a whole new direction while still, with the use of the Kennedy reference, appealing to its all-important American market.

At first, and following the usual tradition, the Chairman's wife, Lady Brocklebank, assumed responsibility for the Q4's interior design. Although conservative by instinct, she was, nonetheless, well-travelled and an informed observer of lifestyle trends and expectations of the travelling public, with a practical point of view and the ability to understand and work with technical drawings and other material from Cunard's design department and the shipbuilders.

To begin with, Lady Brocklebank selected Jean Monro, Evelyn Pinching and Michael Inchbald to decorate the onboard spaces, based upon their forthcoming work for Cunard redoing the interiors during the *Saxonia* and *Ivernia* transformations to *Carmania* and *Franconia*.

Sir Hugh Casson, who was well known for his work on the Royal Yacht *Britannia* and for his contribution to the highly-acclaimed *Canberra*, attempted to persuade Lady Brocklebank that, at least, some more progressive British

architects and designers ought also to be involved. After all, the proposed Q4 was potentially a vast project and, irrespective of style, it was doubtful whether Monro, Pinching and Inchbald would be capable of handling the work alone.

Following Casson's advice, Lady Brocklebank formed an in-house design committee with Cunard's Vice Chairman, Anthony Hume, and Dan Wallace. They began to assemble a diverse team of architects and designers to handle various parts of the ship. Casson suggested that, for starters, his friend Dennis Lennon would be a good choice. Soon the eclectic seven-strong interior design team included the progressive Jon Bannenberg, the society interior decorator David Hicks and the Austrian émigré designer Gaby Schreiber. It was hoped that this diverse group of architects and designers would give the liner's public rooms and cabins the necessary variety of atmospheres to stimulate and delight passengers – and to attract a broad clientele of various ages, social and cultural backgrounds.

The Design Team: July 1965

Dennis Lennon

First Class Restaurant
First Class Cocktail Bar
First Class Verandah Lounge
Cabin / Tourist Class Restaurant
Cabin Class Cocktail Lounge
Entrances / Stairways (including fronts of Purser's Offices and Shops etc.)

Michael Inchbald

First Class Grill Room and Bar
First Class Lounge
First Class Smoking Room

Jon Bannenberg

First Class Lido Lounge
First Class Library
First Class Indoor Pool
First / Cabin / Tourist Teenage Rooms

Jean Monro

Cabin Class Verandah Lounge
Cabin Class Lounge
Cabin Class Library
Casino

Gaby Schreiber

Tourist Class Cocktail Lounge
Tourist Class Verandah Lounge
Tourist Class Library
Conference Room

John Wright or David Hicks

Tourist Class Lounge
Evelyn Pinching
Tourist Class Observation Lounge
Tourist Class Indoor Pool
Unallocated Spaces
Shops
Children's Rooms and Beauty Parlours

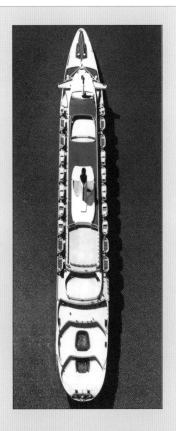

Various studies of Gardner's design for **Q4** including one before the final funnel design was established (middle right) and a balsawood studio model of the rear deck structure (bottom right). *(Author's collection)*

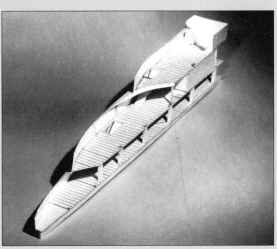

Monro, Schreiber, Inchbald, Lennon and Bannenberg were each asked to submit designs for two pairs of suiterooms (i.e. four cabins in all) while Bannenberg was given responsibility for First Class cabins leaving Cabin and Tourist Class room to Jean Monro or Evelyn Pinching

The Council of Industrial Design lobbied hard for progressive architects and designers to be more centrally involved and considered some of the designers selected by Lady Brocklebank were *"a pretty useless bunch of people."*

On 29 April 1965, Roy Mason, the Minister of Trade for Shipping in Harold Wilson's government, told the House of Commons that:

"Discussions between Cunard and the Council of Industrial Design are ongoing. The company is well aware of the government's concern that arrangements for supervising the interior design of the new ship should ensure that the result achieved will be of the highest possible standard. With this object in view, the President of the Board of Trade will continue to keep in the closest touch with the company and the Council of Industrial Design."

One month later a meeting between Lady Brocklebank, Dan Wallace and the Council of Industrial Design took place in Liverpool which would result in a new team being in place by October 1965.

Dennis Lennon

First Class Restaurant
First Class Cocktail Bar
First Class Verandah Lounge
Cabin / Tourist Class Restaurant
Cabin Class Cocktail Lounge
Entrances / Stairways (including fronts of Purser's Offices and Shops etc.)

Michael Inchbald

First Class Grill Room and Bar
First Class Lounge
First Class Smoking Room

Jon Bannenberg

First Class Lido Lounge
First Class Library
First Class Indoor Pool
First / Cabin / Tourist Teenage Rooms
First Class Staterooms

Jean Monro

Cabin Class Verandah Lounge
Cabin Class Lounge
Cabin Class Library
Casino
Cabin and Tourist Class Staterooms

Gaby Schreiber

Tourist Class Cocktail Lounge
Tourist Class Verandah Lounge
Tourist Class Library
Theatre

Conference Room

David Hicks

Tourist Class Lounge

Evelyn Pinching

Tourist Class Observation Lounge
Tourist Class Indoor Pool
Officers' and Crew Accommodation

Messrs. Tabb and Haslehurst were engaged by Cunard to assist the company and designers in the development of designs and to advise the designers regarding marine constructional methods, Lloyd's and Board of Trade Rules and general shipyard practice as well as work with the designers to stay to budget.

Unallocated Spaces

Shops
Children's Rooms
Beauty Parlours
Suiterooms

A month later, after suffering ill health, Sir John Brocklebank took early retirement in November 1965, aged only 50, and, with him, Lady Brocklebank withdrew her involvement in the design of Cunard's new flagship.

The new Cunard chairman, Sir Basil Smallpeice, brought to Cunard both a modern jet age approach to management and an appreciation of the importance of modern corporate design.

Shortly thereafter, Smallpeice invited James Gardner for afternoon tea at the Athenaeum, a gentleman's club in London's Pall Mall, which Gardner described as being *"a marble mausoleum watering hole where Establishment dinosaurs gather to sip port and fart gently after lunch."'*

Smallpeice wanted to find out about progress on Q4's above-the-waterline external styling and to discuss how the interiors might best be co-ordinated. Gardner, however, was frustrated by the interference and obstruction of Cunard's traditionalist Vice Chairman, Anthony Hume, and so he told Smallpeice of his irritation in no uncertain terms. Consequently, Hume was forcibly retired. As Smallpeice reassured Gardner at another meeting of the two in the Athenaeum, *"Don't concern yourself. When an executive reads of his retirement in The Times, it's a fait accompli."*

Meanwhile, the traditionalist interior decorators chosen by Lady Brocklebank - most notably Jean Monro and Evelyn Pinching – were sidelined and Dennis Lennon was effectively given overall control and those who survived the initial re-structuring of the design team were placed under stricter control.

Upon being appointed to mastermind Q4's interiors, Lennon faced two immediate challenges. Firstly, he instinctively believed that Q4 should be a two-class ship – and this went against the view of Cunard's directorate, which was still determined that there should be three classes. Secondly, Lennon had to persuade Dan Wallace that he should be taken seriously, as he correctly feared that the all-powerful naval architect would resent what might have been viewed as his 'interference' with the overall planning of the ship.

In a memo dated 23 December 1965 regarding arrangements for interior design on the New Cunarder, Sir Basil Smallpeice wrote:

"Time is already short if we are to complete the ship on schedule and, now that real progress can be hastened with the work of interior design, I think it desirable to define the procedure which it seems necessary for us to adopt as from the beginning of 1966.

"Mr A H Hume, a Deputy Chairman of the Company, is responsible to me for all our work as shipowners in connection with the construction of the ship, including control of costs, and he may be referred to at any time.

"Mr D N Wallace, as Naval Architect of the Company, is responsible for the ship as a structure and his requirements in that connection must be satisfied. Minor modifications are possible on some details, but can only be incorporated with his agreement.

"Mr Hume and Mr Wallace together with Lady Brocklebank, who is retained by Cunard as an adviser, constitute a point of reference within the Company with whom the Designers will consult from time to time.

"Lady Brocklebank will place at their disposal her intimate knowledge and understanding of our passengers, their interests and preferences during a voyage.

"I have now appointed Mr James Gardner and Mr Dennis Lennon as Joint Co-ordinators for the design and decoration throughout the ship. The aim is not only to make the fullest use of the talents of our different Designers but also to ensure that, while each area will have its own particular character, its treatment will be related to the whole, which must have a coherence and an overall character and style.

"Mr Gardner and Mr Lennon are jointly responsible for the overall visual character and design treatment and they must both be satisfied that the designs are satisfactory in this respect before they are submitted to the Company. They will, in fact, be responsible for recommending to the Company which design schemes should be accepted; responsibility for acceptance by the Company will rest with myself and the two Deputy Chairman, Mr A H Hume and Mr R H Senior.

"Mr Gardner is in particular responsible, with Mr Wallace, for the upper deck and exterior treatments.

"To enable Designers to visualise the ship as a whole, Mr Lennon's proposed treatments for the general circulation areas and the public rooms, for which his office is directly responsible, will be available at any time for the Designers to view, along with the work of the other Designers as it is developed.

"Mr Lennon will also make available from his own office the full-time services of Mr Gibbon for liaison with the Designers individually in matters of day-to-day detailing and progressing. He will be responsible for programming the design work in close collaboration with the Naval Architect and Messrs Tabb and Haslehurst.

"Messrs Tabb and Haslehurst have been engaged by the Company to provide, in conjunction with the Naval Architect, technical assistance and information to all Designers regarding marine constructional methods, Lloyd's and Board of Trade Rules, and general shipyard practice.

"Agreed standard components and samples of materials, all of which were possible must be of British manufacture, and other relevant information will be available at Mr Lennon's office for the Designers to view when considering the common interest.

"In laying down a formal co-ordinating machinery I am sure that Designers will appreciate the need for the ship to have an overall character. I would be grateful if they would, from now on, make their own personal arrangements with Mr Lennon's office when they wish to attend there."

Dennis Lennon (Interior Design Coordinator)

Grill Room and Grill Room Bar
Columbia Restaurant
Britannia Restaurant
Midships Lobby
Aft Lobby
Forward Lobby and Bureau
Theatre Bar
Upper Deck Library
Midships Bar
Promenade Spaces
Cabin Corridors, Connecting Hallways and Staircases
First Class Cabins
Tourist Class Cabins
Captain's Cabin
Crew Cabins

James Gardner

One Deck (Tourist Class) Swimming Pool

(Theo) Crosby / (Alan) Fletcher / (Colin) Forbes

The Look Out

Tony Heaton and Elizabeth Beloe

Coffee Shop
Children's Playroom

Stefan Buzas and Alan Irvine

Boat Deck Shopping Arcade
The London Gallery
736 Club
Two Deck First Class Suites

Jon Bannenberg

Double Room
Quarter Deck Card Room
Six Deck (first class) Indoor Swimming Pool
Seven Deck (tourist class) Indoor Swimming Pool
First Class Cabins

Gaby Schreiber

Theatre
Two Deck Suites aft of Midships Lobb
Conference Room

Michael Inchbald

Queens Room
Quarter Deck Library

David Hicks

Q4 Room

Professor Misha Black

Synagogue

Jo Patrick

Crew Accommodation
Crew Messes and Recreation Rooms
Hospital, Dental Surgery, Morgue

Lord Queensbury

Tableware

On 19 August 1964 Cunard invited the following shipyards to tender for *Q4*: John Brown and Co., Clydebank; Cammell Laird and Co., Birkenhead; the Fairfield Shipbuilding and Engineering Company, Glasgow; Harland and Wolf, Belfast; Swan, Hunter and Wigham Richardson, Wallsend-on-Tyne and Vickers-Armstrongs Shipbuilders, Wallsend.

The last two firms had formed a consortium to tender for *Q3* but as that was for a larger vessel it was initially felt they would tender alone for *Q4* but again joined forces to bid for the ship and they were considered the favourite for *Q4* given their success in potentially attracting *Q3*. But the John Brown yard was the most confident. Its order book was the least full of all the shipyards expected to tender and the disruption of *Q4* on Clydebank would be virtually non-existent. This confidence also stemmed from the long-association the yard had with Cunard which dated back to 1902 delivery of *Pannonia* and the fact they had built 15 ships, including *Lusitania, Aquitania* and the Queens, for the company since then.

The tender document Cunard issued to the yards on 9 September 1964 consisted of 550 closely-typed foolscap pages of plans and specifications for a centre-engined liner of nearly Queen length at 963 feet and of unprecedented height above the waterline. The drawings were accompanied by a model which showed a more slender hull that her predecessors, and a rather demure appearance due to her lack, at this stage, of a funnel. The companies would tender on the specifications. Their bids, as invited in the tender documents, including their own views on certain basic features of the deign such a speed, power and the number of propeller blades. Thus the 'owners' design' was supplemented by a 'builder's design' and an amalgam of these paper ships would form the basis of the building contract. The final price was to be Cunard's main consideration and the deadline for the shipyards was Monday 30 November.

In mid-October Cammell Laird advised Cunard that *"regretfully"* they would not be tendering for the new Cunarder. The yard's order book and delivery commitments were such that it could not commence work on the new ship until nearly a year later than the date necessary to meet Cunard's delivery requirements. The chairman and managing director pointed out that the yard had been successful in obtaining several new orders in 1964 including two Polaris submarines, one conventional submarine, a large tanker, a large bulk carrier, two ferries, three cargo liners and important conversion contracts and stated:

"Our decision is all the more regretful as we built the Mauretania in 1938 and at present we are working closely with Cunard in strengthening their North Atlantic cargo fleet by building three fast cargo liners for long-term charter to them."

A month later the Fairfield yard announced it was also dropping out of the competition stipulating its order book and commitments for not pursuing *Q4*. It had recently secured a large bulk carrier from the P&O Group and that would require its largest berth.

The main John Brown board met at The Sanctuary, John Brown's London office, to discuss and approve the terms of the quotation for *Q4*. Despite losing *Q3* there was an air of confidence within John Brown's given the Company's record of building many famous Cunarders. In consideration of the great prestige of the contract, it was agreed to cover full costs and full charges but include no profit, although this was kept secret at the time. The board felt that 'extras', by way of changes to the contract during construction, would ensure no loss. It was their view that the contract for this ship simply must be won.

The tender from Harland and Wolf arrived at Cunard's Liverpool Head Office on 28 November some 48 hours before the deadline. The next tender to arrive that day was from John Brown. Both the Clyde and Belfast yards had sent their tenders by messenger. The final tender was personally delivered by Sir John Hunter, Chairman of Swan Hunter, and George Houlden, Chairman of Vickers-Armstrong, to Sir John Brocklebank on 30 November.

On 30 November 1964 the tenders from the remaining three shipbuilders were opened. Since all three Builders were quoting a price based on detailed drawings and specification which were common to each and since there were only comparatively slight differences due to subcontracted items, weights and other technical information, it was considered that a decision as to which offer would be accepted should be based on (a) tender cost, (b) delivery date and (c) guaranteed power.

In order to simplify the work involved in assessing the tender the Builders were given a list of main subcontractors and instructed that were there was more than one subcontractor, the first-named should have been included in the tender price. They were asked to include with the tender a statement showing the variations in price for alternative contractors including – where necessary, subcontractors other than those in the Cunard Schedule and listed in the Machinery Specification. This procedure ensured that the basic tender price of the ship included the same subcontractors and therefore variations due to accepting an alternative subcontractor would be easily assessed since they would be reasonably common to all three Builders. There was no restriction in the competitive element by adopting this practice since it was known that the subcontractor's price to the Builders never varied greatly, although occasionally there was a slight disadvantage to a yard such as Harland & Wolff where an extra was indicated because of the additional transport.

When the tenders were received, all three Builders

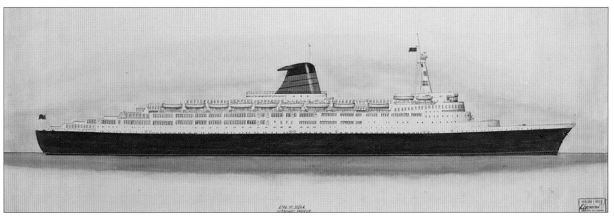

Harland & Wolff's proposed profile for *Q4* as contained in their tender submission. *(Author's collection)*

enclosed a Schedule showing that their price was based on the Cunard specified contractors, except in a few cases. Harland & Wolff did not indicate the variations due to using alternative subcontractors but for the purpose of assessment it was assumed that the variations shown by the other two Builders would apply. Vickers Armstrong Swan Hunter stated that five hull items in their price were not in accordance with the Cunard specified contractor and inspection of John Brown & Company's Schedule showed that they had also departed from the Cunard Schedule in five cases (two of which were the same as the Tyne yard) because they considered that the quotations received did not comply with the Cunard Hull specification. Examination of the variations indicated that the only departure from the specified list which would make an appreciable difference in cost was that the lifeboats included by John Brown did not comply with the Cunard specification and should have had about £50,000 added to their tender price to be comparable to Vickers Armstrong Swan Hunter.

Where alternative subcontractors or alternative proposals indicated a possible variation in price, a detailed examination was made. This examination showed that in many cases the subcontractors had departed considerably from the Cunard Specification but for the purpose of the tender assessment this was ignored.

On weight the Builders were provided with detailed drawings and specifications and were required to quote their price based exactly on this information. This ensured that they could not quite a lower price by allowing for a lower standard than their competitors. They were instructed to submit alternative technical proposals which would reduce costs, weight or shaft horsepower.

The Builders were not asked to produce a design for the layout of the vessel since this had been prepared by Cunard based on their own specialised knowledge.

They were also required to submit a Schedule showing estimated weights, centre of gravity, estimated horsepower etc. All three estimates of weights and centre of gravity were in reasonably close agreement, the only important difference being the Tyne yard estimate of centre of gravity was 2.4' lower than the Clyde yard. The Cunard and Harland & Wolff estimates were midway between these.

A comparison of the main features of the tenders

	John Brown	Vickers / Swan	Harland & Wolff
Tender Cost	£21,677,000	£22,547,428	£23,825,000
Hull	£16,431,000	£16,904,648	£17,765,000
Machinery	£5,246,000	£5,642,786	£6,060,000
Delivery Date	May 1968	October 1968*	end 1968
Lightweight	36,950 tons	36,650 tons	37,800 tons
Vertical Centre of Gravity	50.2 feet	47.80 feet	49 feet
Guaranteed Power			
for Service Speed	96,000 SHP	96,500 SHP	100,000 SHP
Charges for extras	33% Hull and	60% Hull Labour	To be agreed at a later date
Elec. on wages	55% Machinery on wages	95% Machinery Labour	
	5% on total added cost (material and labour)	Material Hull 5% Eng. 5%	

*(subject to contract being awarded by the end of January 1965)

Cunard employee Ronald Marshbank guarding the plans and specifications for **Q4** prior to them to be issued to the shipyards, Wednesday 9 September 1964. *(Author's collection)*

Since detailed arrangement drawings, midship section and specification had been provided, it was felt that the variation was due to differences in estimates and not to any improvement in construction of design. The methods by which Vickers Armstrong Swan Hunter estimates had been prepared were known to Cunard since Vickers had assisted in the preliminary design study. It was Cunard's opinion that the Vickers Armstrong Swan Hunter estimate was slightly on the low side, even allowing for their obvious advantage in having recently built *Oriana* with an aluminium superstructure. On the other hand, it was known, after discussion with John Brown's, that their estimates were slightly on the high side. For this reason it was felt that this was not a competitive factor but served to indicate that Cunard's own estimate of weight and centre of gravity had been confirmed.

The Vickers tender letter mentioned various methods of reducing weights and costs, some of which Cunard were already aware of and some were not considered acceptable. For example they proposed certain scantlings shown on the midship section could be reduced but Cunard had in the original design allowed these as margin to be deleted when more detailed information was obtained regarding the bending moment. The Vickers tender also proposed the re-allocation of oil fuel distribution with a view to reducing stress and this was also regarded by Cunard as not being a practicable proposition taking into account the various sailing conditions.

The three Builders were provided with a Body Plan which had been prepared for Cunard by the National Physical Laboratory at Feltham. The tender letter specified that the Builders should guarantee the power based on this plan and also to submit – should they so desire – an alternative form if this would allow them to guarantee a lower power for the same speed. Both John Brown and Vickers Armstrong Swan Hunter submitted alternative forms and were prepared to guarantee a shaft horsepower for their form lower than that specified in the invitation to tender.

The Builders were asked to include in their tender a statement of charges for modifications to the contract, particularly for additional work. The Tyne yard quoted charges higher than John Brown while Harland & Wolff stated these charges would be agreed at a later date.

The shipyards had been asked to quote a fixed price but all three stated that particularly due to the long building period they were unable to do so. At the time it was difficult to obtain fixed prices from the shipbuilders for any type of ship. John Brown did indicate that their price allowed for a very recent increase in Joiners' wages and allowed for the forthcoming increase in National Insurance contributions. Cunard assumed the latter would increase the price offered by the other two yards. Likewise there was no penalty clause for late delivery of the ship – this had been discussed during the preparation of the tender for *Q3* when all the available builders indicated that they would not accept any penalty clause.

John Brown's price was the lowest (£870,000 less than Vickers and £2,148,000 less than Harland & Wolff) and its delivery date, of May 1968, the earliest. However, Sir John Brocklebank and his staff were shocked to note that all three tenders were in excess of the £22 million set aside for the ship.

None of the Builders was willing to quote a guaranteed delivery date but Cunard favoured John Brown's May 1968 for the obvious reason that the ship would be in service in time for the important summer season and an investigation was undertaken which underlined the financial advantage to Cunard of having the new ship in service in time for summer. Cunard's past experience with the Clyde yard was that it had an exceptionally good record for maintaining delivery dates and the company saw no reason why the yard should not deliver on time in this case and the fact it was already building a passenger ship for Swedish America Line was an asset as the team built for that ship could be transferred to the Cunard vessel.

Since Harland & Wolff quoted the highest price and the latest delivery date and no guaranteed reduction in power further consideration of their tender was eliminated at an early stage in the assessment.

John Brown's offer was the best, their earlier delivery date was more favourable and terms for overheads etc. were also more acceptable but its price was still £2 million more than Cunard had estimated the cost of a new vessel would be.

On receipt of the tenders there were several urgent meetings with Cunard management adamant that *Q4* was still too expensive and may have to be cancelled. The problem for management was that the ageing Queens would soon need to be taken out of commission which would leave *Caronia* and the four Canadian ships in service with the result being a severe reduction in staff.

John Brown was advised that their tender was the lowest but that the price would have to be cut down further before a contract could be signed. Cunard asked the yard to reduce the cost of the ship by approximately £1.5 million. To qualify in time and obtain the benefits of the loan under the government's Shipbuilding Credit Scheme it would be necessary for the ship to be paid for before 31 December 1964. That meant that within a period of two weeks the building agreement had to be prepared, agreed and signed. It

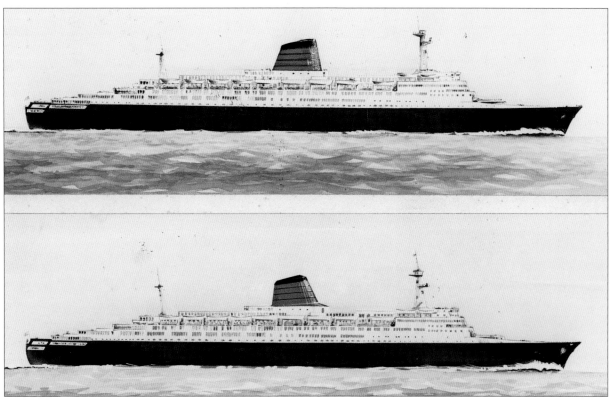

Two proposed profiles for *Q4* developed by Vickers and Swan Hunter and contained in their tender submission. *(Author's collection)*

was essential that the final figure be reached quickly.

A team of Cunard personnel, led by Dan Wallace and Tom Kameen, went to Clydebank to meet with John Starks, John Brown's Technical Director, and George Strachan, the Director of the Engine Department. Over the course of several days, with beer and sandwiches at weekends, the cuts were made. Wallace would later refer to an *"extremely hectic seven or eight days."*

The whole tender was studied again and again and suppliers were asked to re-submit prices based on amended tenders. Even things such as the reduction in specification requirements for cabin furnishing (saving £62,000) to using white instead of colour sanitary units in passenger cabins (saving £9,000) were incorporated.

On 13 December 1964 a list detailing the most significant deletions and alterations was produced.

Perhaps the most significant deletion was one of the boilers which was removed to also save weight and space. The new ship was originally to have had four boilers which could maintain full service speed with only three of these in use, allowing one to be shut down for maintenance without serious loss of headway. The deletion of the fourth boiler would prove to be a false economy as the lack of spare boiler capacity would seriously compromise the liner's reliable operation in service as a steam ship as well as curtail maintenance possibilities.

	Saving (£)
• Stern anchor.	
• The sliding roof on the Sports Deck.	27,300
• A set of stabilizers (four fins instead of six).	43,420
• One auto tensioning winch.	8,000

• Cathodic Protection.	6,600
• Two aft cranes.	32,000
• The aft MacGregor hatch and trunk.	27,000
• The aft lateral thrust units.	46,000
• Mental Ward and Mortuary.	1,600
• Verandah Grill from funnel base	35,000
• Fur Store.	2,000
• Breakwater.	1,000
• Six lifts.	40,500
• Two gangway handling winches.	1,700
• Special cruising gangways.	500
• Twin boiler casings.	3,500
• Insulation in the way of the steam pipe passage.	

Alterations

• The cruise launches were modified.	
• The forward cranes to be Stothert & Pitt.	
• The boat davits to be steel in lieu of aluminium.	69,000
• Omit the painting of aluminium behind the Linings.	12,000
• Enamel beds for crew instead of aluminium.	10,000
• The relocation of insulated cargo from aft to forward.	1,000
• The Boiler Seatings were reduced in number.	

The men were also able to re-arrange the ship by pointing out anomalies in the passenger departments' requirements

Sir John Brocklebank (left) and Lord Aberconway sign the building contract for Q4, Wednesday 30 December 1964. *(Author's collection)*

regarding Pullman berths etc. and this secured berth for an additional 200 Tourist Class passengers by deleting the after-hatch trunk, deleting the steam pipe passage and reducing crew numbers.

In total the machinery (main and auxiliary) costs were reduced by £580,820 and the hull and electrical price by £1,012,920.

When it was decided that it would be possible to fit three boilers instead of four it was realized that this would enable the Engine Toom and Boiler Room to be arranged adjacent to each other due to the fact that the Boiler Room length was now reduced (in the September 1964 design this was not possible since the combined length of the Engine Room and Boiler Room exceeded the length which could be allowed in the side damage calculations). This re-arrangement of machinery space required less volume and consequently the arrangement of tanks, evaporators, refrigerated machinery etc. was revised. This in turn reduced the bending moment of the vessel and finally led to a slight reduction in scantlings.

While reducing costs and improving stability there was a reduction in the lengths of the superstructure which involved

The senior management of Cunard and John Brown (Clydebank) gather at the Bank of England for the contract signing. John Rannie is standing second from right. *(Author's collection)*

the elimination of the Verandah Grill below the funnel, the lowering of the Wheelhouse and a slight reduction in the lengths of the remaining superstructure. The Verandah Grill was transferred to an area adjoining the main First Class Restaurant with a consequent reduction in the Verandah Grill kitchen space.

Some items, such as the stern anchor (reinstated in September 1967 at a cost of £25,000) and the Mortuary would be reinstated.

On 18 December Cunard wrote to the Board of Trade:

"With reference to our recent meeting with the Minister of State regarding the tenders received from the three Shipbuilders, it is our considered opinion that the most favourable tender if that received from John Brown & Co. (Clydebank) Limited.

"Our opinion stems not only from the fact that their tender provides the lowest cost but also the earlier delivery date offered. This is of considerable significance as the peak Atlantic passenger movement arises in the summer months and the earlier in the year the ship is delivered the greater the share of this peak traffic which the ship will attract.

"As you are aware, subsequent to receipt of the tenders we have been considering certain modifications in design. As these modifications would be common to all those Builders, we are satisfied from the replies received that the price advantage in John Brown & Co. (Clydebank) Limited's tender would not be materially affected.

"We are at present engaged in considerable negotiations regarding the financing of the construction and it would be of great assistance f we could have the consent of the Minister to John Brown & Co. (Clydebank) Limited being invited to take part in these discussions without prejudice and his confirmation that, assuming the negotiations are brought to a successful conclusion, he will approve of the order being placed with John Brown & Co. (Clydebank) Limited."

Just after 1500 hours on 30 December 1964 Lord Aberconway and Sir John Brocklebank signed the contract for *Q4* – the biggest passenger ship contract ever clinched in Britain. The contract was signed within the solid walls of the Bank of England. Sir John had telephone the unsuccessful yards earlier that morning to advise them of the company's decision. Both owner and shipyard were in a race against the clock because of the Government decision to implement a Corporation Tax, fated from 1965 and payable on 1 January 1966. The new ship would be the third largest ocean liner ever built in Britain – a position *QE2* holds to this day after *Queen Elizabeth* and *Queen Mary*.

When the news broke on the Clyde, church bells rang out and there was much jubilation in the yard and on the Clyde as work for a large number of people on the world's most prestigious shipbuilding contract had been secured for three years. Cunard, too, was delighted that the old partnership was in business once again. Tom Kameen recalls that John Brown's was held in very high regard by Cunard, based, partly, on the technical excellence of the two original Queens and, partly, on the *"terrific support and assistance given to Cunard in running their fleet."*

Lord Aberconway:

Shipyard workers celebrate and cheer the announcement that the contract had been signed. *(Author's collection)*

"Clydeside will have its happiest Hogmanay for years. There will be no need to lay on a special celebration."

Immediately the news was flashed around the world to the whole fleet of Cunard ships at sea in the form of a personal message from Sir John Brocklebank:

"This confirms our intention to stay in the forefront of the North Atlantic trade. This ship will be the match of any foreseeable competitor and of any cruising liner.

"I am sure that we will be proud of a ship which will not only be profitable to the company but will also be a credit to Britain."

Although Cunard stated they had not made any arrangements to name the liner pressure was mounting from America for a 'Queen' name while Princess Anne was the favourite in England.

The Daily Express, said: *"One suggestion: Queen Victoria. Another suggestion: Jacqueline Kennedy. Best Bet: Princess Anne."*

Two newspapers launched 'name the ship' competitions with the Manchester Evening News asking its readers to express pride in Britain and in the new ship and the Sunday Express offering a £100 prize for the most apt and original name and a slogan of not more than nine words to persuade people to travel by sea.

In less than an hour Cunard were already receiving bookings for the new liner; 100 people, mainly Americans, registered on 30 December.

As required by the provisions of the loan agreement under the Government Shipbuilding Credit Scheme, approval of the Government was obtained to the contract. Finance to cover the construction period was arranged in the City of London by Finance Corporation for Industry Limited and a consortium of 11 clearing banks and the five Scottish banks led by Glyn Mills & Co. and Ship Mortgage Finance Co. Ltd.

Rather than the last gasp of a dying mode of transport Cunard saw their new ship as the next step in the evolution of design and usage. Cunard was going cruising but, in December 1964, no one could have foreseen the troubles and struggle that lay ahead.

On Tuesday 4 April 1967 Cunard unveiled **Q4** for the first time simultaneously on both sides of the Atlantic - at the Royal Festival Hall in London and in the Main Lounge on Queen Mary in New York (shown here). *(Author's collection)*

CHAPTER THREE

736: Keel laying to launch

The shipyard's order book number for the new Cunarder was No. 736 and the ship would be known as 736, *Q4* or the "New Cunarder" until, in time honoured fashion, her name would be revealed at the launch which was set for April 1967.

During January 1965, a new General Arrangement plan, embodying the various economies and changes in passenger accommodation, was developed. This work would continue for the first six months of 1965 but progress in the drawing office was rather slow. Sir John Brocklebank revealed that the new liner would require only three main boilers and that remote control would be extensively employed and temperature and humidity in all parts of the ship would be controlled automatically. The use of light alloys and the inclusion of water distillation equipment were other features mentioned by Sir John.

In a report written early in 1965, Lord Aberconway noted that:

"The winning of the order for the large new Cunarder at the end of December last was a great triumph, and a fitting reward for the hard work put into the project and tender by our management and staff. We are particularly proud that our offer was accepted and the contract signed only thirty days after we submitted the tender. We have long experience of the fine co-operation that we know we shall continue to receive from Cunard and with this we are confident that the ship will be a worthy product of British design and workmanship."

A huge amount of work was undertaken in terms of calculations, drawings, estimates and planning and the numerous network charts were developed. These were designed to avoid hold-ups and would show in numerical and time form what job had to be done, in which order and when. Time was of the essence and a tight organisation was crucial to the financial success of the project from the standpoint of both shipyard and shipowner. Much of the material required was ordered in advance and organisation was greatly assisted by the ability of computers to keep track of the whereabouts and status of such things as the 100,000 different pieces of pipe the ship would need. A workshop for the preparation of the aluminium plates was specially built with a floor that was treated with a special sealant to prevent any foreign particles affecting the metal.

During 1965, other substantial contracts were booked, or in progress, at Clydebank. These included the 12,000 ton cargo liner *Glenfinlas* for the Glen Line, the 18,000 ton bulk carrier *Cape St Vincent* for charter to Lyle Shipping Co., and the partial conversion of the *Queen Elizabeth* for cruising, to be carried out during 1966. The latter contract enabled continuity of employment to be maintained for finishing trades after the departure of the *Kungsholm*. Additionally, three jack-up drilling rigs for the North Sea were ordered by International Drilling Co. Ltd, the first North Sea orders to be placed with any shipbuilder in the UK. Work in hand included *Kungsholm*, the lumber carrier Vennachar, the assault ship Intrepid, the partial conversion of the intermediate liner *Sylvania* and a second 70,000ton tanker for BP, *British Confidence*.

Kungsholm was launched on 15 April 1965 and taken the short distance to the basin for fitting out to begin. The late arrival of drawings for the *Intrepid* delayed her completion which meant that both vessels were now in contention for the limited number of men of the finishing trades, a position which management had sought to avoid in their original production schedules. Much to the irritation of the Royal Navy overseer at Clydebank, more men were put on *Kungsholm* than on the assault ship. Given the penalties for late delivery on the liner, there was a simple and compelling logic behind this. The Navy could wait. At the same time, the yard was hit by a rash of disputes and the completion of *Kungsholm* was subjected to no fewer than eight stoppages by finishing trades, principally plumbers and electricians

The effect of this was to delay *Kungsholm*'s delivery until 11 March 1966, resulting in significant penalty payments. More importantly, the actual cost of building the ship had risen out of all proportion to the original tender of only a few years earlier. By January 1966, the loss on *Kungsholm*, excluding penalties, was a staggering £2,474,000 and the yard had no option but to swallow this bitter pill. At the end of the contract, losses had accelerated beyond £3 million. but Clydebank produced a magnificent ship and the Swedish American Line was delighted with the ship they received.

In 1965, a number of events occurred that would have repercussions up and down the Clyde and beyond. At the beginning of that year, government concerns over the future of shipbuilding in Britain prompted Roy Mason, Minister of State for Shipping, to lead a fact finding delegation to Japan, now the world's largest and most successful shipbuilder. He visited eight yards and had discussions with the Japanese Shipbuilders Association. The short report published as a result of this visit listed points that suggested why the Japanese industry was so successful: a permanent labour force organised in one shipyard union, paid at marginally lower rates than in the UK; a management structure which contained large numbers of men at middle management level with control of individual shops; a middle management was invariably technically qualified graduates with practical experience in the work for which they were responsible; the widespread use of planning and production control techniques and of computers in these fields as well as in ship design and in every case where facilities were being

In his book 'Destiny's Daughter: the tragedy of RMS *Queen Elizabeth*, Russell Galbraith wrote: Sir Basil Smallpeice thought it would be wrong to look upon the new Cunarder as the last of a great line of passenger transport vehicles. He wanted people to think of the **QE2** as the first of a line of great ships which would be engaged in the floating hotel or resort business. This way Cunard could look forward to a prosperous future instead of facing the bleak prospect of scraping a living in the last decade or two of passenger sea transport. *"It is only when we fully grasp the significance of the altered role of passenger shipping in an air-dominated world that we see the dawn of hope for the future"*, Sir Basil argued. *(Author's collection)*

extended, construction docks in preference to slipways.

It was against this background of concern for the industry that the President of the Board of Trade, Douglas Jay, set up the Shipbuilding Inquiry Committee in February 1965, under the chairmanship of Reay Geddes. The Geddes Committee was given one year in which to report on the changes necessary to restore the British shipbuilding and marine engineering industries to prosperity.

On 1 June Sir John Brocklebank revealed a contract price of £25,427,000 for the new liner, which had been paid in advance to get the benefit of *"substantial investment allowances."*

By the end of June 1965 the shipyard had developed a monthly steel erection programme, including a construction schedule for the various trades concerned in the building of units for the double bottom, oil tanks, decks and side shell were in progress and over 1,000 tons of steel had been delivered to the shipyard.

Cunard had to design a ship that used more power for each propeller than any other passenger liner afloat. The difficulty was not in making sufficiently powerful engines but in absorbing that power efficiently. It was done by taking advantage of all the recent work on the design of propellers and using, for the first time on a passenger liner, propellers with six blades instead of the more usual four. Some naval ships did use even more power per propeller but only for short bursts whereas Q4 would have to run at full power all the time. An exhaustive series of resistance and propulsion tests, involving four and six bladed propellers, had been carried out at the Clydebank Experimental Tank and at the Ship Division of the National Physical Laboratory. The latter had also been involved in extensive maneuverability trials in proving the aft underwater hull form. Cavitation tests on models of the propellers were to be carried out shortly at Newcastle University. Vibration studies had been carried out in conjunction with the British Ship Research Association (B.S.R.A), N.P.L and Pametrada.

A model of the liner, complete with superstructure, had been built for testing in the National Physical Laboratory wind tunnel. These tests would assist in determining the optimum shape and height of the funnel to ensure that exhaust gases would be carried well clear of the decks.

Planning would be crucial to ensure onetime delivery. 3,000 men would work on the construction of the new Cunarder – a figure that would increase by another 500 at the peak fitting-out period. Each stage of the building was phased into cardinal dates from the laying of the keel to the final handing over. A skeleton programme with a few fundamental details was initially established. Time, labour, materials, equipment, delivery dates and costs would then be integrated into a grand plan from which the ship would take shape. Monthly targets would be fixed, many items such as 1½ million feet of Formica and units ordered from suppliers, long delivery dates fixed for major items such as main engines and turbo-alternators. Labour resources and materials had to be related to avoid snags and delays. A computer would analyze the number of men required at any given time for a particular job while forecasting progress.

This advanced computer complex was put into action by the shipyard in a completely new technique to keep check on the cost and progress if the new Cunarder at any stage of its

construction. The system would provide information to enable spot checks to be made at any stage of the contract and an accurate cost assessment - all at a glance in the records from the computer. All the key departments where calculations had to be progressively applied – estimating, planning, buying, production, assessment, costing and budget control – were co-ordinated in the vast network.

The liner was broken down into 64 blocks each of which was handled as if it were a small ship on its own. There would be 150,000 pipes in the new Cunarder, each one of which would go through five stages – drawing, manufacture, fitting on board, attachment of valves and testing – and the computer would keep track of each pipe.

On 15 June it was announced that the keel for No. 736 was due to be laid on Friday 2 July 1965 at 1000 hours just two days before the 125th anniversary of the Maiden Voyage of Britannia, Cunard's first ship, from Liverpool to Boston, on 4 July 1840.

The keel for Cunard's 172nd ship was to be laid on a short length of wooden blocks on No.4 slipway in the East Yard of John Brown and Co, the same slipway that Queen Mary and Queen Elizabeth and a host of many other famous Cunarders had been built. The blocks consisted of six baulks of timber placed horizontally at right angles to, and erected level with, the top of the blocks. To one side of the building blocks a prefabricated section of the new ship's keel. This consisted of three 60-ton sections that, in total, would weigh 180-tons, be 117-feet long, 23 feet wide and 6 feet 3 inches high.

It had been decided that the prefabricated section being built in the workshops should weigh forty tons. This would be within the combined lifting capabilities of two tower cranes adjoining the slip, with the aid of a powerful winch fixed to the concrete base of a long gone derrick crane, would lift and pull the keel section into place.

A rehearsal of the ceremony on the Wednesday evening before had gone very well but this was not the case on 2 July.

Lady Aberconway, the wife of John Brown's Chairman, had agreed to perform the ceremony, scheduled to take place at 1000 hours, in front of several press and television cameramen and about 30 journalists from London and Glasgow who had been invited along to witness the occasion. Also present was Lord Aberconway and Sir John and Lady Brocklebank. Sir John Brocklebank said:

"This is a very proud day for the Cunard Line and for the British shipping and shipbuilding industry. It is particularly appropriate that we should be laying the keel of the 172nd Cunarder which will be the largest passenger ship built in Britain since the Queen Elizabeth, only two days before we celebrate our 125th anniversary. And it is equally appropriate that it should be taking place here in John Brown's shipyard, the birthplace of the conspicuously successful Queens.

"In fact, she will be the first large British ship to be planned and designed from the start to capture the cream of the North Atlantic trade in the season and the cream of the cruise market in the winter.

"The final result, we are sure, will be a ship to match any foreseeable competitor, attractive to passengers and an economically sound investment."

Above: Lord Aberconway and Sir John Brocklebank, accompanied by their wives, inspecting the keel before the planned Keel Laying Ceremony, Friday 2 July 1965.

Middle: Sir John Brocklebank (left) and Lord Aberconway in front of the keel block, Friday 2 July 1965.

Below: The keel block is finally hoisted into place, Monday 5 July 1965.

(All photographs author's collection)

The keel for **Q4** in position on Slipway No. 4 with the **Kungsholm** fitting out behind it. *(Author's collection)*

Sir John confirmed that the new liner would be launched in 1967 and that she would in service in the spring of 1968 and that even at that stage the company had received more than 2,000 applications for accommodation on her Maiden Voyage. Cunard claimed this was how well the liner had captured the public imagination and augured well for her future. The company also claimed that had received "thousands" of suggestions for names from the public and two former Cunard liner names – Aquitania and Berengaria were mentioned as strong possibilities.

Sir John claimed she was a "fresh concept ship" and stressed:

"…she is far from being a scaled-down Queen liner. She will be different from anything that has gone before, not in the sense that she will contain innovations for innovation's sake, but because her design concept looks ahead into the 1970s and beyond."

At the appointed time the cranes took the strain of the steel section and the winch commenced to take in the slack on the wire cables. Unfortunately the cranes were designed to lift their maximum load of 20 tons each in a vertical direction and not at the angle induced by the pull on the winch.

After moving slightly the keel section refused to move any further which placed an enormous strain on the winch. Consequently, as the winch continued to pull in its cable, the concrete blocks used for anchoring the lifting tackle began to shift when the strain was applied. It was thought a spell of dry weather had dried the earth and was the cause of the trouble. A steel hawser was secured to the concrete blocks in the ground and was being used to slide the section into

place. As the strain was taken by one of the cranes, the keel section refused to move and instead the anchor blocks began to lift. Shipyard officials hurriedly arranged for the lifting tackle to be secured to another block and to the base of one of the cranes. This time, when the strain was applied, the keel section lurched several inches at one end.

The ceremony thus came to a hasty and slightly undignified halt and the journalists were quickly ushered into the Model Room where they were liberally entertained. Fortunately press coverage was sympathetic.

The keel section was move quietly into position onto the building blocks on Monday 5 July, by a carefully chosen gang of men who had delayed their start of the local 'Clydebank Fair'; the shipyard was normally closed-down during the fortnight of this annual holiday. Later that day Sir John would send the following to all ship's Captains:

"Actual keel-laying at Clydebank today deferred for two weeks because of technical hitch with crane but ceremony carried out today as planned. This event brings nearer the day when this great and forward-looking ship will join our fleet which we are all keenly anticipating. I am confident today's news will be stimulating to your whole ship's company."

Dan Wallace would later put the Keel Laying problems down to *"builders inefficiency."* Interestingly the shipyard would still use 2 July as the official Keel Laying date for the ship.

Just four months after the keel laying one of Britain's foremost shipbuilders, the Fairfield Shipbuilding & Engineering Co Ltd, collapsed despite a £34 million order book. The Fairfield yard had been Clydebank's great rival during the late nineteenth century, while both yards were considered to be the most important on the upper reaches of the river. The failure of this leading yard added momentum to government efforts to find a remedy for the increasing problems bedevilling British shipbuilding.

On 8 November 1965 Sir John Brocklebank resigned as Chairman of Cunard citing "ill health" (he had been severely troubled by a leg complaint):

"When Colonel Denis Bates died suddenly in 1959, the Board asked me to succeed him in the Chair. I have seen the Company through to a point where a decision has been taken and terms have been agreed for the building of the New Cunarder, but I have been away through illness for several months this year and realise that, if I am to avoid a repetition of this, I must take things much more easily in future. This is quite impossible in the Chairmanship of a company of this size and importance, and so I have decided that the right thing for me to so is resign."

Sir John had approached Sir Basil Smallpeice about taking over the Chairmanship about two weeks earlier. This was a big decision for Sir John as it would be the first time that the chair had been offered to someone outside the Liverpool shipowning families and it severed a direct Brocklebank connection with shipping that had stretched back 200 years.

Sir Basil had left BOAC as Managing Director in 1963 after 13 years with the airline and Cunard, already familiar with him thanks to the BOAC-Cunard venture was quick to approach him initially in December that year but he did not join the Cunard Board until April 1964 with responsibility for Cunard's London operation with a trip to Liverpool once a week for management and board meetings. When Bill Donald retired as Deputy Chairman in June 1965 Sir Basil was offered that position. On the retirement of Sir John Brocklebank he was appointed Chairman.

Now Sir Basil's biggest challenge was the successful construction, delivery and entry into service of the new ship – a ship many were already saying was a huge gamble and a *"white elephant"* that would probably have to be laid up after six months in service. But Sir Basil also had to fix Cunard and before that new ship even finally appeared the company would have to go through a prolonged and difficult period of *"do or die."*

At this time the Cunard passenger fleet consisted of the *Queen Elizabeth*, the largest passenger ship in the world (a distinction she would hold until the introduction of the Carnival Destiny in 1996), the *Queen Mary*, the Caronia (the 'Green Goddess'), the *Mauretania* (her withdrawal from service in November 1965 had already been announced), the *Carmania* (formerly the *Saxonia*), the *Franconia* (formerly the *Ivernia*), the *Carinthia* and the *Sylvania*.

Sir Basil firmly believed that Cunard was *"fighting for its life"* and could only survive and flourish by *"selling floating holidays instead of just a form of transport."* He was committed to his mission to *"save Cunard, not only for its stockholders but even more for the sake of those who worked in it."* His challenge was a daunting one as Cunard's total volume of business had remained static for the previous ten years or so and between 1961 and 1964 the company's

passenger business had lost £16 million

With regard to the new ship, one of his first moves, after consultation with the Council of Industrial Design, was to appoint James Gardner and Dennis Lennon as the design coordinators for the project.

On 17 December 1965 Sir Basil attended the monthly progress meeting as Cunard was concerned with the slow progress but the builders still maintained that their estimated launch date would be April 1967. In their defence of the slow progress John Brown also intimated that *Q4* progress was always going to be slow at this time due to other work in the yard.

It is interesting to note that from December 1965 to March 1966 *Queen Elizabeth*, undergoing a £1.5 million refit handled by John Brown & Co (Clydebank) Limited, would be on Clyde at Greenock just 18 miles away from the shipyard and her future namesake and replacement.

Throughout the first six months of 1966 Cunard continually raised their concerns that while good progress was being made in the drawing office the steelwork progress was disappointing.

The Geddes Report was published in March 1966 and this recommended the creation of large shipbuilding groups on Britain's main shipbuilding rivers and districts. Rationalisation was implicit. The theory was that, through merger, shipbuilding firms would reduce costs by directing resources - such as marketing, design, purchasing, personnel, training, and management services - via one organisation. The report did not subscribe to the view that large building docks were necessarily the way forward, commenting that improvements in industrial relations might, on their own, be more useful. Thus, John Brown's scheme for a super yard would not be supported. With government finance to back the report's recommendations, merger discussions began on the basis that a large shipbuilding group would be formed on the upper reaches of the Clyde. In one scheme under discussion, employment in the group would be reduced from 13,000 to 7,500. Understandably, the trade unions and the workforce generally viewed these events with considerable concern.

A result of the Geddes Report would be the name John Brown disappearing from shipbuilding with the yard becoming part of the Upper Clyde Shipbuilders group from January 1968. In the midst of these discussions, the hull and superstructure of *Q4* continued to take shape.

During his frequent visits to Clydebank, James Gardner wryly observed the severe conditions of shipyard life there, which had not changed significantly since the early twentieth century:

"'Through the spiked shipyard gates - another world. Teams of tough Glaswegians… treat the game of 'workers-v-bosses' as they would knock-out football and… a man who becomes worn out is replaced by his son. Visitors who are not 'shipmen' are considered twerps and discouraged – and that goes for pale-faced intruders from down south…"

Gardner was, however, impressed by the skill and organisation of the yard:

"While the smooth-sided hull was slowly growing on the slipway, it was starting to see a chunk of superstructure,

Building work in September 1965. *(Author's collection)*

larger than a house, swing from a giant crane, to be wielded neatly into place. Delicate lines drawn with a 2H pencil became muscular men fighting the stiff resistance of steel. At one point, where the observation deck swept in forward of the bridge, there was, what John Brown's chief draughtsman termed, a 'discrepancy.' A tapered section of steel plate sailed two feet outboard when it should have met another plate in an uninterrupted curve. "What the hell are you going to do about that?' I asked. Then I forgot about it. Why? The tough gang had sprung that heavy plate inboard and then welded it for good. Not a kink, yet sufficient tension there to knock a bus over."

Private discussions between Cunard and the shipyard in March 1966 had concluded that the new liner was already six months behind schedule – the shortage of steel workers in the Clyde area being primarily responsible for the delay.

The Board of John Brown's met in mid-April and Cunard was advised that the launch was now scheduled for September 1967 and delivery in November 1968 – some six months delay in both cases.

By May the situation regarding the delay had worsened:

JOHN BROWN REASONS FOR DELAY

John Brown: The completion date quoted in November 1964 was based on the clear understanding that the design and arrangements of the ship were reasonably fixed and final. When, in December 1964, the need for many amendments was raised by Cunard, Clydebank emphasised the necessity for prompt action to avoid delay in construction.

Cunard Response: Agree. Due to the change in General Arrangement it was accepted by both sides that a combined supreme effort, backed by complete mutual trust, was essential to ensure that rapid progress would be made.

John Brown: The amendments and rearrangements have, in a number and in magnitude; far exceeded those visualized when the contract was signed. Since then 16 months have passed as compared with the six envisaged above

Cunard: Completely disagree. At examination of the General Arrangements dated 13 December 1964 (which had

been hastily prepared by us since receipt of the Tenders on 30 November) shows that our revised requirements were known at the time of signing the contract.

John Brown: The Drawing Office work involved in dealing with the rearrangement of the ship has seriously delayed the production of working plans, on which little progress can be made until the arrangements are made final.

Cunard: Disagree that the Drawing Office have been involved in dealing with rearrangements. It was always our policy to ensure that development of the General Arrangements would not delay structure.

John Brown: The work involved in the changes has proved far in excess of what either side visualized; and despite intensive efforts both by the Cunard technical officers and by the Clydebank staff, the plans of the ship are broadly six months behind what was originally foreseen. This period cannot be recovered

Cunard: Completely disagree. Most of the changes in design were apparent when the contract was signed and it is ridiculous to state that the plans are six months behind.

John Brown: The repositioning and rearrangements for the main and auxiliary machinery seriously affected steelwork plans and it took about six months to finalise the size and positions of associated tanks, seatings, casings and trunking with consequent delay in producing the accommodation plans.

Cunard: The rearrangements of machinery spaces was known in 1964 and naturally caused some additional work.

John Brown: The projected programme for public rooms has not been maintained. There have been changes in their disposition, and uncertainty has been created by Cunard's current reconsideration of the number of classes to be catered for.

Cunard: The Builders have never produced a programme for public rooms and it is presumed the programme mentioned is that prepared by me as a guide mainly to the designers.

John Brown: The position has recently deteriorated markedly by the quite unforeseen changed of crew furniture from wood to metal.

Cunard: Agree in general with this paragraph although it is only the chests-of-drawers and wardrobe doors which are in question.

John Brown: The design of passenger accommodation is most important, and here the greatest concern must lie. Clydebank had hoped to have sample passenger cabins approved long ago but not one cabin has yet been settled despite block cabins having been ready since August 1965 to facilitate decisions.

Cunard: It was with some difficult last July that we

obtained the Builders agreement to commence erecting preliminary sample cabins and these were commenced in August 1965 and were developed by us until their final approval on 12 January 1966.

John Brown: Uncertainty as to how many classes of passengers to cater for, poses alternative design features which involved consequential changes which could have far reaching effects.

Cunard: The uncertainty as to the number of classes has had some delaying effect since last December but the change of public rooms made in February 1966 to anticipate a 2-class vessel involved practically no change of structure.

John Brown: Steelwork on the berth has fallen behind the original schedule.

Cunard: The Builders admitted as a progress meeting last August and subsequently as a progress meeting in December that they have fallen behind their schedule.

Correspondence between Sir Basil and Lord Aberconway throughout May 1966 concluded that the best excuse for the delay would be shortage of labour and, in order to avoid any embarrassment to the builders, undue stress would be placed on the fact that the delay was due to alterations to the ship.

The vexed question of two or three classes having been settled also resulted in some re-arrangements of the decorative designers with some leaving and some new designers being brought in. Cunard accepted this would cause interruption to progress but Dan Wallace considered that the yard would only be "slightly inconvenienced."

A statement issued on 27 May 1966 said:

"In a joint statement today, The Cunard Steamship Company Limited and John Brown & Company (Clydebank) Limited, announced that the delivery date for the new Cunarder is now planned for November 1968 with the launch in September 1967.

[as opposed to a May 1968 delivery and a launch in April 1967]

"Since the contract was signed in December 1964, the employment situation in the shipbuilding industry has changed materially. Shortage of labour has had and is having a delaying effect on the ship's progress. It has also been decided to revise the layout of certain passenger accommodation in the ship as well as to modify the arrangements for interior design.

"As a result of the work that has been done, the new Cunarder will, when she goes into service, embody all the features essential to successful operation and will, we believe, be acclaimed by all those who travel in her."

The loss of the lucrative summer 1968 season was a great blow to Cunard – transatlantic revenue would have been in the region of £200,000 per week.

Dan Wallace was still unconvinced of a November 1968

The new ship was assembled on the ship from pre-fabricated units, limited in size only by shed and crane capacity. *(Author's collection)*

delivery and he suggested privately it may be March 1969 before the ship would be delivered. In a memorandum to Sir Basil he stated:

"…it may be realistic to aim for a November 1968 completion but the actual date is more likely to be about March 1969.

"The main reason for delay is that the available shipyard labour became scarce very soon after the contract was signed; this was a national shipyard problem and would probably have affected delivery no matter which shipyard had received the contract.

"It should be noted that the Vicker's delivery date was October 1968 and Harland & Wolff December 1968. The proposed earlier delivery date of May 1968 was one of the major features in the contract being awarded to Messrs. John Brown & Company but was commonly regarded in the industry as being almost impossible."

"We battle for our survival" was the blunt message delivered to shareholders by Sir Basil Smallpeice at the 1966 Annual General Meeting in one of the frankest statements given by a Cunard Chairman at such an occasion. With regard to the new ship Sir Basil claimed she would be the "finest in the world":

"Into the building, fitting and furnishings of Q4 will go new materials and new techniques.

"They are being used on the Rolls-Royce principle of using the best possible modern methods – but without experimenting just for the sake of doing so.

"Q4 will be about six months later than planned, due to labour shortages and some redesigning. But she will be worth waiting for."

Within months of running Cunard, Sir Basil had put together a new management team of six, with an average age of 43, before he appointed consultants Urwick Orr and Partners to improve the organisation with a widespread brief. The Economic Intelligence Unit was asked to thoroughly review the cruise market and the prospects for the new ship. As he swept through the troubled company with the intention of leaving no stone unturned, Sir Basil told shareholders:

"The time has come to give younger men their heads – men who realise that for them it is do or die."

The construction of *Q4* at Clydebank took place against a background of industrial decline, economic and social turmoil. As work progressed, the financial position of the John Brown shipyard continued to deteriorate. Yard Number 736 had been laid down before the true scale of losses on *Kungsholm* had been learned. By 1966, the picture was clear, prompting Lord Aberconway in his report for that year to include the following chilling statement about *Q4*:

> *"The outcome of this contract, decisive perhaps for the continuance of Clydebank as a shipyard and for the future livelihood of those who work there, depends greatly on how well our team of management, staff and workpeople work. I cannot emphasise to each of them too strongly how much it is in his own interest that he should strain every nerve to make this contract come out on the right side, and not let it come out on the wrong side."*

In the wake of the *Kungsholm* disaster the forecast results of losses were:

Year to 31 March 1967	£269,000
(The actual loss was £932,175)	
Year to 31 March 1968	£391,000
Year to 31 March 1969	£1,230,000

with *Q4* making no profit and the yard empty.

It seemed certain that the shipyard would close after the *Q4* had left.

In July 1966 the yard confirmed to Cunard that the launch date would take place in September 1967.

Sir Basil claimed the new liner would not be a Queen:

> *"We shall have to find a name which will reflect this modern age and not recall the days of Henry Hall's band"*

He agreed that the name was of greatest importance and close attention would have to be paid to the feelings of the Americans. The name reflected directly on the selling value of the ship. Sir Basil said he would resolve himself into a committee of one to choose the name claiming that if he had his way the name would not be chosen until the actual launching but felt that it might not be possible to keep it back until then.

By September over 6,000 tons of steel had been erected and work on major engineering components was underway in the engineering works. The stern frame had been erected by the end of the month.

In October 1966, in preparation for future eventualities, the shipyard and engine works were split into two separate businesses. This was in recognition that the shipyard would probably fail or be merged with other Clyde yards, in line with the recommendations of the Shipbuilding Inquiry Committees Report. The engine works, which a few years earlier had seemed to be in terminal decline through the contraction of marine work, was showing all the signs of making a dramatic recovery, courtesy of General Electric and industrial gas turbines. Renamed John Brown Engineering (Clydebank) Limited, the works, unlike the shipyard, would remain firmly under the wing of the John Brown parent. Therefore on 1 October 1966 certain engineering interests at Clydebank were transferred to a separate company, John Brown Engineering (Clydebank) Limited

On 23 November 1966, a party of 16 Labour and Conservative MPs visited the new vessel, which now towered 80-feet over the berth, followed by the joiners shop and engineering works. The MPs were accompanied in the yard by Sir Basil and Lord Mancroft, Deputy Chairman of Cunard, and then later that evening the Lord Provost of Glasgow hosted a Civic Reception at the City Chambers.

At Cunard's first-ever Masters' Conference held in Winchester on 8 December 1966, in which 17 out of the 27 Cunard captains were present, it was announced that 54-year-old Birkenhead born Captain William 'Bil' Warwick would be Master of the new ship. Bil Warwick had joined Cunard in 1937 as Third Officer on *Lancastria*. His first command had been the cargo ship *Alsatia* in 1954 before he took over his first passenger ship, *Carinthia*, in 1958 and had since commanded almost all of the ships in the Cunard fleet.

Captain Warwick:

> *"It is a great honour, I had no idea I had been selected. I regard this as the chance of a lifetime – I've no doubt she will be the finest ship in the world."*

Captain Warwick was the youngest captain ever to be appointed as master of a Queen liner and was posted ashore immediately to keep a watching brief on the progress of the new ship and to act as liaison chief for all the departments concerned with its construction. He was given an office in London and told to visit the shipyard whenever and how he wanted to keep an eye on progress.

He would later recall that his appointment was *"highly fascinating."*

Interestingly, his son Ronald Warwick went on to become Captain of *QE2* in 1990, and later became Fleet Commodore just as his father had. Moreover, just as Captain Bil Warwick became Master of Cunard's first transatlantic liner for over 30 years, so did Commodore Ron Warwick when he was appointed Master of *Queen Mary 2* in 2003.

By the end of 1966 it was obvious that while the builders were making satisfactory progress on the steelwork they were losing ground on the aluminium superstructure. The builders agreed to work overtime and shift work as necessary in order to regain the original schedule for aluminium erection.

Cunard was also experiencing problems with the interior designers who were very slow to finalise designs for public rooms and cabins and this held up the approval of the sample cabins process for example.

As early as 1966 Cunard had made arrangements for the appointment of Merchandise Agents, Peter Barker Ltd (UK) and Worldwide Licensing (USA), to initiate and administer the widespread use of licences to manufacture for public sale commercial goods associated with the name of the then (unnamed) new ship, such as souvenirs, fashion, fabrics, toys and children's goods. The physical side of the merchandising was done by the Peter Barker firm but the administration was handled by Cunard's sales side. The company had not benefitted financially through the manufacture of hundreds of different gifts related to *Queen Mary* and *Queen Elizabeth* – in fact Cunard had paid to have such items such as *Queen Elizabeth* and *Queen Mary* pencils but the company was

Above: The new ship advances towards the Clyde.

Left top: The stern being built.

Left bottom: Welding in October 1965.

Below: A prefabricated section of the keel with both shaft bossings assembled to the after body.

(All photographs author's collection)

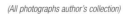

determined this time to benefit and get a commission on such items. The stylised 'Q4' had been the work of Cunard Typographer N J Butterworth who signed over the copyright for the logo to Cunard in August 1967.

Cunard would draw a royalty of two to three per cent on the sale of all such goods, thereby obtaining revenue in addition to a great number of free publicity outlets available to the company. In addition Cunard would have access to many items useful for their own publicity purposes at minimum cost. The design of merchandising as very closely watched over – after all it had to match the ABC1 buying classes to whom Cunard was advertising.

The company had already received many enquiries for permission to produce cut-out models, wall charts, souvenir books etc. and these could be bought into the scope of licensed activity.

The *Q4* and then *QE2* logos would eventually appear on James Buchanan's specially-blended whisky, biscuit tins, jigsaw puzzles (130,000 sold before they were on the market), toys, pencils, books, confectionery, stationery and fabrics. Cunard claimed that they would consider the granting of a licence for any kinds of manufactured article.

Companies were also urged to showcase their products in one of the 49 showcases to be built on the ship and by June 1968, 24 British and seven American companies, with products ranging from cars to perfume to fabrics and antique silver, had done so.

Figures revealed at the end of 1966 showed for the first time that Cunard ships collected £24 million a year from passengers. Sir Basil claimed that to wipe out the yearly losses of between £2.5 and £3 million *"...all we need is a 12.5% improvement. In other words, if the passenger side can cut costs by 2s. 6d. in the pound or make an extra half-crown profit on every pound earned – the losses would go. There ought to be little doubt that this, and more, can be achieved."*

Cunard was going into the 'holidays at sea' market. The new Cunard marketing was certainly bold, with the new 'Go Sun Hunting' slogan replacing the revered 'Getting there is half the fun!' but while the new marketing was bold,

The first bulbous bow fitted to a Cunarder, Monday 13 February 1967. *(Author's collection)*

innovative and fun, the reality was limited success in the cruise market because the ships themselves were not bold, nor innovative and lacked fun. Attempts to modernise the *Caronia* and the *Queen Elizabeth* with new outdoor swimming pools and the earlier transformations of the *Saxonia* into the *Carmania* and the *Ivernia* into the *Franconia* to make them more cruise-friendly were lacklustre at best and failed to appreciate that the future of cruising lay with purpose-built cruise ships.

In 1966 the passenger fleet carried 104,262 passengers, which was more than any other shipping line, and Cunard was able to keep its position at the top of the transatlantic league despite the six-week seamen's strike which had crippled the shipping industry. Its position was also

The hull is almost complete. *(Author's collection)*

A party of 16 Labour and Conservative MPs visited the new vessel, which now towered 80-feet over the berth, followed by the joiners shop and engineering works, Wednesday 23 November 1966. *(Author's collection)*

maintained despite 49 fewer sailings than in 1965. Thirty-seven cruises were operated in 1966, 10 from British ports and 27 from North America and of the 22,962 cruise passengers carried 6,620 sailed on a cruise from the UK and 16,342 from North America.

On 12 January 1967 Buckingham Palace announced that *"The Queen, accompanied by The Duke of Edinburgh, will launch the Cunard Steamship Company's new ship at John Brown's yard, Clydebank on Wednesday 20 September 1967."*

On 21 January, the first pre-fabricated aluminium unit of Upper Deck was lowered into position becoming Cunard's first aluminium deckhouse. The lightness of aluminium allowed great freedom in the size of prefabrication; the only limitation was due to the size of the doors through which they would have to pass to reach the ship. In all 130 separate multi-ton pieces would be welded together to create the superstructure. The new ship now loomed over her surroundings just as the earlier Queens had during their construction but there was one key difference as the booming noises resulting from installing six million rivets into their hulls had been eliminated now thanks to the practically all-welded construction of *Q4*.

The first bulbous bow fitted to a Cunarder was installed on 13 February and on 22 February the most powerful forced draught fan ever built for a merchant navy ship went under test in Belfast. The fan was one of three which would supply combustion air to the three giant boilers of the ship.

The shipyard experienced a formal lockout of a number of its workpeople which started on 8 March 1967 and lasted until 10½ weeks until 15 May. The lockout, the result of a dispute elsewhere, was at national level and involved all persons, except apprentices, who were members of the Draughtsmen's and Allied Technicians' Association. The shipyard advised Cunard on 23 March that the lockout occurrence *"may cause delay in the delivery of the vessel, particularly if not resolved at an early date."* The lockout did seriously curtail the preparation of orders, plans and drawings as for over ten week the drawing, design and other

associated offices were only manned by senior managers, non-union members and apprentices. On 23 May the yard reported to Cunard that *"the effect of this on progress in the yard will not be felt for some months, and while we shall take every step to mitigate this by increasing drawing office effort where possible, it must be necessarily be that many plans will not be prepared by the previously programmed dates."* The stoppage, together with the distrust it generated, contributed greatly to the overall lack of progress on construction and the eventual late delivery.

Given the fact it had given Cunard the earliest delivery date then any stoppage could have a serious implication to the schedule and strikes and stoppages would plague the construction of *Q4* which is not surprising when the management of the yard had to deal with 18 unions covering the 5,500-total workforce.

On Tuesday 4 April 1967 Cunard unveiled *Q4* for the first time simultaneously on both sides of the Atlantic. At the Royal Festival Hall in London Sir Basil Smallpeice, supported by Managing Director Philip Bates, Dan Wallace, Tom Kameen and James Gardner, unveiled a five-foot model. The event emphasised the technical achievements of *Q4*. At exactly the same time, in the Main Lounge on *Queen Mary* in New York, Deputy Chairman Lord Mancroft, supported by Captain Warwick, unveiled an identical model which had been enclosed and was revealed on a spot-lit rotating plinth as individual panels unfolded just like a flower opening. This event focused on the commercial attractions of *Q4*.

The first external artist's impressions were unveiled with the caption:

"The world's fastest and most powerful twin screw liner, Cunard's Q4 will have more open deck space than any other passenger ship. Two thirds the tonnage of the Queens, she will carry the same number of passengers in greater comfort and at the same cruising speed – but will do it on half the fuel consumption. The new Cunarder will be the largest ship capable of passing through the Panama and Suez canals for worldwide cruising. Restaurants high in the ship with sea views for all the 2,000 passengers is one of the liner's unique features."

Dan Wallace was modestly quoted:

"We tried to design the largest and most powerful ship that could be driven by twin screws."

The press pack advised that *Q4* was not a gimmick ship – *"gimmicks date, but good design doesn't"* – and how she was to keep 'new' for her working life. One release, titled 'Evolution of Q4: The most efficient ship', stated:

"When it became necessary in the early 1950s for Cunard to plan a replacement for the new 81,000-ton Queen Mary, the initial thinking was that the new ship would need to be a third Queen of similar size – the Q3.

"The Government prepared and passed the North Atlantic Shipping Bill to permit a grant of up to £3¼m towards the cost of the new ship.

"But by October 1961 Cunard had realized that the highly successful Queens could not be repeated as such

because the need for an all-the-year-round Atlantic service had gone. With it had gone the traditional role of a passenger liner as ship operating on a regular route for virtually her entire life.

"With the change in market requirements for a liner, any ship would have to be two ships in one. The ship would have to be dual-purpose in the fullest sense. An Atlantic liner merely adaptable as a cruise ship would not do.

"For this reason that handy name the press originated, Q4, is really a misnomer, for the 'Q' implies another queen. In everything except comfort, service and speed the thinking behind the new ship is completely different.

"The Q4 is literally the first ship of her kind and size the world has seen. The ship that began to take shape in the drawing office of Cunard's naval architects' and technical departments in Liverpool was planned and designed from the start to capture the cream of the North Atlantic traffic from both sides of the ocean in the season, and the cream of the international cruise market in the winter.

"In addition to Cunard's long experience of cruising over many years, the planning of the new ship was considerably helped by experience with the company's Carmania and Franconia. Built in the middle 1950s for the Canadian route, they were converted to dual-purpose ships which carried passengers on the North Atlantic scheduled services for part of the year and spent the rest of their time largely on Caribbean cruise, which particularly appealed to the important American cruise market.

"The result is that the Q4 is the most carefully planned ship ever built. The traditional method of building a liner was to allow the naval architects and the engineers of the shipowner and the shipbuilder to design and build the ship and then for the commercial, hotel and catering departments to adapt it for their use at later stages.

"The Q4 has been designed from the start in full partnership with all the departments who will have to operate the ship, plan its uses and cater for its passengers. This has been done since the first lines went down on the drawing board.

"Consequently, the Q4 will achieve the greatest efficiency ever known in a passenger ship.

"The name of the new ship will not be announced until she is launched at Clydebank by HM The Queen on September 20."

After unveiling the model, Sir Basil was asked about the name of the ship and he responded:

"In accordance with the best management practice we've scheduled the jobs by critical path analysis and the necessity for taking this decision doesn't arise until next August."

On 8 May 1967 the devastating announcement was made that Queens would be withdrawn from service with *Queen Mary* leaving the fleet in October that year followed by *Queen Elizabeth* a year later despite it being planned to have her in service with Q4 for the new ship's initial years. It was confirmed that the Cunard fleet of 1969 would consist of six ships: Q4, *Caronia*, *Carmania*, *Franconia*, *Carinthia* and

The hull of the new ship towered nearly 100-feet over the berth in this view taken at the end of 1966. *(Author's collection)*

The aft shaft bossings before completion and propeller attachment. *(Author's collection)*

Sylvania. The reality was only *Carmania* and *Franconia* would be in Cunard service when *Q4* finally entered service.

Cunard advised that they were studying how to redeploy as many of its officers, petty officers and ratings as possible and during 1968 hoped to assemble most of *Q4*'s prospective crew in *Queen Elizabeth*.

One week later, on 15 May 1967 *Q4*'s rudder – bigger than a double-decker bus – was winched slowly into position.

286 electricians at the shipyard withdrew their labour on 20 June over the men's unwillingness to implement a district agreement and did not return as expected after the works' annual holiday which ended on 17 July.

On 14 July 1967 HRH The Duke of Edinburgh toured the uncompleted liner and lunched with Cunard Chairman and John Brown Chairman. This would be the first of many visits by member of the British Royal family during *QE2*'s service and The Duke himself would visit five times including a farewell visit to the ship on 11 November 2008 – her last day in the UK!

This royal visit was followed on 21 July 1967 by the Prime Minister Harold Wilson at the yard and during the three-hour visit he inspected progress on the new ship before having lunch with the directors of Cunard and the yard.

The only UK Prime Minister to visit *QE2* in service would be Margaret Thatcher who, after leaving office would attend two functions on board – one to mark the 20th anniversary of the Falklands Campaign in 2002 and one when The Queen paid her farewell visit in 2008.

Q4 was to feature the most sophisticated computer system ever to be installed in a merchant ship; it was the first to combine technical, operational and commercial functions at sea. Based on the Ferranti Argus 400 computer, the installation cost just over £100,000. The micro-miniature Argus 400 was one of the smallest and most advanced computers in the world and was the result of two years investigation and research in which Cunard co-operated with the British Ship research Association, the National Research Development Corporation, Ferranti and the shipbuilders. The computer system would have six main functions: data logging, alarm scanning, machinery control, weather routing, prediction of fresh water requirements and stock control.

Approximately 3,000 men were now working on *Q4* and steelwork was now complete on eleven decks.

August 1967 saw several work stoppages involving the boiler shop helpers and labourers which had an adverse effect on the completion of the boilers and other sundry work on the machinery where boilers makers and their helpers were involved.

During the build period so far an average of 300 tons of steel a day had been put into the ship – this was believed to be a record tonnage for a passenger ship. An average of 30 tons of aluminium had been erected weekly from the time the raw material was delivered to the yard. The 1,100 ton aluminium superstructure was the first all-welded unit to be erected in a passenger ship and 750 tons would be erected by the time the ship was launched. This was the largest amount of aluminium (including some of the biggest plates) ever to be used in the construction of a British liner. In total 30 separate multi-ton pieces were welded together to create the superstructure for the new liner. The aluminium was supplied by Alcan and they built a special training centre within the shipyard as well as a workshop which had its floor specially treated with a sealent to prevent any foreign particles affecting the metal. The aluminium was primed with a special anti-corrosion paint as soon as it was prepared.

To prevent any corrosive electrolytic interaction between the steel of the hull and the aluminium a special epoxy compound was spread along the joints between the two metals and then steel rivets were used for the final connection.

Pre-fabricated sections had been widely used. The heaviest, such as the double-bottom, bow and stern units weigh 40 tons. The biggest of the pre-fabricated aluminium sections was 15 tons. The massive stern frame, installed on 29 September 1966, was a solid cast steel unit of 65 tons. Each propeller bracket weighed 65 tons and the rudder 75 tons.

In order that everyone concerned with the selling and the operation of the ship a confidential report was issued by the Passenger Director on 18 September 1967. He stressed that the ship should be looked upon and talked about as something new in passenger ships. No 736 was a new conception – as a ship and as a resort hotel. Her design and internal layout broke fresh ground and owed little to past tradition. The company's intention was to anticipate the needs of the passenger of the future and by that they meant the 1980s not the 1970s. Flexibility was the absolute key when it came to 736 and this flexibility was amply demonstrated:

• The ship could be a two-class ship, with many

The Prime Minister Harold Wilson at the yard for a three-hour visit when he inspected progress on the new ship before having lunch with the directors of Cunard and the yard, Friday 21 July 1967. *(Author's collection)*

combinations of passenger numbers, for example – from 276 to 576 in first class and from 1,441 to 1,600 in tourist class.

- The ship could effectively become one-class or classless ship of the resort hotel concept of her accommodation layout.

- Three quarters of the passenger complement could be accommodated in outside rooms.

- On cruising service 1,400 passengers can be accommodated in outside rooms and dine at a single sitting.

On 13 September about 350 ship platers, members of the Amalgamated Society of Boilermakers, Shipwrights, Blacksmiths and Structural Workers, claimed that the management had brought forward the date when 80 boilermakers were to be laid off from 30 October to 6 October. They claimed the decision was reached without consultation with ship stewards or the union's full-time officials. After a lunchtime meeting outside the yard the men decided to return to work the next day to meet management. It was thought unlikely the dispute would hold up the launch.

As the 20 September launch approached 17,500 tons of steel from Colvilles of Glasgow, worth more than £1 million had been used, as had £500,000 worth of aluminium from Alcan. Generators and other electrical equipment ordered from AEI were worth another £500,000 and air-conditioning from Carrier was worth another £750,000.

Clydebank resident Lynda Bradford would later recall the town lampposts were given a new coat of paint in readiness for the arrival of The Queen as part of a general tidying up of Clydebank and bunting being hung in the shop windows.

On 17 September a special sailing of the Clyde steamer Duchess of Hamilton from Largs at Rothesay allowed passengers to see the *Q4* on her launching berth three days before she was launched by The Queen.

Cunard's financial situation had worsened during 1967, a disastrous period for the company which had begun with the

1966 seaman's strike, and the company forecast a further £3½ million loss of the passenger ships for that year. This was compounded by the news from John Browns in July that the contract price for *Q4* of £25½ million would probably be increased by a further £3 million. Even if *Q4*'s cost had not risen the additional losses on the passenger ships would mean that the Government's financial aid would not be adequate. Cunard warned the Board of Trade that the project was in danger of being abandoned, with major political repercussions, unless the Government would agree to increase the loan.

As Scotland prepared for what was arguably the biggest event in the long, proud history of shipbuilding on the Clyde, the public remained blissfully unaware that the Government was putting together a desperate rescue package for Cunard.

Sir Basil reported:

"I have seen the Board of Trade about the new loan and they are considering our request. It is to cover the increases in shipyard wages and materials since the £25,500,000 contract for the Q4 was signed in 1964.

"When the Government loan was arranged it was to cover 80 per cent of the estimated cost of the hull and machinery, but it did not take into account a substantial escalation of in cost levels. Even now it is impossible to tell what the final price of the Q4 will be when she comes into service early in 1969."

A stern view of the new ship in July 1967. *(Author's collection)*

There then followed a period of intensive negotiations between Cunard and the Government throughout August and September with Cunard stressing that a final decision would have to have been made by the time of their next Board Meeting on 14 September – if the worse had come to the worse the company felt they would have to give the Queen at least five days' notice of a cancellation!

Prime Ministerial papers show that Sir Basil did not hesitate to break royal protocol rules by involving the unquestionable embarrassment to the Monarch of such a decision as a weapon to steam-roller Harold Wilson's Government into providing a loan to save hi company.

In a letter to the Prime Minister, just 12 days before the launch, Sir Basil threatened to call off the ceremony:

"I am becoming increasingly concerned at the situation to which we are in danger of exposing The Queen, should a proper arrangement not be reached regarding the future of the Cunard company.

I have been speaking on the telephone to Sir Michael Adeane (The Queen's then Private Secretary) at Balmoral Castle this morning and he is anxious on The Queen's behalf that there should be no misunderstanding."

Sir Basil warned that a decision would have to be made that October whether or not to liquidate the company in the absence of some *"politically and commercially acceptable form or Government participation in or support for it"* the launch would have to be abandoned.

Sir Basil said that in the absence of a rescue package, his board would have no option but to take steps to liquidate the Cunard company and his letter to the Prime Minister continued:

"For such a decision to be made public so soon after The Queen had launched this ship would, I am sure you will agree, place Her Majesty in so embarrassing situation that it must be avoided.

I feel that my duty will be to advise The Queen that the company's future is so uncertain that the arrangements for the Royal launching of the ship must be reconsidered, in which case the reason for any change in arrangements would have to be made public.

"I need hardly point out to you the national and, indeed, international implications of the decision that is taken about Cunard's future; I believe I am not exaggerating the importance of the company when I say that Cunard is widely regarded as a symbol of Britain and all that Britain stands for."

The letter came as a bombshell to the Prime Minister who knew Cunard had financial difficulties but had not realized how severe they were.

Harold Wilson, who had said the new Cunarder must be a *"showpiece of modern Britain"*, took three decisions: the launch had to go ahead as planned; the ship had to be completed and even if Cunard eventually went under, the new liner would not go into foreign hands, at least in the short term.

It was rumoured the ship would be sold to Greek shipowners or even scrapped after the launch.

In his autobiography 'Of Comets and Queens' Sir Basil would later write:

"We had no indication of what the Government were prepared to do by the afternoon of the 13th. Geoffrey Seligman (of S G Warburg, our merchant bankers) and I asked to see Harold Lever, the Financial Secretary to the Treasury, that evening. We met him in his flat in Eaton Square. This gave us the opportunity to present our case to him in a simple and straightforward manner, not through officials. Without a larger loan from Government, we

Those flying to and from Prestwick Airport in Glasgow enjoyed spectacular views of the new ship which dominated the shipyard and all around. *(Author's collection)*

should almost certainly have to stop building the ship; her new cost was much higher than quoted in 1964 and we could not meet it in full. He listened with evident sympathy and asked questions to fill gaps in his knowledge. He promised to let me have a written answer before or during our board meeting next morning. And with that, which was all we could have expected, Geoffrey and I retired to our respective homes and Harold Lever left – late – for a dinner engagement.

"While waiting for the Financial Secretary's letter, we had time at our board meeting to consider what we would do if the Government's response proved negative. Geoffrey Seligman was with us, and so were Sir Henry Benson and Anthony Pinkney, our auditors. It was a grim prospect. We might even have to put Cunard into liquidation. At last the long-awaited letter arrived. To our great and undisguised relief, we found that our basic requirements had been substantially met."

On the eve of the launch, 19 September, Cunard announced that agreements had been reached in the discussions with the Board of Trade concerning the provision of additional finance for the completion and putting into service of Q4.

The existing loan agreement under which the Government would make available a loan of £17.6 million on delivery of the ship by the shipyard to Cunard was to be replaced with a new arrangement. Under it the Government was now prepared to lend in the neighbourhood of £24 million which Cunard could draw as may have been necessary in advance if delivery.

The original arrangements for Cunard borrowing from a consortium of banks to enable progress payments for to be made while the ship was under construction was therefore to be brought to an end as soon as practicable.

The new Government loan was to be in two parts. Cunard intended to set up a separate subsidiary company to own the passenger ship fleet (including Q4) and other assets necessary for the operation of the transatlantic and other passenger services. At the option of the Cunard board, up to £14 million (including £2 million for working capital) could be lent to this subsidiary company. The security for this part of the loan was confined to the assets of the passenger subsidiary company, and would not require any guarantee by Cunard or any other member of the Cunard group.

The terms of this part of the loan provided for interest of 4½ per annum until the end of three years from delivery of Q4 and thereafter at a rate to be agreed; for repayment to be completed by the end of 12 years from delivery.

The remaining £10 million of the loan was made to the Cunard Steamship Co. Ltd. The rate of interest was 4½ per annum throughout and repayments of the loan would not necessarily be in equal amounts but would be completed within five years of the first drawing.

This new loan arrangement relieved Cunard at a time of continuing trading difficulties, of the strain in its cash resources involved in putting Q4 into service.

A secret internal memo dated 28 July 1967 discussed those who should attend the launch. For financial reasons, invitations to company staff to attend the launch were being severely restricted and would be restricted to all Cunard Line

Directors and their wives and senior members of the shore and sea staff from the three main areas: Southampton (12 invitees), London (two invitees) and Liverpool two invitees). The senior managers (whose wives would also be invited) would be balloted and would also have to meet the criteria of being in receipt of a salary of £2,250 and above and have 15 or more years' service with the company! To the disgruntlement of several of the designers an invitation would not be extended to them.

It was planned that Q4 would glide toward the river at 22 miles an hour with the last shore fetters, the massive drag links, running out in a thunderous roar.

There were ten bundles of them on each side of the ship. Each weighed 70 ton – 1,400 tons in all to steady the liner's journey to the river and so to the sea. The ship was expected to be traveling at 19 miles per hour as she hit the water pushing away 20,000 tons of water – her own launching weight. 150 men would be aboard the empty shell that was Q4 ready for any emergency while 161 would work ashore to ensure a smooth launch.

The intricate launching calculations had been worked out by a computer – a week's work reduced to 30 minutes compared with the normal methods with the slightest error having to be eliminated. Many factors had to be considered for the river was narrow and the ship was long.

The problems of a launch of this size were enormous. Very early on in the proceedings, John Browns had to decide the width and slope of the slipway on which the liner would slide down to the water. The effects of temperature on the launch lubricant grease mixture had to be considered and a host of other factors had all to be checked, evaluated and re-checked.

John Starks, assistant managing director heading John Brown's design team:

"The first step is, obviously, to make sure that it will move. When it starts to move the first things that starts to happen is that the stern begins to lift. As it does so pressure on the forward end of the slipway is increased very considerably as it is taking the whole weight of the ship, apart from any buoyancy that the water is taking. One must, therefore, make sure that the ship is then strong enough to take the stress at the forward end.

"You also have to ensure by calculation that the ship will float off the slipway as opposed to dropping off and you also have to make sure that it is waterborne while it is reasonable clear of the slipway. The next thing that you have to decide is how far the ship can be expected to travel and you have to decide what drag chains you are going to attaché at what points to prevent the ship from going too far.

"What most people do not appreciate is that the ship takes a very rough ride during its launch. She bends during the course of the launch and we have to make sure that all her structure is absolutely sound. We, therefore, inspect the ship very carefully. She probably gets far more local stresses during the launch than she ever will during the course of her working life.

"The most critical factor by far in the launch is the depth of water available at the aft end of the slipways. The River Clyde is extremely temperamental; sometimes the

Construction of the launching platform has commenced at the foot of the bow of the freshly-painted new ship. *(Author's collection)*

water is deficient and sometimes is it excessive. If we have too much water, the danger is that the ship will really be afloat before she is clear at the end of the slipway and the danger is that, since high water is usually associated with high wind, if she is not clear at the end of the ways she could damage herself on one of the cranes. The problem usually solves itself because if the wind and water are that high, it is obviously no condition in which to launch a ship. This happens very infrequently and is obviously something to be avoided, but nevertheless the problem is still there.

"We, therefore, watch the weather forecasts very carefully before the day. We also measure the heights of the tides for a good many days before the launch to check whether the river is running true to form, under prediction or over prediction. We also measure the river in Greenock and Glasgow as a precaution and we are halfway between the two we can get a very good idea of what the river is doing. Having obtained this information we then can, within certain limits, ballast the ship to aim off for weather conditions, but obviously in a ship of this size the resources pen to us are limited."

The man responsible for the slipway was Robert Craig, head foreman shipwright. He had worked at John Brown's since he left school in 1918 and *Q4* would be his 47th launch. He built the slipway from the information given to him. Its declivity (downward inclination towards the river) was ½ inch to the foot. Every square foot of the sliding and standing (fixed) ways to bear a weight of more than two tons – he claimed for *Q4* it was 2,089 tons.

He used 16,300 feet of 12" square timber to build the supporting poppets (cradles) at each end of the ship. Once the ship rested on 300 keel blocks but these had now been knocked away; the berth had been stripped of the huge shores like tress trunks, bilge blocks and wedges.

Q4 rested on two sliding ways, each formed of 25 lengths of timber 30 feet long, six feet wide and 12 inches thick. The sliding and standing ways had been greased with a concoction of nine tons of tallow compound, 70 gallons of sperm oil, 14 cwt. of soft black soap and seven gallons of fine spindle oil. Robert Craig took responsibility for this.

Q4 was held by six mighty triggers, each with its eight inch wooded tongue set into the sliding ways. Wires trailed from a tiny electrical device to the button on the high platform where the Queen would perform the launching ceremony. As the Queen pressed the button the powerful trigger arms would snap back in their pits with a report like an artillery salute. Then *Q4* would glide towards the river; and just in case the liner is reluctant to leave the berth, two hydraulic rams would give her a nudge – a push with the power of 1,200 lbs. per square inch behind it.

In the river six tugs would be waiting to handle the ship – three at the fore and three at the aft. Another will be standing by for any emergency. Lines would be rocketed from the tugs to the new Cunarder and towing lines would be secured and the new ship would move towards her fitting-out berth.

Prior to launch George Parker, shipyard director, said:

"I am personally very proud to have had some part to play in the building of this liner, an intimate part to play, being connected with directing the construction of the liner. Secondly,

I'm very proud not only to be connected with building the ship but also to perpetuate this very long tradition of John Brown's. It is my belief; it is my aim, to make this Cunarder the best one that Brown's ever built over a long, long number of years of this close connection with Cunard."

The final selection of names had been decided in May by Sir Basil and his deputy Ronald Senior. They met to agree the final choice in Cunard's London offices on the evening of Monday 18 September where Sir Basil and took three names from a safe: *Queen Elizabeth*, *Princess Margaret* and *Princess Anne*. Elizabeth had joined the list last after the decision to retire the *Queen Elizabeth* had been made.

When the choice was made, a message was sent by scrambler telephone to the Queen through her private secretary, Sir Michael Adeane, in Balmoral. They were the only four to know the name.

A sealed envelope containing the name was dispatched to the New York office – it was to be opened if there were any problems with the live transmission on the day.

Princess Margaret became the 4-1 favourite on the eve of the launch when it was announced at the last moment that she would also be attending the ceremony and she duly arrived at the yard the day before the launch. Workers had chalked the Princess Anne on the liner's hull – that was the name Captain Warwick liked. Prince Charles carried the shortest odds.

Captain Warwick said:

"I have already said in the past that I would not like the name 'Queen' to be given to this ship."

Captain Warwick, when interviewed earlier in the year and asked about the name, stated:

"I dare say they're mulling it over in the boardroom, but if they're reached a decision they certainly haven't told me. Why should they? I'm not concerned with names. I'm a sailor."

In January 1966 the Daily Mirror columnist, Cassandra, wrote:

"The next question for romanticists such as myself is to speculate on what they are going to call the new maritime giant, which is known simply as No. 736. I predict that there will be enormous pressure to christen the new Cunarder a Queen. But which queen?

"We are short of reigning queens in English history. The Normans, the Plantagenets, the Tudors, the Stuarts, the Hanovarians, the Saxe-Coburgs and the Windsors have only produced half-a-dozen in the past thousand years.

"Two Marys, two Elizabeths, one Anne and one Victoria. Queen Anne was a colourless nobody and Queen Victoria was a colourful somebody.

"So RMS Queen Victoria is a distinct possibility for that dumpy little old lady who was a real character who ruled for sixty-four years at the height of British imperial wealth and power.

"The Americans who will be the main clients foe the ship would, I am sure, settle for RMS Winston Churchill.

They are very fond of that old Anglo-American party.

"My own suggestion doesn't stand a hope in high water. It is that the new ship be called John Brown. A fine solid British name that any commoner should be proud of.

"Nobody would know which John Brown. The chap who founded the firm that will build the ship. The whisky drinking Scottish ghillie who for nineteen years dominated Queen Victoria. The John Brown whose soul goes marching on. John Brown the celebrated Northumberland poet. John Brown who wrote the famous Dictionary of the Bible. John Brown the celebrated Edinburgh theologian of any of the thirty eight John Browns who are listed in the London telephone directory.

"It would provide endless argument as to which John Brown was meant that would rage in every bar in the country, including the bars onboard RMS John Brown.

"I just want to be helpful."

More than 15,000 bets had been placed with the bookmakers and a Glasgow bookmaker was offering the following odds:

3 – 1	*Sir Winston Churchill*
4 – 1	*Prince of Wales*
	Prince Charles
	Princess Margaret
5 – 1	*Britannia*
6 – 1	*Princess Anne*
	John F Kennedy
8 – 1	*Queen Victoria*
10 – 1	*Aquitania*
12 – 1	*Mauretania*
14 – 1	*Queen Elizabeth* II
	Prince Philip
	Atlantic Princess
25 – 1	*Clyde Princess*
	British Princess

Other suggestions included Queen of the United States, New Britain, Queen of Britain, British Queen, Great Britain, Ocean Queen, The Crown and Anchor, Rose of England, Twiggy, The New Elizabethan, G*loriana*, Windsor Wave and Donald Campbell (he had been killed a few weeks earlier). Housewife Helen Gormley suggested 'Helen Gormley'. Over 400 names were suggested with the last suggestion, Francis Chichester, arriving in the last 48 hours.

The many uncertainties surrounding the shipyard's future were temporarily forgotten as thousands of people flocked to the yard and the opposite bank of the river in time honoured fashion to take one last look at the liner on the slipway.

The Prime Minister Harold Wilson issued the following message:

"This is a proud moment in the history of Clydeside and of British shipping.

"Cunard's Q4 represents the best in modern shipbuilding, technology and design. It is a credit to John Brown's yard and to its many specialists, advisers and suppliers of components.

"As everyone knows, Q4 could not have been built without financial help from the Government. Cunard

The Queen inspects the new ship and the launching arrangements. *(Author's collection)*

The view from the stern towards the launching platform. *(Author's collection)*

received a £17,600,000 loan under the Shipbuilding Credit Act, 1964, and yesterday the Government announced agreement in principle to provide a further £6 million as a basis of new arrangements for financing and operating Q4.

"This represents effective and timely assistance for this long-established famous company, whose new ship is to be launched and named by Her Majesty The Queen this afternoon.

"I am confident that Q4 will justify this help and for years to come will add to the prestige of British shipbuilding and sip operations."

The jackup rig *Gulftide* was removed from the fitting out basin and held midriver by the three Clyde Shipping tugs *Flying Mist, Flying Spray* and *Flying Foam* to make it easier to maneouvre the new liner into her fitting out berth after the launch.

Renfrew Town Council closed the right-of-way from Fishers Road, at the end of Meadowside Street, to Inchinnan Road, on the right bank of the River Cart from daylight to 1600 hours on 20 September as the right-of-way had flooded when the *Queen Mary* was launched in 1934. A farm on the opposite side of the River Cart had no right-of-way and was not opened for the public. During the launch, there would also be restrictions imposed on all aircraft entering or leaving Glasgow Airport.

Several Clyde steamers, including the *Duchess of Hamilton* and the *Caledonia*, offered pleasure cruises

downriver to view the launch. The steamers and tugs were dressed overall with signal flags for the occasion and would carry around 2,000 passengers from Bridge Wharf in Glasgow with the *Caledonia* berthing at Rothesay Dock beside the shipyard.

The Queen was about to become the first reigning British Monarch to launch a ship and had her first view of the liner as she flew overhead prior to landing at Abbotsinch Airport, Glasgow, at 1140 hours. She was then driven to the shipbuilder's offices. There she met by Admiral Sir Angus Cunninghame Graham, Lord Lieutenant of Dunbartonshire who presented Sir Basil Smallpeice and Lord Aberconway to Her Majesty. At a private luncheon party she and Prince Philip joined 120 other guests and dined on prawn cocktail, Scots Saddle of lamb, fruit and cream and coffee. The Queen then made the two-minute car journey to the launching berth where she and the Duke spent 20 minutes inspecting the slipway arrangements including the launching trigger which she would soon be remotely activating. The Queen looked *"supremely happy"* and was laughing and joking while walking among the crowd.

The Royal Party consisted of The Queen, the Duke of Edinburgh, Princess Margaret (who had arrived the day before – an arrival that increased speculation that the new ship would be named after her), Sir Angus, Sir Basil, Lord Aberconway, Lady Aberconway and John Rannie. Lord Aberconway's eight year old son, Michael McLaren, presented the Queen with a bouquet.

The party ascended to the platform at the bow of the ship

The crowds gather for the long-awaited announcement of the new ship's name. *(Author's collection)*

The Queen in animated conversation with Sir Basil Smallpeice and Lord Aberconway and they make their way to the launch platform. *(Author's collection)*

and The Queen refused an envelope containing a sheet of paper on which was written the proposed name of the new ship: *"I won't be needing that"* she joked.

The rigger on board the liner shouted down to The Queen below *"Call it Prince Charles!"*

At precisely 1428 hours on a sunny afternoon Her Majesty stepped forward on the launching platform and said:
"I name this ship Queen Elizabeth the Second. May God Bless her…May God Bless her and all who sail in her."

There was a thin cheer in the yard from the 30,000 or so spectators as the Queen announced the name and as it was shouted outside through the yard gates and relayed by police to the crowds, the first reaction was of disbelief and then disappointment. The cheers stopped as people turned to each other to ask for confirmation. A journalist in the crowd would later report than only two out of every six who were asked for their reaction to the name were happy with it.

Her Majesty then cut the ribbon using the same gold scissors that her mother had used to launch *Queen Elizabeth* in 1938 and her grandmother to launch *Queen Mary* in 1934 which released the bottle of Australian wine which duly smashed onto the side of the newly named liner.

For many of its launches Cunard had traditionally used wine from the Empire and had declined a request from the shipyard to use whisky to launch the New Cunarder. This was apparently in response to the shipyard declining a hope from Cunard that the Beatles would perform a specially-commissioned song for the ship at the launch.

The Queen then pressed the button that electrically released the launching trigger.

Then nothing happened. For 70 seconds it seemed as if the ship did not move. The Queen looked amazed; the smile slowly faded from Prince Philip's face. Workmen high up on her deck leaned and shouted *"Give us a shove!"* Shipyard director George Parker joined in the spirit of the request and bowler-hatted, he sprang to the bows and gave the liner a shove. He jubilantly waved his bowler when, by a coincidence, she began to move. In a little over two minutes after the Queen had named her the new Elizabeth had slid smoothly into the Clyde. Newspapers the next day claimed the Queen had wept as the new ship entered the Clyde and that Prince Philip took a white handkerchief from his pocket and handed it to her. The Queen exclaimed "Look, oh look at her! She's beautiful" which was picked up by the still-live microphone.

The Illustrated London News described the scene:

"For a full minute after the launching button was pressed, the new queen of the seas appeared not to move − as if regally pondering he coming to life and considering the name she is expected to bear with honour. Then the liner, her personality imprinted on the cheering thousands, moved swiftly and gracefully down to the water edge…"

Afterwards Cunard remained buoyant and claimed there was nothing unusual in the delay and the ship began to move as soon as The Queen had pressed the button but she

The Royal Party just before The Queen announced to everyone, including Cunard, the name of the new ship and cutting the ribbon which released the bottle of Australian wine. *(Author's collection)*

moved only a fraction of an inch at a time.

Buccaneer aircraft from the No 736 Squadron of the Fleet Air Arm flew over the ship in an anchor formation as an aerial salute. The officers and chief petty officers would later attend a ceremony on board the finished ship on 7 August 1969 when the commander would present a squadron badge to the Captain.

As the hull began to move the crowds gathered in the fields opposite initially pulled back taking heed of the police warnings that a mini tidal wave may have been generated as the liner entered the water but no such wave was generated such was the graceful entry into the Clyde by the new ship.

Whistles were sounded by the shipyards and ships on the Clyde as the launch was underway.

The tug *Cruiser* moved in to hold the vessel steady while the hawsers to various other tugs were made fast and she was joined at the stern by *Strongbow* and *Campaigner*. The six tugs would move the new ship inch by inch into the fitting out basin where she would remain for just over a year.

The Queen and the official launch party then went for a champagne afternoon tea in the specially refurbished Mould Loft. During the tea, which consisted of sandwiches with various fillings, cake and biscuits for 700, toasts were given with 150 bottles of Krug Privee Curee, demi-sec, vintage 1961.

In his speech, Lord Aberconway reminded those present that the launch had signaled the beginning of the end of John Brown's shipyard as an independent entity and that the new ship was the last ship of note that could be called a "John Brown" ship:

"Many great ships will be built and fitted out at Clydebank in the years to come, to the same standards as in the last seventy 'John Brown' years; they will be worthy successors to the Queen Mary, the Queen Elizabeth and the Queen Elizabeth the Second."

In her response, The Queen said:

"Lord Aberconway
"I am most grateful to you for the very kind and generous words you have used in proposing my health and that of my family. But the people who really deserve a toast today are the designers and builders of John Brown's last great ship for the Cunard fleet. Today's launch marks the culmination of the first stage in an immense team effort, involving many skills and highly complex organization. We hear so much about the new technological age and all the new industrial methods but we seldom have an opportunity to see all the most advanced techniques brought together in the shape of one single product.

"This new ship is designed and built to carry passengers, but to the world she represents the present day standards of British engineering, management, and workmanship. I have every confidence that she will be a worthy representative. There is much more to be done before she goes into service but I take this opportunity to offer my warmest congratulations to every individual man and woman in office and workshop who has made a contribution to the design and construction of the new ship.

"I particularly welcome the opportunity you have given me to launch this splendid successor to those two famous Cunarders Queen Mary and Queen Elizabeth. I suppose these two ships were better known and loved, both in peace and war by all of us living in these lands, than any other merchantman in our history. I have always had a very special affection for them because they were named after my grandmother and my mother, and it does not seem very long ago that I was present with my sister when my mother launched the Queen Elizabeth in 1938.

"Every great enterprise has an element of risk and uncertainty about it, and I am sure that no one can predict the future career of the new Cunarder. However, I am equally certain that in the experienced and capable hands of the Cunard Company she will stand the very best chance of a happy and profitable lifetime.

"We have all read, with a touch of nostalgia, that the name of John Brown is to disappear from the list of great ship builders. However, this does not mean that the very special skill and spirit of this yard will be lost to Clydeside or to British shipbuilding. In wishing Queen Elizabeth 2 a long life and good fortune on all her voyages I add my very best wishes for success and prosperity to the new consortium of Clydeside ship builders."

Instead of the usual piece of jewelry The Queen was presented with a 15-foot blue and white speedboat for use as a pleasure craft on the royal yacht Britannia. A delighted Queen thanked Lord Aberconway and suggested it may be appropriate to call it John Brown and have it painted in Cunard colours. A voice, said by some to be that of Prince Philip, commented: "Why not call it Cunard and paint it brown?"

The speedboat had been a secret not even The Queen had been advised about. John Rannie commissioned the Glastron Sutura Chrysler-engined (with spare engine) craft from Glasgow firm Clyde Chandlers and ordered "a boat for a very special customer."

The Queen's personal Christmas Card for 1969 showed her and The Duke of Edinburgh with their four children surrounding the speedboat presented to her at the launch on board the Royal Yacht Britannia during an unofficial visit to Norway in August 1969

Earlier in July that year plans had been put in place by Cunard to ensure the offices in Montreal and New York were advised of the name just as soon as it was known. Each office would have a model of Q4 and the company proposed to keep a hotline from Glasgow to Montreal and New York. The moment the name was announced by the Queen both offices would be informed of the name and perform a little ceremony round their own respective models. Staff in the offices would immediately place the name of the ship on her

'Queen Elizabeth the Second' entering the Clyde for the first time. *(Author's collection)*

stern, crack a suitably miniature bottle of champagne on her bows with, the company hoped, the guests cheering!

Later that night the sealed envelope was removed from the New York office safe and opened to reveal the words *Queen Elizabeth*. The fact the hotline link had worked saved possible embarrassment with the wrong name being announced in New York.

Fred Turfus, Vice President Commercial and Sales, issued a memo to staff in New York stating:

"As you are aware, the Q4 was launched today, and I am pleased to be able to advise you that the name of the ship will be Queen Elizabeth II."

The name 'Queen Elizabeth the Second' immediately caused controversy. *"Unimaginative"* was the typical English reaction but in Scotland: *"insulting"*, *"provocative"*, and *"disgraceful"* were typical responses from the Scottish Nationalists who took it as an insult to the people of Scotland and claimed it was *"an ignorant and thoughtless choice"* and *"quite irrelevant to Scotland and showing scant respect."* To them The Queen was Elizabeth the First. Arthur Donaldson, chairman of the Scottish Nationalist Party, said: *"It could not be a bigger insult to the people of Scotland'.*

Lord Aberconway told journalists he had been *"completely in the dark"* about the name but thought it *"absolutely wonderful."*

John Rannie had written his choice of name – 'The Queen'

– on a piece of paper more than a year earlier and put it in his safe until the big day. After saying goodbye to the Royal Party he took the piece of paper from his pocket, and with a wry grin, tore it up.

Many small punters won at 10-1 when the name was announced but the big money was on the names *Princess Margaret, Mauretania, Churchill, Prince Charles* and *Britannia*. As a result Glasgow bookmaker, John Banks, cleared £383 15s which went to a nautical charity.

More than 500 calls were made to the various offices of Cunard in the UK to congratulate the company on the choice.

Celebrations took place across the fleet and on the *Queen Mary* – making her 1,001st and final Atlantic crossing – Captain Treasure Jones toasted the new ship and led the singing of Auld Lang Syne in the first-class lounge. During its 'The Launching of the Q4' live broadcast (1345 – 1640 hours and followed by Jackanory) the BBC had a live radio link with the *Queen Mary* which was 146 miles south of Halifax and in crystal clear tones the Captain told how pleased they were when they heard the new ship's name and he said there were scenes of "gaiety." There was also a radio link with the *Queen Elizabeth*.

Afterwards when asked why all the secrecy, Sir Basil said:

"It just seemed rather fun. People seemed to having a marvelous time trying to work out what it would be called. We decided to let them carry on. We were anxious to continue our tradition of royal names for our ships. I did not, by the way, have a bet with the bookmaker."

This cameraman was told to film the drag chains as the ship went down the slipway – that's all he saw. *(Author's collection)*

Afloat at last and looking magnificent after making a delayed, but graceful, entry into the Clyde. *(Author's collection)*

When asked about the other names, Sir Basil's responses were:

Churchill?
There is already a schooner of that name. And Cunard has not forgotten the day it picked Queen Mary for a name only to find a Clyde steamer already owned it. The name had to be bought and the steamer became QMII.
Prince Philip or Prince Charles?
The tradition of merchant ships in this country is that they always take the name of women.

In his autobiography 'Of Comets and Queens' Sir Basil would later write:

"In thinking about the name for Q4, I could not ask the Queen to give it her own name, because only battleships had ever been allowed to take the name of a reigning monarch. On the other hand, it was to be a successor Queen ship, as the cipher Q4 indicated. I talked the matter over with the Queen's Private Secretary, Sir Michael (now Lord) Adeane. In the end we decided to recommend that it should simply be named Queen Elizabeth - just as, for example, we had had two Mauretanias and two Caronias. After all, the new ship would be coming into service almost immediately after the first Queen Elizabeth was withdrawn, and the two Queen Elizabeths would not be in service on the high seas at the same time.

"Her Majesty had the same sure instinct about a name as her grandfather had had. As was customary at all launching ceremonies, John Brown's managing director, John Rannie, had handed the Queen a slip of paper with the name written on it – Queen Elizabeth. But those of

us standing near noticed she never looked at it. I could hardly contain my delight when, in launching the ship, the Queen announced without a moment's hesitation: "I name this ship Queen Elizabeth the Second."

"It was what I wanted but had not dared ask for. No name could have assured the ship of more worldwide renown. It remained only to decide how to write the name. I did not feel we should use 'Queen Elizabeth II', which is the official designation of the Queen as sovereign; it would be wrong to use that style in all our advertising and publicity.

"I thought the use of an Arabic 2 instead of a Roman II might make a sufficient distinction, and I was pleased to hear from Michael Adeane that the Queen had approved the styling of the ship Queen Elizabeth 2."

The *QE2*, as she became universally known and certainly the most famous initials in travel, would cause debate over the exact origins of her name throughout her life. The use of 2 was obvious whenever the *QE2* was berthed alongside the *Queen Elizabeth* II Terminal in Southampton - she was 'named' after the first *Queen Elizabeth* ship while the Terminal was named after The Queen. Even today lazy radio presenters or journalists talk about traffic congestion on the *QE2* Bridge at Dartford which is incorrect - they should announce traffic congestion on the *Queen Elizabeth* the Second Bridge as the Bridge is named after The Queen. The same mis-naming applies as well today to that Terminal, the *Queen Elizabeth* II Conference Centre or the *Queen Elizabeth* II Hospital in London.

On 21 September the following from Sir Basil was delivered to those on *Queen Mary*:

"The decision to retire the Queen Mary was difficult to make.

As the hull began to move the crowds gathered in the fields opposite initially pulled back taking heed of the police warnings that a mini tidal wave may have been generated as the liner entered the water but no such wave was generated such was the graceful entry into the Clyde by the new ship. *(Author's collection)*

With the new ship afloat all that remained on the building berth was the smoking remains of the launching ways that had supported the huge hull. Even though these had been well greased they were still hot enough to cause smoke after the incredible friction of the launch. *(Author's collection)*

Safely berthed alongside the fitting-out jetty after a successful launch. *(Author's collection)*

"Very few ships…if any… have won the particular affection and esteem she has enjoyed. Her claim to precedence has been more than a royal name painted on her bow. It is impossible to define the certain quality which causes one ship to proceed at full steam to capture and hold the public's love, leaving all others in her wake.

"We may not be able to define that quality, but it seems we have created it again. Yesterday a new Cunard luxury liner slipped down the ways at Clydebank and clove the seas for the first time. To those of us who were there, it was apparent that whatever it is that the Queen Mary has had…has been passed on."

That same day Anthony Hepper met the five Chairmen of the proposed Upper Reaches consortium for the first time. The meeting, at the Fairfield shipyard in Govan, discussed two items – finalising a preliminary agreement among the shipbuilders that all tenders from then on would be submitted on a group basis and deciding whether Yarrows or Fairfields would tender on behalf of the group for the new £6 million order from the American navy for two ocean-going tugs.

Within a few months after the launch, to prepare for the merger with other Clyde shipyards, the Clydebank yard was first de-coupled from John Brown & Co. (Clydebank) Ltd., to become John Brown & Co. (Shipbuilders) Ltd on 25 January 1968. However, the new company was only a stepping stone to the wider merger and had an existence of just two weeks. On 5 February 1968, John Brown & Co. (Shipbuilders) was sold to Upper Clyde Shipbuilders (UCS) in exchange for

1,199,999 £1 shares in the new company.

The shipbuilding map of the Clyde had been redrawn and the former John Brown shipyard was now known as the Clydebank Division of Upper Clyde Shipbuilders Limited, with other shipyards at Linthouse, Scotstoun and Govan. The new company set about the introduction of methods to raise productivity, but labour relations only deteriorated.

Lord Aberconway had been relieved of a loss-making subsidiary, but had gained a major shareholding in the government-supported UCS. Anthony Hepper became Chairman of the Clydebank division of UCS and John Rannie became Special Director in direct control of *QE2* for the shipyard.

"Clyde built, well built

"Although there were certainly problems and issues with the shipyard workers at the John Brown yard there can be no doubting that *QE2* was built by a skilled labour force that had been responsible for building some of the greatest - and strongest - ships ever to go to sea. The shipbuilding industry on the River Clyde, the eighth-longest river in the United Kingdom, and the second-longest in Scotland, was truly the envy of the world and was constructing around a fifth of all ships launched in the early 1900s. An estimated 30,000 naval, merchant and passenger ships have been built on the Clyde and its tributaries since the Scott family set up in Greenock in 1711. Conditions for the workers were tough but that did not diminish the pride and passion they displayed when building the latest ship – 'their' ship. Shipbuilding was

Tugs head to assist the newly-launched hull. *(Author's collection)*

Even though Cunard had wanted the Beatles to play a specially composed pop tune at the launch to attract useful publicity the event attracted significant worldwide attention. *(Author's collection)*

in the blood and the results of their skills would be seen the world over. Industrial relations were not good which added to the overall situation for the men not being good and while there were elements of militancy there were faults on the sides of both the management and workers. What is never in question is the overall quality of the finished product of a new ship its owner would receive *QE2*, and other famous ships built and launched on the Clyde, would certainly live up to the saying *"Clyde built, well built!"* Such was the strength built into *QE2* that her hull was probably as good in 2008 when she arrived in Dubai as it was in 1968 when she arrived in Greenock. That strength was there for all to see when

replacing the bathrooms in the passenger cabins in 1994 caused serious delays in the completion of the refit as removing what had been built at the yard proved far more difficult than planned! The skills and pride displayed by the workers of John Brown was on a whole new level with *QE2*. They knew that she was probably going to be their last chance to build something special. *QE2* was to be their legacy. And she is. That pride was on display whenever *QE2* returned to Greenock. For each visit retired Grandfathers and Fathers would be seen on the quayside showing their Grandchildren and children the greatest ship ever leave the Clyde.

A sight never to be seen again after the launch – a great ocean liner rising on a slipway and a sensational backdrop to a lunchtime football match. *(Author's collection)*

At the end of another day the much maligned, but highly-skilled, workforce of the yard head home. *(Author's collection)*

'Magic Ride'

One of the strangest promotional films ever produced for a ship, or indeed many other travel experiences, was 'Magic Ride' – a 24-minute film released from 1969.

Cunard and James Archibald and Associates signed an agreement in September 1966 for a film about the design and construction of the new Cunarder. This was to portray the achievements in building the ship in an exciting way, largely through the people concerned with her at all levels, and was designed for commercial distribution both on television and theatrically.

The film was shot in 35 mm colour at a cost of £16,000 of which £10,000 was contributed by Cunard over the production period, and £6,000 was provided by the producers. The producers would be reimbursed out of the commercial takings of the film up to the amount of their contribution, after which any further revenue would revert to Cunard. It was thought that the interest would be such that the total cost to Cunard would be negligible, or that the film would even produce a small profit.

Cunard wanted to have a film made about how a ship grows up. Just, in fact, they thought, like a modern teenager. James Archibald would say that the story was *"…a sort of Alice in Cunarder Land."* The film traced how a young girl grows up with the liner.

The two 'stars' of the film were Anna Bentinck and Murray Head and the film was written and directed by Don Higgins. The pop group 'Applejacks' were featured singing 'Rosemary' and Commodore Bil Warwick was also featured.

Anna Bentinck joined *QE2* in 2007 and 2008 for the ship's 40th anniversary of the launch cruise and final Round Britain and would reveal that she had not been on *QE2* since May 1969, it was the first time she had seen the film and was surprised by it and its popularity and she requested a copy to show her children! During her talks on board prior to introducing the film Anna told of the auditions at the time. Once she had been chosen she was to assist in selecting the right male for the part as it was important she and actor clicked and had chemistry. One of the auditioners turned up looking quite scruffy and was rejected because he *"didn't look right for the part."* That was David Bowie!

For the launch sequence the Director wanted Anna to be on the foredeck as the ship slid down the slipway but the male-dominated world of shipbuilding would not allow a woman to be on board during the launch so Anna had to be filmed in the main grandstand during the launch and can clearly be seen 'acting' for the film standing a few steps behind The Queen and Princess Margaret.

The film company paid for all of her driving lessons as she had to drive a classic car in the role.

Anna went on to mainly narrate various programmes and broadcasts while Murray Head became an actor and singer best known for the international hit 'One Night in Bangkok'.

CHAPTER FOUR

The Class Argument

As the hull of *Q4* took shape on the building berth in the months that followed the Keel Laying, the ship's internal design still had a long way to go before it was finalised. Cunard remained firmly committed to *Q3*'s three-class Atlantic service despite a strong case put forward by, among others, Dan Wallace. While the class structure would remain sacrosanct, virtually every other design aspect of *Q4* was questioned and evaluated.

In a statement issued in February 1962 Cunard stated:

"Cunard are aware there have been moves towards two class ships, but are convinced that in a ship of 'Q4's' size, three classes are justified. The safeguard is that the internal design is sufficiently flexible to make adaptation to two classes a simple operation if the trade should warrant it. There are several factors: (1) consistent and continuing demand for Cabin Class; (2) higher revenue from a three class ship; (3) the large public who cannot afford First Class and are unwilling to go Tourist; (4) American travel agents consider that a three class ship is right. Their opinion is important because 70% of Cunard passenger business originates in North America.

"Q4 will have unparalleled flexibility between First, Cabin and Tourist, so that almost any combination of passenger numbers can be carried. She will be a complete break from the tradition of the present 'Queens', where in comparison with First Class, tourist has little or no space."

Sir John Brocklebank, whose main expertise was cargo shipping, felt that a three-class vessel would be more profitable and have greater passenger appeal. While he acknowledged that two classes could be successful in medium sized liners, such as Cunard's own *Carmania* and *Franconia*, he continued to believe that passengers preferred three classes in larger vessels such as Italy's *Michelangelo* and *Raffaello* on *"which three classes are more attractive on all counts."* But these liners were operating on a very different route, with their lower class being virtually emigrant traffic and, as history proved, these ships, with their heavily subdivided accommodations, had limited potential for cruise service and, in fact, lasted in service for only a decade.

In Cunard tradition its new liner would offer three classes - First, Cabin and Tourist - but the various Cunard departments could not decide the make-up of the passenger carry. Some preferred a maximum First-Class passenger total while others wanted a maximum Tourist Class complement.

Two schemes were proposed:

First Class	630	or	250
Cabin Class	700	or	300
Tourist Class	530	or	1,450

As designs were being compiled, these departments / offices continued to disagree. The London office thought C Deck was very low so should be assigned to Tourist Class. One office complained there were not enough First Class single cabins and some wanted a retractable roof over the First and Cabin Class outdoor swimming pools as *"both pools are overlooked by passengers of a lower class which could cause dissatisfaction."* Some complained that there was no outdoor pool for Tourist Class.

Q4 would follow the original *Queen Mary* plan of First Class in the middle and on top, Cabin at the rear and Tourist at the front. Main Deck was reserved mainly for First Class with a few Cabin Class cabins aft, Foyer Deck was again First Class with some Cabin Class aft and Tourist Class forward, as was A Deck. B Deck was all Cabin or Tourist while C Deck was all Tourist. First Class passengers were to occupy all outside staterooms, just over one-third of Cabin Class passengers would occupy inside cabins while less than half

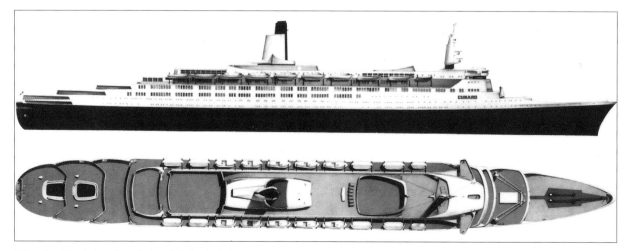

QE2 profile and top decks by James Gardner. *(Author's collection)*

Above: QE2's funnel was probably the most technically advanced funnel ever fitted to a passenger ship and perhaps the most controversial!

Left : To increase her appeal as a cruise vessel, vast lido areas were created on the aft decks complete with outdoor swimming pools.

Below: On Tuesday 4 April 1967, *QE2*, the world's fastest and most powerful twin screw liner, was formally unveiled.

(All photographs author's collection)

of Tourist Class was inside cabins.

The design included a large number of interchangeable cabins and some common public rooms and facilities; at best, this would have made it possible superficially to retract class barriers for cruises. With work well in hand, and a stringent deadline for the ship's completion to be met, she may well have entered service that way.

Three Class Division

First Class	Promenade Deck (Quarter Deck)
Cabin Class	Verandah Deck (Upper Deck)
Tourist Class	Verandah Deck and 50% of
	Boat Deck(Upper and Boat Decks)

First Class

Sports Deck	Outdoor space
Verandah Deck	Teenagers Room
Promenade Deck	Restaurant
	Grill Room
	Library
	Card room

The Synagogue on Three Deck by Professor Misha Black. *(Author's collection)*

	Nightclub
	Bar
	Outdoor pool / Lido
Foyer Deck	Lobby
Passenger	
Accommodation	Main, Foyer and A
	Decks (centre)

Cabin Class

Verandah Deck	Restaurant (shared with Tourist Class)
	Cocktail Lounge
	Bar
	Lounge
	Library
	Shop
	Teenagers Room
	Promenade
Main Deck	Outdoor pool / Lido

Foyer Deck	Lobby
Passenger	
Accommodation	Main (aft), Foyer (aft), A (aft) and
	B (interchangeable with Tourist) Decks.

Cabin Class

Verandah Deck	Observation Lounge
	Restaurant (shared with Cabin Class)
	Promenade
	Teenagers Room

Foyer Deck	Lobby
Passenger Accommodation	Foyer (forward), A (forward), B (interchangeable with Cabin Class) and C (all of) Decks
Shared Facilities	
Cinema /Nightclub	Verandah and Boat Decks
Indoor pools	C and D Decks
Coffee Shop	Boat Deck

The initial concept for the Juke Box Room on Boat Deck. *(Author's collection)*

Art Gallery	Boat Deck
Teenagers Room	Boat Deck
Nightclub	Boat Deck
Main Lobbies for Embarkation / Disembarkation	
First Class	midships on Foyer Deck
Cabin Class	aft on Foyer Deck
Tourist Class	forward on Foyer Deck
Main Staircases	

These would connect with their main lobbies:

First Class	what became D Stairway
Cabin Class	what became G Stairway
Tourist Class	what became A Stairway

A fierce debate raged within Cunard between those in favour of three-classes (notably the New York office) and those who felt that because the future of the ship lay in cruising as well as the North Atlantic, she should be a two-class ship. The principal advantage of two classes over three was that the public rooms of a two-class ship could be so much larger. The feeling in America had been that in a ship carrying First, Cabin and Tourist, it was still possible to sell the Cabin Class accommodation in sufficient numbers to warrant carving the liner up three ways.

One of the most comprehensive and detailed anti-three class documents was prepared in March 1963 by Cunard's Naval Architect's Department. They analysed the number of passengers possible in a three-class ship and a two-class ship: in a three-class vessel it was possible to have 1,816 passengers or 1,990; for a two-class vessel the passenger capacity could be 1,960, but this would not take into account space-saving from having a single kitchen and reduction in crew. This could increase the estimate of passengers to 2,030.

The report highlighted that in a three-class ship:

- If the lowest class has to compete with modern tourist Class, the standard would approach so closely the Cabin standard that it would be difficult to give the cabin Class an advantage over Tourist commensurate with the difference in fare. In other words, the three-class ship would

the ends of the accommodation decks with interchangeable rooms on the lower decks, where the first contact between the two classes would take place. To give a high interchangeable number resulted in passengers being very far from their vertical access to public rooms and open decks. General working access was difficult to achieve (and often unsatisfactory) when arranged. The forward class in particular would be forced to the highest parts of the ship for deck space, which was difficult to screen and was a long distance away from staterooms. Each of these classes had a high proportion of accommodation subject to movement and noise.

The report went on to say that cruising requirements were difficult to satisfy in a three-class design. There would be a number of public rooms which would not be used for cruising, while the two-class vessel would have fewer rooms, at least one of which would be big enough for use as a cruise lounge. Other savings which a two-class design would produce would be numerous: deletion of Cabin Class menu, furnishings, linen, crockery, cutlery, printing and stationery etc and a reduction of shore staff administration for Cabin Class

The One Deck Shop. *(Author's collection)*

call for a low rated Tourist Class of the economy type.

- The space savings in the two-class ship affected first build costs and then running costs:

- fewer public rooms and associated pantries, bars, lavatories etc

- common kitchen with less equipment

- fewer entrances

- Common use between the classes of:

> Library
> Shopping Centre
> Theatre
> Beauty Parlour
> Treatment Baths
> Launderette

- Designers were forced to locate the two lower classes at

Initially, even this clear analysis did not persuade Cunard management who claimed, after a series of evaluation meetings, that:

"…the data and design and economic studies made 'demonstrated conclusively that a ship of three-class arrangement was not only more profitable but of greater passenger appeal, in that it resulted in a more evenly scaled grading of accommodation from Tourist through Cabin to First Class"'.

The significant factors which weighed heavily in favour of a three-class vessel were:

- A consistent and continuing demand for cabin-class.
- The higher revenue that would be derived from a three-class ship.
- The proven fact that there was a large public who could not afford first-class and would welcome a middle-class.

• The views of the company's sales organisations on both sides of the Atlantic

The American side of Cunard won the battle. They insisted that the American market demanded three classes and as Americans provided over 70% of Cunard business, it was not surprising which way the Cunard Board was swayed.

On 21 October 1963, when Cunard announced that they were proceeding with Q4, Sir John Brocklebank confirmed that a two-class operation was under review but three classes were doing good business and it would take a lot of convincing to get two classes adopted. He advised that there would be plenty of time to make a final decision.

"The question of whether the new ship will carry two or three classes has for some time been the subject of detailed examination, but as it is not immediately necessary for us to take a final decision these studies are continuing. I may say, however, that as regards to First Class, her restaurant, similarly to the 'Queens', will be sufficiently spacious to take care of all her First Class passengers at one sitting."

Conference rules prohibit one-class ships, there has been a trend towards building ships with the smallest possible first-class accommodation, the bulk of the space being allocated to tourist class.

"The Israeli shipping line, Zim, for example, made it clear recently that it would have preferred to have operated its new transatlantic liner Shalom ('Peace'), as a one-class ship, but was barred by rulings of the Atlantic Passenger Liner Conference.

"Among the smaller ships on the route, Holland America line's Statendam, has first-class accommodation amounting to only 10 per cent of the total accommodation.

"But the bitterest controversy must arise over the reasons for Cunard's decision to remain loyal to the three-class travel idea. These reasons are not based upon tradition, as might have been the case ten years ago, but upon the results of a searching inquiry on both sides of the Atlantic into the type of accommodation and degree of class segregation sought by potential passengers.

"It is believed that the Cunard's US sales staff were the

The Officers Dining Room adjacent to their Wardroom forward on Boat Deck. *(Author's collection)*

Earlier (unissued) drafts of the same statement declared: *"…the situation [two versus three classes] will be resolved before the specification has to be completed."*

This confirmation from the Chairman would cause further controversy when it came to the class debate.

The Evening Press reported:

"Cunard's final decision to build three passenger classes – first, cabin and tourist – into its new £22 million transatlantic express liner, has roused more controversy in the passenger liner trade than any other development in liner design in the last decade.

"The notable point about the decision is that it sails boldly against the post-war tide flowing towards the smallest possible number of segregated classes aboard a ship.

"On some routes one-class ships have been introduced with great success; while on the transatlantic run, where

strongest supporters of a three-class ship; and American opinion is important because most of Cunard's passenger business originates in North America.

"The consensus of Cunard opinion, however, is that there is a consistent and continuing demand for an intermediate cabin class, and that there is a higher revenue to be won from three classes.

"Cunard certainly cannot be accused of being old-fashioned in its other plans for the new 58,000-tons liner. Again against most of the modern liner trends the new Cunarder will have her three restaurants high up in the ship with passengers being able to look out on the undulating sea through large windows; a welcome contrast to feeding low in the hull with only portholes.

"With the increased efficiency of anti-roll stabilisers this should be an effective selling point.

"Nevertheless, advocates of the one-class vessel claim that three and even two classes are unnecessary in liners today. In a one-class ship, they assert, duplication and even

triplication of public rooms are eliminated, with a corresponding increase in the number of fare-paying cabins made available.

"So far as 'classes' in the social sense are concerned, they believe that even this can be tackled successfully within a one-class structure through the use of 'atmospheric' design of public rooms.

"If there is sufficient choice of public spaces within a one-class liner, they argue, passengers will naturally drift towards the rooms which are more appropriately designed and decorated for their tastes. Birds of a feather will flock together...

"This is one form of class war which will certainly be bloodless!"

Cunard confirmed that the investigation into the class debate had been thorough and it was convinced that a ship of Q4's size should be a three-class vessel.

Fairplay reported:

"Has Cunard taken the right decision? If the company has, does this mean that all other lines on the North Atlantic are wrong in operating two-class ships and in their general wish to move to one class? Modern passenger liners in trade have tourist classes providing so high a standard of cabin accommodation, public rooms and service that it is difficult to see how three classes can be right for a ship of Q4's size; the two class France is some 10,000 tons larger. It is to be hoped that Cunard's decision was taken after a most thorough economic investigation and does not represent outdated Anglo-Saxon attitudes"

In January 1964, the Shipbuilding Committee of Cunard decided that a three-class ship would cost £500,000 more than a two-class ship and that manning would involve 50 more men.

At the same time the Committee advised that 600 First Class passengers could only be carried if the restaurants were on the upper decks, thus giving the designers greater freedom of space and a through run of passenger decks.

The Cunard Board was further informed that if tenders were to be invited by the end of August 1964 a decision on the number of classes had to be made by the end of January 1964.

Despite the strong factors supporting two-classes, in February 1964, the Naval Architect was instructed to design a three-class ship with the restaurants on the higher decks. It was agreed that stabilisers had reached such a high degree of efficiency that rolling would not act to the detriment of passengers eating so high. This would mean a higher First Class passenger total and greater flexibility of inter-changeability of accommodation and larger stateroom layout for Cabin and Tourist Class amidships.

Carmania's Captain, William Law, wrote in February 1964:

"Cabin Class has no place in the future. The argument is often put forward that the Cabin Class in the Queens is well booked; this is merely due to the fact that the Tourist Class is well below standard and that a number of people who cannot afford First Class fare feel that they desire something that is better than the present tourist Class. In

a new ship with a well-designed, attractive Tourist Class there will be no need for the 'middle of the road' passenger to look for anything beyond Tourist Class"

Law went on to discuss the fact that America had changed so much since the Second World War that the result was virtually a classless society wherein almost anyone in the vast middle segment could afford a substantial level of comfort.

Another telling argument was that, as a three-class ship, Q4 could accommodate between 1,860 and 2,000 passengers, depending upon the division of the three classes. As a two-class ship, the liner would be able to carry as many as 2,030 and, in spite of the increase payload, the number of staff needed would be less.

In April 1964 Cunard announced that Q4 would be a three-class vessel and that on-board innovations would include the positioning of her three restaurants above the main passenger deck rather than on a lower deck in the hull. All passenger cabins would have private facilities and there would be a very high flexibility between First, Cabin and Tourist classes. Another innovation would be the planning of the accommodation so that in each class passengers will have the run of the full length and breadth of the ship:

"There will be three classes but the division of the ship will be entirely different from the Queens. It will be lengthwise rather than horizontal and there will be tourist-class cabins amidships rather than at both ends."

The company also added that, although plans for the new liner had not been finalised, there would be greater distribution of deck space for the three classes.

In June, an article in the Canadian 'Seaports and Transport World' stated:

"The decision to carry First, Cabin and Tourist Class passengers was reached following detailed discussions between Cunard teams on both sides of the Atlantic.

"The investigation has been thorough, bringing conviction that in a ship of her size this is the right configuration. Design studies were a fact prepared for both a two class ad a three class arrangement.

"There are several significant economic factors that weigh heavily in favour of a three-class ship. These include a consistent and continuing demand for Cabin Class; the higher revenue that can be earned from a three-class ship; the proved fact that there is a large public who cannot afford First Class and would welcome a middle class; views on both sides of the Atlantic are that three classes are right in a vessel of this size and capacity.

"American opinion is important because a preponderance of Cunard passenger business originates in North America."

Colonel Frank Bustard OBE (retired Passenger Superintendent of the White Star Line) offered a few observations to Cunard he thought "may be helpful to Cunard" when he wrote in the August 1964 edition of 'Modern Transport':

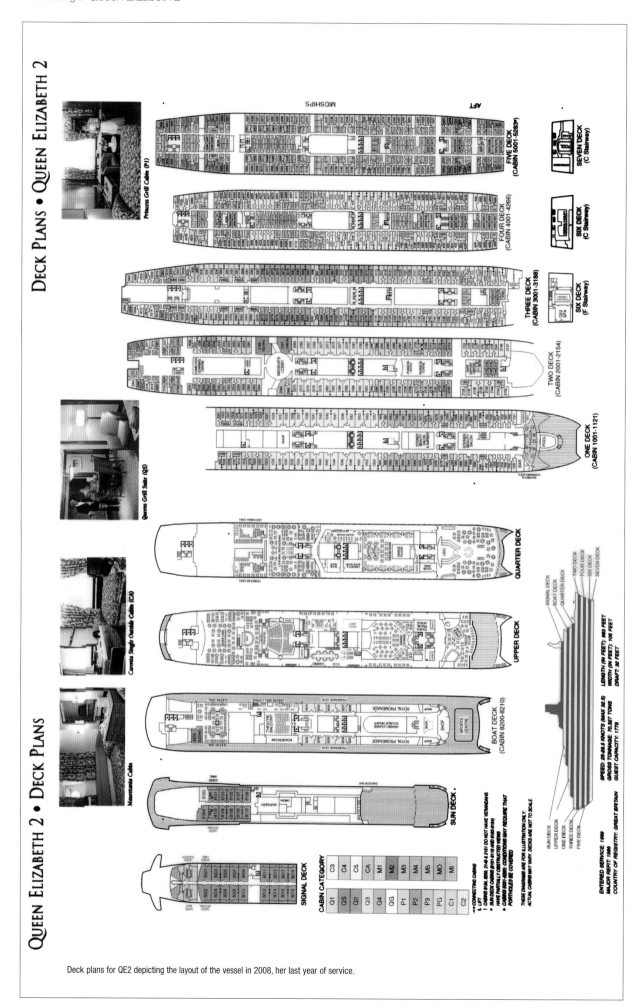

Deck plans for QE2 depicting the layout of the vessel in 2008, her last year of service.

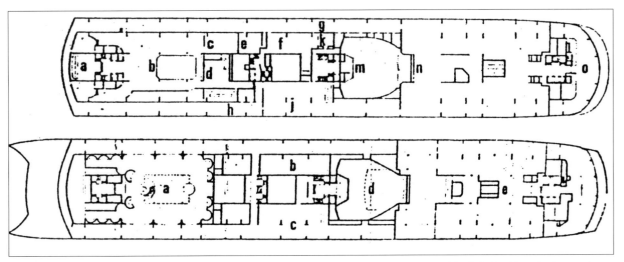

Plans of what would become Upper Deck showing the progression of the deck layout from a three-class layout to two-classes and the elimination of the enclosed promenades.

Verandah Deck – three classes (top)

a – Cabin Class bar; b – Cabin Class lounge; c – Cabin Class library; d – Cabin Class shop; e – Cabin Class teenagers room; f – Tourist Class teenagers room; g – Tourist Class enclosed promenade; h – Cabin Class enclosed promenade; j – Cabin Class cocktail lounge; k – First Class teenagers room; m – Theatre; n – Cabin / Tourist restaurant; o – Tourist observation lounge.

Upper Deck - two classes (bottom)

a – lounge (Double Room); b – library; c – cocktail bar (Theatre Bar); d – Theatre; e – dining room (Britannia Restaurant); f – observation lounge (The Look Out)

"The information recently released that Q4 will be a three-class ship is almost unbelievable. This takes us back 53 years to the Olympic, first of the so-called monster ships. Since then the railways, air transport and practically all shipping companies have discarded three-class carriage as seeming entirely out of date to the travelling public and proving uneconomic to the transport operator.

"Applied to a North Atlantic liner, it means three separate arrangements of public rooms, with separate catering staffs. There is no virtue in travelling Second Class (call it Cabin Class if you wish) beyond it being cheaper than First Class and more comfortable than Third Class (Tourist). The answer to this is to make the first-class fares cheaper and / or the third class (or Tourist) more comfortable. Keep in mind, too, that it gives tourist passengers a possible inferiority complex to realise there are two classes on top of them, restricting their deck pace and creating the thought that they are, after all, a steerage or emigrant class – anachronism indeed.

Colonel Bustard went on to write that accommodation in future Western Ocean liners should be sold on the hotel basis of bed and breakfast and that the new Cunarder should be about three-fifths of the proposed new tonnage, between 33,000 and 35,000 tons, and should cost £15 million or less. He claimed that a good deal of forward thinking was needed.

It was seen as an attack on the ship as a commercial prospect.

The Journal of Commerce commented on 26 August 1964:

"It is, therefore, hard to imagine Col. Bustard's advice being greeted with enthusiasm at the Pier Head.

"What Col. Bustard wants is a clean break from the "unbelievable" – his phrase – announcement that the Q4 is to be a three-class ship. That means that Col. Bustard feels the general pattern of North Atlantic passenger liner building should have guided Cunard, rather than the people in whom the company have in fact put their trust – passengers, agents, and members of the organisation.

"What undermines faith in Col. Bustard's thesis is that it looks like taking into too little account the energy Cunard have put into projecting the market for their ship, and too much account of current liner practice.

"There is no doubt at all that a two-class ship would accord with such practice. But, despite their admiration for the France, a two-class ship on the luxury run, Cunard feel three classes are in tune with their custom. If Cunard are right, the customer is necessarily right – and Col. Bustard is wrong.

"Still, much of Col. Bustard says is interesting. The disparity in fares in a ship in her transport and in her cruising roles is surprising, even when it is acknowledged that all too many liners are being cruises because they cannot earn all the transport passengers they need. And the idea of giving passengers a greater say in the cost of their meals – so that some may spend more on accommodation and less on food if they wish- is attractive. It may mean increased catering overheads. But at least they would be borne by the big eater. There's a rough justice in that."

Colonel Bustard continued to put his views across and a lengthy letter by him was featured in The Financial Times on 11 September 1964:

"Sir, - The plans – should they be made public, for Cunard's proposed 58,000-ton liner will be examined with much interest by the tax-payer, shareholder and all interested in the future maintenance of British shipping.

"Cunard say she will be a three-class liner. This seems incredible, as it takes us back over 50 years to the

Olympic (sister to the ill-fated Titanic) the first of the so-called "monster" ships. IN recent years the railways and practically all shipping companies have discarded three-class carriage as entirely out-of-date. Air transport and hotels have never even considered it.

"Naturally is Q4 has a second-class it will fill during the first years of service – as would any new super Atlantic liner – but this is a short-term view to take of ship that may be in service 28 years from now. The vital period is in 18 years hence, by then, if she is not paying her way the ship will only have negligible break-up value, as there is no other trade in the world that can afford an ageing "monster" of 58,000 tons.

"The ideal North Atlantic liner should not exceed 35,000 tons, be capable of doing 30 knots, and with accommodation for 500 First-Class and 1,000 Tourist-Class, that is a total of 1,500 berths – all readily convertible to a capacity of 1,000 when cruising or carrying convention parties – so popular with American businessmen. There should also be car (or cargo) space for, say, 200 vehicles with roll-on, roll-off facilities.

"Feeding should be on the accepted hotel basis of paying for your meals separately from your accommodation, with the use for First-Class of a small Ritz-Carlton type of restaurant, a grill room and a winter garden café. The Tourist-Class to be similarly provided for, but naturally with no deluxe restaurant.

"The cost of such a ship should be in excess of £15 million, a radical reduction on Cunard's present anticipated outlay of £22 million, making it possible to envisage the laying down in, say, five years' time of a Q5 to replace the ageing Queen Elizabeth which, by then, will be 29 years old.

"The present basis of North Atlantic sea-fares is complicated, confusing and undoubtedly restrictive if the potential tourist mass-travel that we have heard so much about over the past 30 years. Why should it be necessary to charge on the Queen Mary for a 5-day Atlantic voyage, minimum fares which work out at: £34 a day First Class, £21 a day Cabin Class, $17 a day Tourist Class, whereas on the same ship on a 6-day Cruise voyage one pays the minimum of only £11 per day First Class.

"The present-day scale of North Atlantic fares is fantastic and needs radical reconsideration in relation to other overseas trades and the ever-increasing air competition. This never can be done so long as the fare-structure has to meet the heavy capital and operating costs of the "monster" type of ship evolved half-a-century ago to carry the – now departed – hordes of Continental emigrants in Third-Class quarters."

Cunard responded by reiterating the line that the debates had come down strongly in favour of three classes and it was the Americans who provided the largest amount of business on "the top travel route" between New York and Europe.

The company also claimed that the new ship would spend at least four months cruising each year and during that time she would be one class only. The transformation would not be difficult because the specifications, by now in the hands of five British shipyards, showed that the old horizontal division of passenger accommodation had been completely changed.

All classes would have a fair share of the upper deck space.

The criticism that the liner would need three sets of public rooms and three sets of kitchens was tackled by Cunard:

"All sets of public rooms will fit into the idea of a one-class cruising ship and there will be only one galley to serve the three dining rooms."

On 23 October 1964 it was reported in Commerce that a Cunard spokesman had confirmed to the publication that the new liner would be convertible form her planned three class to two class operation. He added that major public rooms had been designed so that, with the removal of bulkheads, cabin and tourist class salons could be united. There would, the spokesman said, be no space wasted in such a configuration, compared with the same facilities built for exclusively two-class operation.

Commerce commented:

"So the company are having it both ways. If their market research is correct and three classes are wanted on the North Atlantic, so be it. If the two class trend holds, well, so be that, too.

"The convertibility of the Q4 is a neat example of advanced British design work, and worth a round of applause from past critics."

PUBLIC ROOM LOCATIONS (December 1964)

Bridge Deck

Grill Room
Casino
Passage and Stair

Sports Deck

Passage and Stair
Forward Passage
Tourist Class Entrance
Tourist Class Stair

Mezzanine Deck

Tourist Class Observation Lounge
Entrance Hall
Stairway

Boat Deck

Tourist Class Cocktail Lounge
Tourist Class Bar
Tourist Class Library
Bowling Alley
Teenagers Room
Verandah Lounge
Playroom
Nursery and Crèche
Entrance and Passage Stairs x 2
Tourist Class Lounge
Beauty Parlour and Barbers
Forward Passage and Entrance
Stairway Forward
Shop
Synagogue

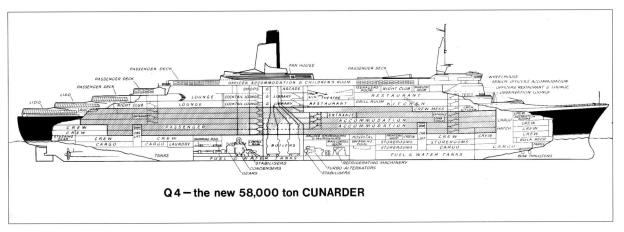

Q 4 – the new 58,000 ton CUNARDER

A profile issued for the new ship with no classes designated. *(Author's collection)*

Verandah Deck

Cabin Class Cocktail Bar
Cabin Class Lounge
Stair and Vestibule
Cabin Class Library
Conference Room
Passage, port side
Theatre (auditorium balcony)
First / Cabin Class Teenagers Room
Cabin Class Cocktail Bar and Lounge
First Class Playroom
Cabin Class Playroom and Crèche
Children's Dining Room
Stairs x 2
Cabin / Tourist Class Restaurant

Promenade Deck

First Class Nightclub
Stairway x 2
Entrance
First Class Lounge
Enclosed Promenade (port and starboard)
First Class Cocktail Lounge and Bar
First Class Smoking Room
First Class Library
Entrance Hall
First Class Club Room
Stairway (aft)
Stairs (forward) x 2
First Class Restaurant (raised roof over foyer)
Tourist Class Stair (forward)

Main Deck

Cabin Class Beauty Parlour
Cabin Class Barber
First Class Beauty Parlour
First Class Barber
First Class Entrance (amidships)
Stairways x 2
Tourist Class Entrance (forward)
Staircase

Foyer Deck

Cabin Class Entrances (aft)
Shop

Cabin Class Stair
First Class Entrance (amidships)
First Class Shop
First Class Stairway
Tourist Class Entrance (forward)
Tourist Class Stairway

A Deck

First Class Entrance (amidships)
First Class Shop
Tourist Class Entrance (forward)
Tourist Class Stairway

B Deck

Cabin and Tourist Class Entrance (amidships)
Cabin and Tourist Class Stairway (amidships)
Cabin and Class Tourist Entrance (forward)
Cabin and Tourist Class Stairway (forward)

C Deck

Tourist Class Entrance (forward)
Tourist Class Stairway (forward)

D Deck

First and Cabin Class Swimming Pool, Bar and Treatment Rooms

E Deck

Tourist Class Swimming Pool and Bar

PUBLIC ROOM LOCATIONS (May 1965)

Boat Deck

First Class Playroom
First Class Nursery
Cabin Class Crèche
Cabin Class Nursery
Cabin Class Playroom
Tourist Class Beauty Parlour and Barbers
Tourist Class Shop
Tourist Class Cocktail Lounge
Tourist Class Playroom
Tourist Class Nursery
Tourist Class Crèche
Tourist Class Verandah Lounge

Tourist Class Library
Tourist Class Lounge
Conference Room – all classes
Theatre (balcony) – all classes

Intermediate Deck

Verandah Deck

First Class Teenagers Room
Cabin Class Cocktail Lounge
Cabin Class Teenagers Room
Cabin Class Library
Cabin Class Shop
Cabin Class Lounge
Cabin Class Verandah Bar
Cabin and Tourist Class Restaurant
Tourist Class Observation Lounge
Tourist Class Teenagers' Room
Theatre – all classes

Promenade Deck

First Class Grill Room
First Class Restaurant
First Class Verandah Lounges (port and starboard)
First Class Casino
First Class Smoking Room
First Class Cocktail Bar
First Class Lounge
First Class Library
First Class Lido Lounge and Night Club

Main Deck

First Class Grill Room Bar
First Class Shop
First Class Beauty Parlour
First Class Barbers Shop
Cabin Class Beauty Parlour
Cabin Class Barbers Shop
Cabin and Tourist Class Shop

Foyer Deck

Main Entrances	Forward (Tourist Class)
	Midships (First Class)
	Aft (Cabin Class)

A Deck

B Deck

C Deck

| **D Deck** | First Class Swimming Pool, Massage, Vapour Rooms |

| **E Deck** | Cabin and Tourist Class Swimming Pool |

In November 1965 Sir John Brocklebank resigned from Cunard on the grounds of ill health. His successor was Sir Basil Smallpeice and within weeks of taking charge Sir Basil announced that although she was originally designed as a three-class liner, *Q4* was now more likely to turn out to be a two-class ship. He confirmed that further market research was being carried out to prove or disprove the suggestion by Cunard's sales staff in the US that American customers insist upon a middle-class 'Cabin-Class'.

Dennis Lennon's appointment by Sir Basil to mastermind *Q4*'s interiors strengthened the case for two classes. Lennon instinctively believed that *Q4* should be a two-class ship, going against the view of the Cunard directorate.

Research undertaken by the Economic Intelligence Unit and a report on future traffic during which 83,000 people in America had been questioned about their ideas on sea travel concluded that the original three-class plan was potentially less profitable.

On 7 February 1966 Cunard's Naval Architect submitted a memorandum to the New Cunarder Committee with plans suggesting certain modifications to public rooms which would produce improvements for a two-class ship and yet would have little detrimental effect if three classes were carried. The modifications included:

Promenade Deck

- The Library and Casino were interchanged.

- The Smokeroom was designed as a Card Room.

  Verandah Deck

- The Teenagers' Rooms were removed and replaced by a Library. This Library would be larger than originally planned to enable it to be used as a quiet room on cruises. If the vessel was completed as a two-class ship then it was large enough to accommodate the combined Cabin and Tourist Class numbers. The former Cabin Class Library would become a Conference Room / Cruise Office.

- In the revised arrangement First Class would not have direct access to the Conference Room.

- The Cabin Shop was moved to Sports Deck.

- The Cabin Class Lounge was extended to the ship's side.

  Boat Deck

- The Tourist Shop was moved aft and a new shopping centre was provided. This revised layout provided a central shopping area suitable for three-class, two-class or cruising.

- The extent of the Nurseries was curtailed on the assumption that they would be combined for all classes except a separate First Class Nursery could be provided when required. The Nursery would be arranged to give separate access to all classes.

- Bowling alleys and other similar facilities were to be provided in each of the three classes but it was now proposed that a single Teenagers' Room be arranged. This room was directly accessible only to Tourist Class. Cabin and First Class passengers would need to walk through the Tourist Verandah area to access it.

- It had already been agreed to provide an opening in the Tourist Class Lounge so that this room could be linked with the Cabin Class Lounge below. The possibility was established of arranging a portable cover to this opening to ensure that as a three-class vessel the rooms were segregated. Further investigations confirmed that it was feasible to have a portable dance floor which could cover the opening when the vessel was three-class that could be raised to the ceiling when the vessel was cruising or two-class. Dennis Lennon and James Gardner objected to the portable dance floor.

The Naval Architect's Department stressed a decision on these proposed changes was required urgently as *"consultations with the designers have now reached a stage when progress is being delayed until a decision is made."*

PUBLIC ROOM LOCATIONS (February 1966)

Sports Deck

Children's Room

Boat Deck

Tourist Class Cocktail Lounge
Tourist Class Verandah Lounge
Tourist Class Lounge
Conference Room

Verandah Deck

Tourist Class Observation Lounge
Cabin Class and Tourist Class Restaurant
Cabin Class Cocktail Lounge
Cabin Class Lounge
Cabin Class Verandah Bar
Theatre
Tourist Class Teenagers' Room

Promenade Deck

Grill Room
First Class Restaurant
First Class Smokeroom
First Class Cocktail Lounge
First Class Lounge
First Class Side Lounge

Main Deck

Foyer Deck

Main Entrances	Forward (Tourist Class)
	Midships (First Class)
	Aft (Cabin Class)

A Deck

B Deck

C Deck

| **D Deck** | First Class Swimming Pool |
| **E Deck** | Cabin Class and Tourist Class Swimming Pool |

PUBLIC ROOM LOCATIONS (May 1966)

| **Sports Deck** | Children's Room |

The initial concept for the passageway adjacent to the Juke Box and leading to the Coffee Shop on Boat Deck

Boat Deck	Tourist Class Cocktail Lounge
	Teenagers Room
	Theatre Balcony
	Shops
	Upper Main Lounge
Verandah Deck	
	Tourist Class Observation Lounge
	Cabin Class and Tourist Class Restaurant
	Theatre
	Cabin Class Cocktail Lounge
	Main Lounge
Promenade Deck	
	Grill Room
	First Class Restaurant
	First Class Library
	First Class Smoking Room
	First Class Cocktail Lounge
	First Class Lounge
	First Class Lido Lounge
Main Deck	
	Grill Room Bar
	Shops
	First Class Beauty Parlour
	Cabin Class Beauty Parlour
Foyer Deck	
Main Entrances	Forward (Tourist Class)
	Midships (First Class)
	Aft (Cabin Class)

"The Most Exciting Thing Since Apollo 1". *(Author's collection)*

A Deck

B Deck

C Deck

D Deck   First Class Swimming Pool

E Deck   Cabin and Tourist Class Swimming Pool

Cabin and Tourist classes were to share the dining room on Verandah Deck as a consequence of the amalgamation of catering services in a single galley complex on Promenade Deck.

All passengers were to have use of the same theatre, following the example of *Rotterdam*, *France*, *Michelangelo* and *Raffaello*. However, despite these concessions to the changing times, the smaller specialised spaces such as libraries and teenagers' rooms were still be have been rigidly segregated.

On 11 May 1966 Lord Aberconway wrote to Sir Basil Smallpeice to advise him that delivery of the vessel would be delayed to November 1968 instead of May 1968 because of a shortage of skilled steel workers. About two-thirds of the hull of *Q4* was completed at this time, and had reached a fairly advanced stage of construction, with some items of machinery already in place and work on the lower strata of cabins begun, but there was still time for change.

While this meant that the already financially beleaguered owners would lose the lucrative 1968 summer Atlantic season, at an estimated cost of £200,000 per week in lost revenue, it allowed enough extra time for some very important changes to *Q4*'s design and these improvements to the ship would pay off in the long run.

During April and May 1966 the discussions regarding the vexed question of two or three classes was brought to finality.

Those who wanted a two-class vessel had won the day.

The new ship would be a loosely-defined two-class vessel on the Atlantic and a single-class cruiser.

In the 'Statement of the Chairman' issued on 18 May 1966 as part of the 1965 Annual Report, Sir Basil Smallpeice stated:

The New Cunarder:

Shortage of labour has had a delaying effect on the work of steel erection on the new ship (No. 736) now being built for us as John Brown's yard at Clydebank. We have also chosen to revise the layout of certain passenger accommodation in the ship as well as to modify the arrangements for interior design, so as to ensure that it confirms with the new marketing policy we have evolved for our passenger business. The New Cunarder is now designed basically as either a two-class ship or an open ship with the ability to reserve a whole deck of public rooms for the exclusive use of passengers who have purchased the most expensive stateroom accommodation.

The new ship is expected to earn about one-third of our total passenger ship revenues and will therefore play a major part in the future development of the Company. With its improvements in design and economics as compared with existing ships, it should prove a profitable investment. But I regard it as essential that we should put our existing ships on at least a break-even basis before the Q4 is delivered in 1968 and not just rely on the new ship to get us out of our difficulties.

In a statement announcing the delay in completion (issued on 27 May 1966), it was stated:

"It had also been decided, in view of the results of the Economist Intelligence Unit's market researches, that certain modifications to the ship as originally planned are desirable.

"In particular, a firm decision has been taken to make

the new Cunarder a two-class ship. Although her original design allowed easy conversion from three classes to two classes or one, various facilities on the ship would have remained separated and the modifications are intended to concentrate these facilities where they will be most convenient. The work will include re-siting or concentrating the shopping, children's and teenage areas, and combining the original cabin and tourist lounges into one large public room with a balcony."

Cunard Chairman Sir Basil Smallpeice reported:

"We have chosen to revise the layout of certain passenger accommodation in the ship as well as to modify the arrangements for interior design, so as to ensure that it conforms with the new marketing policy we have evolved for our passenger business.

"In travel, separate class accommodations as a reflection of a hierarchical social stature is clearly out-of-date. What is offered is a wide variety of accommodation to suit the widest possible range of demands in terms of quality and where in traditional Cunarders, separate parts of the ship were assigned to different classes, the new ship is entirely open. All passengers can walk from end to end without let or hindrance."

It is also thought that the upgrading of the minimum in Tourist Class to ensuite that led to the British finally overcoming the American objections to move to a two-class layout.

Dan Wallace received the orders to change the ship from three to two classes and it was he who made the philosophical statement that it was easier to re-design the ship with one fewer class than an additional one!

On the Atlantic run, extra rooms and amenities would be available for what would now be known as Premium fare-paying passengers. The old terms First, Cabin and Tourist – so inbred into the 'Old Cunard' structure, were swept away simply by First and Tourist Classes.

The areas affected were primarily the public spaces which the overall design scheme had already relegated to the uppermost strata of the ship's integral hive of passenger spaces.

The traditional practice of giving the highest deck to First Class was completely reversed. This was done to provide the premium-fare passengers with an added measure of comfort by locating their spaces nearest the centre of gravity. Despite the use of stabilisers, Cunard was still worried about the ships' great height, particularly since the topsides public spaces for each class were to include restaurants. On North Atlantic service, First Class passengers would be assigned exclusive use of Promenade Deck rooms while Tourist Class would occupy Verandah and Boat Decks.

Changes to Promenade, Verandah and Boat Deck Layouts

The change to two classes involved a near-total redesign of the public rooms on the uppermost decks. The new arrangement would allow for a virtually open plan / range of passenger facilities for cruising, with provision for the dining rooms and a few other spaces to be segregated by class on North Atlantic service only. A complete rationalisation in the layout of all public spaces, especially those allocated to the two lower classes (Cabin and Tourist), was also undertaken. Extra space was gained because of the resultant reduction in the number of public rooms and associated service required.

Promenade Deck (later Quarter Deck)

- The First Class rooms were retained in their original layout and concept.

Verandah Deck (later Upper Deck)

- The layout of this was completely revised. The separate facilities for Cabin (Verandah Deck) and Tourist Classes (Boat Deck) were amalgamated to either serve Tourist Class in Atlantic service or to complement the first-class facilities below on Promenade Deck while cruising as an open-class vessel.

- In one brilliant stroke two lounges (Cabin on Verandah Deck and Tourist on Boat Deck) became one, two-deck space with both levels connected with a stainless steel and glass stairway. One of the largest and most impressive rooms afloat (eventually to become the 20,000 square-foot Double Room) was created. This plan had been mooted in the early design stage.

- The triplication of First, Cabin and Tourist Teenagers' Rooms was eliminated along with the duplication of shops, bars and other smaller rooms belonging to the two lesser classes.

- The combined Cabin and Tourist Dining Room was re-designed as a Tourist Class Restaurant.

- The portside Tourist Promenade and starboard Cabin Class Promenade were eliminated.

Boat Deck

- The layout of this was completely revised. The separate facilities for Cabin and Tourist Classes were amalgamated to either serve Tourist Class in Atlantic service or to complement the facilities below on Promenade Deck while cruising as an open-class vessel.

- Forward of the new combined double-room lounge, space formerly allocated to other Tourist facilities became the Shopping Centre (First and Tourist Classes).

- Further forward the original Tourist Class rooms were eliminated and replaced with a Coffee Shop, Art Gallery, Teenagers' Room and a Nightclub were placed; all available to all passengers without any class barriers.

- The combination of Cabin and Tourist also enabled the elimination of corridors to serve the First Class Teenagers Room and the movement of Cabin and Tourist Class Teenagers Rooms on the Boat Deck –leaving space for what become the Upper Deck Library.

The most outstanding feature of these re-designed decks was their simplicity of plan, replacing the old-fashioned layouts with their numerous vestibules, galleries and other wasted circulation spaces which had no purpose.

The overall plan, which at various stages of its evolution included traditional open and closed promenades, was further reworked into a fully-enclosed and climate-controlled circulating space around the perimeter of each deck, providing side access to the public rooms, stairways and other central services, as aboard the latest Scandinavian liners *Sagafjord* and *Kungsholm*.

The design and layout of *Q4*'s cabins did not undergo the same extensive rationalisation, except that they were no longer divided among three classes. The existence of mock-up cabins ensured that no real difficulties occurred because of the change in class direction.

The most expensive accommodation was arranged amidships, along the greater part of Main, Foyer and A Decks, comprising the First Class bloc on Atlantic service. However, all cabins, regardless of their category, were designed to uniformly high standards.

Even Cunard's policy on gratuities was developed with the two-class system in mind; First Class passengers were expected to pay gratuities for service while Tourist Class fares would be all-inclusive.

PUBLIC ROOM LOCATIONS (As Built)

Sports Deck

Children's Room

Boat Deck

Tourist Class Nightclub	736 Club
	London Gallery
	The Coffee Shop
	The Juke Box
	Theatre Balcony
	Shops
Tourist Class Main Lounge	Double Room (Double Up)

Upper Deck

Tourist Class Observation Lounge	The Lookout
Tourist Class Restaurant	Britannia Restaurant
	Theatre
Tourist Class Library	Upper Deck Library
Tourist Class Cocktail Bar	Theatre Bar
	Tour Office
Tourist Class Main Lounge	Double Room
Tourist Class Bar	Double Down Bar

Quarter Deck

	The Grill Room
First Class Restaurant	Columbia Restaurant
First Class Library	Card Room
First Class Cocktail Bar	Midships Bar
First Class Main Lounge	Queens Room
	Conference Room
First Class Lido Lounge/Nightclub	Q4 Room

One Deck

First Class Laundry	Grill Room Bar
First Class Shop	One Deck Shop
Beauty Parlour	
Barber Shop	

Two Deck

Main Entrances	Forward Lobby (Tourist Class)
	Midships Lobby (First Class) Aft

Three Deck

	Synagogue
	Main Laundry

Four Deck

Five Deck

Six Deck

	Tourist Class Laundry
	First Class Swimming Pool and Gymnasium

Seven Deck

	Tourist Class Swimming Pool and Gymnasium

CHAPTER FIVE

The new Cunarder

After launching, *QE2* was moved to the fitting out basin, where she was to be completed over the following months. In the engine shops, now known as John Brown Engineering (JBE), the ship's turbine machinery and boilers were well advanced. Pametrada, the Newcastle based designers of the liner's machinery, had ceased to exist in 1967 and so John Brown Engineering recruited the nucleus of Pametrada's design team specifically to work on the liner's machinery contract.

Over a thousand firms and 500 subcontractors would send lorry loads of items from all over the country. The lifeboats of the new liner were built in a Surrey boatyard and were manufactured in glass-fibre and moulded in two parts.

Every public area was made in quarter inch models which were placed together on tables for meetings with the Cunard directors to see how the complete effect would be. Dennis Lennon built part of the Columbia Restaurant in his office basement and he said in the 1980s that *"there are still bits of it around."* Cunard had 14 sample cabins built at the yard and a complete range of sample chairs were tested there.

On 11 October 1967 all joiners in the shipyard withdrew their labour to enforce a claim for increased payments. The joiners returned to work at 0900 hours on Sunday 15 October having been granted an increase in wages in keeping with those awards recently made in the district. Even though this stoppage was of short duration it adversely affected the fitting out progress and therefore the completion of the ship.

Nine days later on 20 October the coppersmiths and plumbers withdrew their labour following a lengthy dispute regarding demands for increased wages. While plumber work was well advanced a prolonged stoppage would also affect the completion. The men returned to work on 29 November.

In all there was nine stoppages of work in 1967.

The news from the yard would have been a mere distraction for Sir Basil Smallpeice who had greater concerns which were revealed on 19 October when he gave a press conference at the Cunard office in Leadenhall Street. Unsupported by any other member of the Board Sir Basil faced around 70 journalists to report a loss of £2,031,000 for the half year to 30 June – some £562,000 more than in the same half of 1966. Passenger traffic had continued to fall and there was an expected £4 million drop in revenue expected

Paint crews at work on the port side in this view taken in summer 1968 where **QE2** looks remarkably complete but still missing her bridge wings. *(Author's collection)*

Top left: E Stairway at Boat Deck.

Above left: D Stairway looking down to Quarter Deck and the entrance to what would become the Columbia Restaurant.

Above rght: The vast cathedral-like space within the ship before the funnel was positioned.

Below rght: The funnel was installed in two halves with the lower portion being swung into place on Thursday 18 April 1968 followed four days later, on 22 April, by the upper section shown here.

(All photographs author's collection)

The Safety Control Room on Two Deck being installed. Its 30 foot by 25 foot walls were crammed with equipment that would ensure *QE2* was as safe as modern technology could make her. *(Author's collection)*

for 1967. More passenger ships would be sold and the cargo side was just about breaking even and it was expected staff numbers both ashore and afloat would be reduced.

Back in Clydebank it appeared the *QE2* had been renamed HMS *Twikker* when that name appeared in pale green letters four-foot high that had appeared in the dead of night over the weekend 18 and 19 October. The name was the work of a group of students from Sheffield University to publicise their Rag Week. Twikker was the name of their student's magazine. The students drove to Glasgow in a Land Rover with a gallon of paint and a large brush. They hired a rowing boat and paddled out to *QE2* and painted the new name on the stern with the paint brush tied to a 15-foot pole.

23-year old economics student Peter Mortimer said:

"We think the publicity will help us towards our Rag Week target of £17,000."

John Rannie responded to press enquires:

"I was a student myself and know what they get up to. As long as there is no malicious damage no action will be taken. The paint on the stern is only for protection during the fitting out. The final coats have still to be put on. The ship is open to the river and easy to get at. I only hope it's not paint from John Brown's they've used…it's harder to come off."

It was also apparent that at some point someone has scrawled Celtic FC in large letters at the stern on Three Deck.

41 crane men, in violation of a union agreement that had recently been concluded and ratified by the Ministry of Labour, went on unofficial strike on 20 November. This

resulted in the yard having to suspend a further 153 men from various trades with a threat that further men would have to be suspended if the stoppage was not ended quickly. The yard was able to advise Cunard that much of the work on the ship would not be affected by this as the 150-ton jib crane, which was manned by A.E. U members would be in continuous use and that covered much of the machinery spaces. The crane man returned to work on 24 November and those suspended returned three days later.

In December Dan Wallace wrote:

"I have advised the builders that in my opinion there must be a co considerable improvement in the general rate of progress if the vessel is to be completed by the end of November 1968. The builders, while not sharing this view, agree the whole matter of progress must be fully reviewed at the next meeting on 21 February."

A model of the new ship was unveiled by Captain Warwick at the International Boat Show at Earls Court on 2 January 1968. Later that year, in October, a large model and several display boards of *QE2* would be placed on *Queen Elizabeth* in her indoor promenade.

On 18 January 1968 *QE2* received minor damage during a gale. An aluminium unit, consisting of deck plating and bulkheads, was badly damaged and required renewal. Two public room windows were smashed and damage was also done to an aluminium bulkhead, five gangways, 30 wooden blocks, a gangway platform and welder's platform. Aluminium superstructure on the starboard side of the Upper Deck aft was buckled and several pieces of liner furniture was damaged when bricks from another building fell through the roof of a joiners shop.

But strikes and acts of God were only part of the toxic mix

The Coffee Shop'

Original plans for QE2 did not include a Coffee Shop which subsequently appeared on Boat Deck immediately aft of the 736 Club. This space was originally to be the Teenagers' Room and Gallery and the Photography Dark Room. Sir Basil Smallpeice insisted late during the build of QE2 on having a Coffee Shop installed. Sir Basil was convinced that this was this was a 'must have' and the facility would emulate the then current trend in American hotels. Cunard's Managing Director, John Whitworth, and others remained unconvinced that people would want to spend money to buy coffees etc. The Coffee Shop was duly built and became known by Whitworth and the doubters as *"the Chairman's folly."*

In January 1968 the contract for the Teenagers' Room was suspended whilst a decision regarding the conversion of the space to a Coffee Shop was made.

The introduction of a Coffee Shop would present several issues regarding manning. Accommodation for 20 female staff would be required in place of male staff. Originally there had been spare capacity for 19 female ratings on A (Three) Deck but in February 1967 this was converted to single rooms for leading catering ratings.

It would be necessary to reconvert this accommodation to stewardesses and move the displaced ratings to ratings' rooms on D (Six) Deck. This latter block would then need to be converted to rooms for single ratings. Fortunately the piping in this block had been provided for the future use of washbasins.

The shipyard indicated to Cunard that they were still prepared to carry out the crew accommodation modifications at this stage – provided a final decision on the Coffee Shop was made immediately. These amendments were calculated to cost £10,000 to £15,000.

On 31 January 1968 a meeting was held with senior Cunard management where it was agreed (and later approved by Sir Basil) that the main Coffee Shop area would be amidships and on the starboard side. This would reduce the teenagers' area which would be now in the bay at the after end of the starboard side with the facility spread into the next bay forward. A pantry would be set up in the existing pantry / dark room area that would be capable of providing coffee shop facilities for 400 maximum with additional seating being available on the port side and coffee shop service being available in the 736 Club. The Dark Room was relocated to the First Class Gymnasium on D (Six) Deck.

A subsequent plan showing seating capacity for 132 in the main area and the forward two bays was accepted on 15 March 1968. It was also agreed that the Stefan Buzas design for the entire port side as a Gallery should be accepted, but that this space would be flexible and could be used as an adjunct to the Coffee Shop with a capacity of about 56 seats when not in use as a Gallery.

This meeting on 15 March 1968 thus confirmed that the Long Gallery would be interchangeable to a Coffee Shop, the former Teenagers' Room would be the Coffee Shop, and the after bay of the former Teenagers' Room would be called the Juke Box.

The extent of the alterations in this area, including the increased cooking facilities and the moving of the Dark Room to Six Deck, involved much more work than was envisaged and the cost of these various alterations was now considered to be £20,000 – £25,000.

conspiring to compound the delays. Another was a Clydebank hobby known euphemistically as 'squirrelling' but which most people would recognize as theft.

'Squirrelling'

In August 1967 Bob Arnott, later to become QE2's longest-serving Captain, was appointed Chief Officer, and his initial duties before the ship came into service were to oversee aspects of construction on Cunard's behalf. He soon became aware of the practice of 'squirrelling', which was explained to him as just being a lucrative perk but, rather like some of the strikes, a means of keeping a good job going longer. That was not how he saw it, though, preferring as he did the epithet *"larceny on a grand scale."*

No doubt QE2 was not the first ship to suffer from the practice, but it was so prevalent that Arnott later recalled that: *"Some of the yard workers were stealing the ship faster than the others could build it!"*

There was a thriving trade around Glasgow of materials removed from the ship, a trade that was so organised that items even had a fixed retail price including delivery. Paint was £1 a gallon, light fittings (including shades) from the

cabins just 5 shillings (25 pence) and Formica sold at 10 shillings (50 pence) for 2.4 metres by 1.2 metres (8 foot by 4 foot) sections.

When rolls or carpet for the public rooms were laid out, they were found to have front room-shaped sections, complete with window bay, but out of them as if by a giant pastry-cutter. The main reception area, the Midships Lobby, had been fitted with a carpet that was in place at the end of the shift but a large square of it disappeared by the next morning. There were certainly some cosy and expensively carpeted living rooms in Clydebank that winter. One dismayed Cunard manager advised a steward *"We won't come here again."*

By way of example, Arnott cited one electrician whose home was raided by the police, who was found to have removed from the ship 27 metres (30 yards) of carpet, two chests-of-drawers, a wall cabinet, three bookcases, three lounge stools, 55 metres (180 feet) of fiberglass, five lamps, 36 litres (8 gallons) of paint, plus crockery and soft furnishings. In mitigation the man's solicitor implied such activity was the norm: *"My client just walked off the ship with the stuff."*

The start of another day on Clydebank. *(Author's collection)*

It was regular practice for workers to walk out of the yard concealing items beneath their clothes – items ranging from copper piping to towels. Ironically, Bob Arnott noted, most of the stolen material had to be carried past the police station adjacent to the dock gates, but the prevailing attitude of the police was that although an ocean liner was being stolen piece by piece in from of them, there was little they could do about it.

On 1 February 1968 Cunard made its first public statement about the name using an Arabic 2 rather than a Roman Numeral:

"The name of the new 58,000 ton Cunarder will appear on the ship as Queen Elizabeth 2 – not Queen Elizabeth II.

"This is the first time a royal name has been written with an Arabic numeral instead of the traditional Roman figure. This decision, like other decisions about the design of the ship, was taken for sound practical reasons.

"As with motorway signs, for clarity at a distance it was necessary to use block lettering for the name on the bow and stern of the ship. Roman numerals cannot all be successfully represented with block lettering – in particular the Roma figure 'II' can only be represented by a repeated Arabic numeral 1 and then unfortunately appears as a figure 11.

"The decision has the advantages of being in keeping with modern design trends (Roman numerals are disappearing even from such traditional manifestations as

clock faces, and the fly leaves of books), and the popular contraction of the ship's name is much more legible and attractive as QE2 than QEII."

QE2 made her first 'trip' since launching when she was winched just 50 feet further into her fitting out basin to bring her stern in from the Clyde. Until this time the stern had been sticking out into the river to enable a heavy crane to lower machinery into the engine room. Engines, condensers and boilers were now in place and about 2,300 men were engaged.

On 21 February 1968 the first glimpses of the interior of QE2 were given at a special exhibition which opened that day at the Design Centre in Haymarket, London. The exhibition was opened the previous evening by Princess Margaret and included full-size mock-ups of two cabins and illustrated with diagrams and models and photographs how the restaurants, bars, lounges and other sections of the ship would look. Examples of the tableware, furniture, carpets, furnishing fabrics, wall coverings and other products to be used on the liner, as well as specially developed sign posting and graphics system, were also displayed. The exhibition ran until 23 March and was arranged jointly by Cunard and the Council of Industrial Design.

Dan Wallace was still very frustrated at the lack of information from the builders and their reluctance to commit plans:

"They consistently underestimate the complicated nature of

the ship and all their programmes tend to leave too much to be completed at the end of the vessel. The fact that crew accommodation and Tourist accommodation is now almost ready for final inspection misleads them into a false sense of progress. The vessel still lacks supervisory staff."

By March 1968 progress was improving and preliminary final inspections of some Tourist and crew accommodation on Four, Five and Six Decks was taking place and areas such as storerooms were rapidly nearing completion which indicated that the lower part of the ship was in a fairly healthy position. Cunard were keen to have the ship handed over by the end of November 1968 while the yard saw the end of November 1968 as a time for the ship to leave the yard for trials.

By April 1968 the Signal, Sports and Boat Decks were well underway and 5 April saw the hoisting of the Bridge, still minus its wings, into position. In future officers on the Bridge would not be troubled by misting-up or icing over of the Bridge windows thanks to electrically heated screens more usually associated with aircraft and cars and had been supplied to warships but never to a passenger ship before.

The funnel was installed in two halves with the lower portion being swung into place on 18 April followed four days later, on 22 April, by the upper section. There was still no mast.

The name *Queen Elizabeth 2* was emblazoned on the hull – formal approval having been received from the Registrar General of the Board of Trade in Cardiff to use *Queen Elizabeth 2* having recently been given. The Registrar General also confirmed the allocation of the signal letters GBTT (originally used by the *Queen Mary*) at the same time. GBTT would serve Cunard from 1936 to 2011 when the third Cunard ship to carry the name *Queen Elizabeth* was re-registered in Bermuda.

Dan Wallace felt that now QE2 was by now *"two to three months behind schedule."*

There was a disagreement between Cunard and the Builders about where the problems lay. The yard felt that the public rooms were more problematic and attention should be focused on them while Cunard felt the accommodation was farthest behind and that is where the focus should be. Dan Wallace was very frustrated and later wrote :

"I was becoming increasingly concerned at this time about Mr Rannie's general handling of the situation but found it difficult to know what to do, remembering at this time that he was still regarded as 'the king of shipbuilders'.

The builder's lack of appreciation of the immense task in commissioning items would be one of the main contributory factors of their final failure. The yard "partially agreed" with Cunard's assessment that QE2 was behind schedule and undertook to re-examine the position with a view to accelerating progress.

In his 25 April report to the Chairman's Construction Committee, Dan Wallace reported:

"The Builders have now extended overtime hours and have agreed to keep the ship open during their annual holiday period to allow subcontractors to continue working in public rooms. The Builders are also arranging for painting of superstructure, laying of deck coverings etc to be carried out during this slack period.

"In spite of this reorganization however, it is understood that at the next Progress Meeting on 6 June the Builders will indicate that they wish to postpone the vessel leaving the shipyard until about 2nd December, with delivery at the end of December.

"Whilst I agree that it is unlikely they would have the accommodation completed before leaving for trials in early December, there is a fair chance that the remainder of the vessel – including the main machinery – could be completed by early November and I would submit that we

Seen from the river in April 1968. *(Author's collection)*

The Funnel

QE2's funnel was probably the most technically advanced funnel ever fitted to a passenger ship and perhaps the most controversial! The design and position of the single funnel added to the graceful appearance of the ship but it was not merely a design feature. The funnel was as functional and efficient in disposing of smoke and boiler gases as science and a long and exhaustive series of tests could make it.

The actual design was not finalised until fairly late in the design stage – the builder's model had no funnel at all at the pre-tender stage – and responsibility for the funnel design fell to James Gardner, the man responsible for styling the exterior appearance of the ship. Gardner would develop the funnel in conjunction with Cunard's technical department after months of testing in the wind tunnel at the National Physical Laboratory at Teddington in Middlesex.

At first it seemed that the task of adapting Gardner's original tall slender stack from the Q3 Project would be simple enough. There was still some resistance to such a design from the more conservative factions within Cunard, but this was no real threat. The greatest difficulty was that none of the various model funnels tested in the National Physical Laboratory's wind tunnel seemed to overcome the old problem of keeping soot and smuts away from the shelter decks.

James Gardner, writing in his autobiography, The ARTful Designer:

"A traditional smokestack proved out of the question after the first wind tunnel test. In a functional stack, performance had to take complete priority, and the final structure comprises (a) a relatively small diameter smokestack, (b) a large air outlet vent and (c) a wind scoop mounted on the fan house which covers the air intake."

Various types were tried – in all 20 different funnel designs were produced and tested before the final design was approved – including thin mast-stacks, fat ovoid forms, some with air vents, others without, and so on. The aerofoil-shaped Strombos type, adopted for Holland America's *Maasdam* and *Ryndam*, as well as the French ships *El Djezair* and *Lyautey*, were also tried. It all really did not seem to make much difference. Under the worst wind conditions the smoke always ran down the back of the funnel and onto the open decks. *"What about 'those ungainly projections on the funnels of the France and the flat mortar-board topes on the Michelangelo"*, asked Gardner? Nobody seemed to know or care; they were foreign anyway.

The real cause of the problem was that smoke had a tendency to flow down the leeward side of the funnel to fill in an area of low pressure there. If the prevailing winds were blowing from either side of the ship, and were strong enough, then a greater low pressure area would occur around the opposite aft quarter of the funnel. Under these conditions, when the winds did not reinforce the ship's own enveloping airstream, the smoke may well lack the velocity to get full clear of the decks. This was observed by one of the shipyard's research people, who then worked with Gardner to find a funnel design that would work properly under such circumstances.

The eventual solution that evolved was based on three elements. The funnel itself was made as tall and thin as possible, somewhat resembling Gardner's original visualisation of it for Q3. The trick was to fill its relatively small low pressure void with used air from the accommodation ventilating and air-conditioning systems. This was done by enclosing the aft half of the stack within a cowling through which the return air was pushed by powerful exhaust fans, where this forced airflow was vented just below the top of the working funnel, it would give the engine exhaust smoke and gases the needed push to carry them away from the ship.

However, further wind tunnel tests of this arrangement showed that under somewhat unfavourable wind conditions the outer cowling created its own low pressure area. At first the two men experimented with various arrangements of windscreens on deck to overcome this. What finally emerged was wide wind scoop on top of the deckhouse. This solved the problem using the Venturi-effect, with the narrowing form of its curved lines increasing the airflow from the deck level and forcing it up around the back of the whole funnel structure, cowl and all.

It was a combination of old and new ideas. The stack itself embodied the old idea of a tall think funnel which would discharge steam, smoke and soot well above the ship, rather like those of, perhaps, *Campania* more than half a century earlier. The outer cowling and wind scoop were modern refinements which made it work more effectively.

Having produced the shape to give the best overall efficiency for differing ship speeds and wind directions, the design shape was then slightly adapted for aesthetic appeal.

In the Cunard Boardroom there were still those who needed convincing and some Cunard directors still had doubts about ditching the old notion of that big red funnel, *"the insignia of the line, you know, Cunard red."* Sir Basil Smallpeice asked that a conventional funnel also be made to show on the model for comparison, and to pacify traditionalists.

Having given Gardner's design work unqualified support up to this point, Sir Basil Smallpeice decided that, on this controversial issue, diplomacy was required and so he decided to pass the buck. In an unexpected bout of conservatism, he elected to ask for The Queen's opinion when showing a model of the Q4 to her at Buckingham Palace at a special private audience, arranged in relation to Her Majesty's invitation to launch the ship in September 1967.

Gardner later recalled how the matter was

irrevocably resolved once and for all:

"A week later he (Sir Basil) rang. Apparently he was a buddy of the Queen and wanted to show her the model (to ask if she would acquiesce to her name being linked with it, I guessed). I was to meet him with it at the side door of the Palace, and, 'oh bring both funnels, please, your first one and the one in Cunard house colours'. So, he would ask the Queen, and my guess was she would plump for the red one; after all to anyone not practised at the objective visual design it would look more like a Cunard funnel is expected to look. At the appointed hour my model maker and I were gingerly steering the fragile model into the hands of a flunky, when Smallpeice asked: 'Where's the red funnel' 'Awfully sorry', I said, 'it fell off this morning and someone trod on it. Absolutely useless, I'm afraid'. Smallpeice just gave me one look."

Months were spent refining the lines of the structure to achieve the perfect relationship of the various parts – and the John Brown engineers had to get an awful lot of ducting and fans into the base of such a slim funnel as well as be sure that it would stand erect, poised off-centre, over a great rectangular hole in the deck (which they eventually did without recourse to staywires). The result was the black and white funnel with a touch of Cunard red in the wind scoop. The two white masses – the funnel and the mast – were the key elements which gave the ship her scale and dignity. The unusual mast was not needed as such but had a purely functional purpose as it served as an exhaust for the kitchens.

There was some lamentation at its distinctive black and white colour scheme which had replaced the traditional Cunard red and black. Gardner had considered the Cunard colours *"too heavy"* and not in keeping with the overall approach he had taken with the external design of the ship.

So for the first time in Cunard history – although it was then current airline practice – the side of the ship would carry the name of the company below and aft of the bridge. The word Cunard was in red on the white superstructure in the distinctive letterform recently adopted by the company for its name. The wording was aluminum plate of about .35" thick and was manufactured and fitted at a cost of £924 at November 1964 prices.

The 'midships location of the funnel was conventional Cunard practice and the position was dictated by the disposition of the boilers, which for convenience was located next to the main machinery and this was sited amidships in order to achieve maximum strength and stability. Another advantage in positioning the funnel amidships was that the maximum shelter deck accommodation in a fast ship would be achieved.

QE2's funnel was Gardner's greatest triumph – an inspired combination of old and new ideas resulting in a form that was sophisticated, highly effective and also iconic.

When the veil of secrecy which had shrouded the design of the liner was lifted in April 1967, the Daily Telegraph wrote:

"She is mainly a traditional ship with an extremely unusual funnel. This stands amidships like a piece of modern metallic sculpture."

The Architectural Review

"The funnel is a triumph. For the first time the design and arrangement of the power plant has enabled a giant liner to be single-funnelled, liberating an extra half-acre of play deck – a premium passenger attraction. The form of the funnel and the sculptured casing which encloses it evolved through a long series of wind tunnel models. It reflects the intuition of James Gardner and the aerodynamic open-mindedness of the engineers, rather than a precise science. The result is a mixture of very old and very new; tall thin smoke stacks for the boiler gases, plus a novel casing to lead up some of the huge exhaust from the air-conditioners to balance pressure behind the stack and help blast the stack gases skyward."

As building work progressed, Dan Wallace started worrying that perhaps the liner's upper decks, mast and funnel were reaching too high up to the sky. He explained that a ship at sea is like an inverted pendulum, and the higher she goes, the wider she swings. To make his point, Wallace took Gardner up on a shipyard hoist. *"Two more decks to come, then the fan house and that eighty-foot funnel of yours"*, said Wallace, motioning skywards with his umbrella. "And the dog kennels", added Gardner, though the wind blew that one away from the naval architect's ears. Point taken though, as a wiser Gardner later pencilled a sketch in his notepad of the ship's unfinished decks rising ever higher into the sky above Clydebank, before whittling away at a piece of cheddar from the fridge as he modelled a refined and slightly lower profile for the bridge housing. However, his elegant tall and slender funnel would stay.

should suggest to the Builders that the ship should leave the yard about 12 November, when there is suitable tide.

"Trials and handing over would still probably not take place until nearly the end of December, i.e. one month late.

Time and time again Dan Wallace would be proved correct in his understanding of the situation.

April 1968 also saw problems with labour when the Otis Elevator Company reported that its workforce had withdrawn their labour and then the shipyard experienced problems when its sheet iron workers went on strike for over two months. As the working of the passenger lifts was essential this area was probably the farthest behind contract on the ship at this point and Cunard wrote to Otis after the strike had finished requesting the company to increase its workforce of 30 on board. These troubles were followed in May by all the Insulators and Pipe-Coverers going on strike

The QE2 in drydock at Greenock. *(Author's collection)*

That same month a secret document circulated within Cunard the initial operating programme for *QE2* which was scheduled for public release on 1 July:

1 – 12 December 1968   Builders Trials

Carrying hotel staff and approximately 500 people of our own nomination, who will be requested fully to test the ship's working, e.g. hotel system, stateroom fittings and amenities.

12 – 22 December Initial arrival at Southampton after handing over. Final fitting out, crew boarding etc. Official ceremonies.

23 – 27 December (Dress Rehearsal) Inaugural shake-down cruise entirely at sea – no ports of call, to be operated under sponsorship of selected Charity which will sell or otherwise assign the accommodation of passengers to be carried. The Charity will return to us operating costs. One class: approximate number of passengers 1,000, nominated by the selected Charity, plus an additional limited number of Cunard personnel or Companies associated with the building of

the vessel. Ship will sail from Southampton on Monday 23 December at 1700 hours and return to Southampton on Friday 27 December at 0800 hours.

21 December – 2 January At Southampton

2 – 14 January (Maiden UK Cruise) Southampton / Gibraltar / Las Palmas / Dakar / St Vincent / Madeira / Southampton. One Class: approximately 1,350 passengers.

17 – 20 January (Maiden Westbound Voyage) Southampton / Le Havre / Las Palmas / Barbados / Kingston / New York. Two Classes: First Class 500; Tourist Class 1,300

31 January At New York. Official functions. The ship will be thrown open for inspection by travel agents during the day.

1 February – 10 March (Maiden US Cruises)

11 – 26 March (Maiden Eastbound Voyage)

E Stairway. *(Author's collection)*

New York / Barbados / Las Palmas / Madeira / Lisbon / Le Havre / Southampton. Two classes: First 500; Tourist 1,300.

George Parker, Clydebank's Divisional Director, reported an 'irresponsible and unrealistic' wage demand from sheet ironworkers. On 6 May, the sheet ironworkers went on strike. They returned on 27 May, having won an additional 4d per hour. John Rannie reported that finishing trades were working well on *QE2*, although a strike of sub-contract pipe coverers, insulators and plumbers was threatening progress. He was, nevertheless, able to assure his board that Cunard had agreed to an increase in the ship's price, caused by the higher wage costs.

On 7 May 1968 Sir Basil wrote to Anthony Hepper:

"I know full well that you are anxious that the ship should be delivered in time because the publicity attached to the ship worldwide is such that a late delivery of it could not rebound on Upper Clyde Shipbuilders. As far as we are concerned, the revenue potential of the ship, even in the

winter, is of the order of £¾ million a month, and even four weeks delay would therefore be a very serious matter from our point of view, to say nothing of your own.

"It would be possible to get the ship to sea with some of the passenger accommodation on the lowest deck uncompleted but what is absolutely necessary is to finish the more expensive accommodation and the public room areas.

"The main thing is to get the ship to sea on time. It is always possible to have certain work done while the ship is at sea so long as it is out of sight and hidden from the view of passengers."

These comments by Sir Basil were a fair record of the Cunard official policy from then until the end of December 1968.

In his Annual Statement to Stockholders on 20 May 1968, Sir Basil said:

"Doubts have been expressed in many quarters about the economic viability of the QE2. In the long run, over the next 15 to 20 years, who can tell? But in the first years, there should be little doubt that, given reasonable economic and political conditions on both sides of the Atlantic, this ship can be made to trade at a profit (how much, no one in their senses would be rash enough to say at the present time). After all, she will be the newest and finest passenger ship in the world, which will give her great drawing power in the market. She will be operating in alternate weeks with the France the direct service across the Atlantic in the summer months when the great transatlantic holiday movement is on, and she will share common terminals and other facilities and services with the French Line. For the rest of the year she will be cruising mainly in the western hemisphere, but partly out of Southampton. And by comparison with her two predecessor Queens, she had a ratio of no more than about 30 gross tons per passengers for really excellent accommodation throughout.

"In hotel terms, the QE2 will have cost just under £15,000 per bed to build and equip, which is substantially higher than the cost for a top class hotel. But we are not comparing like with like, in that no shore-based hotel has to provide lounge, recreational and dining facilities for all its patrons. Also, it must be remembered that, in the case of a ship, the cost includes self-sufficiency for all services (electricity, fresh water, and so on). In addition, she has the advantage of being mobile, so that she is able to follow the sun or public demand. The value of her transport potential of some 700 miles a day is equivalent to at least £15 a day (on the basis of average economy-class air fares) out of the price charged to our passengers. However, her operating costs should be at least 20 per cent less than the first Queen Elizabeth, and this, together with the reduced shore overheads attaching to the ship, should compensate almost entirely for the new ship's financing charges."

On 4 June 1968 30 plumbers and engineers employed by one of the sub-contractors went on strike and did not return until 11 June.

To comply with the American fireproofing regulations which

stipulated a reduction in the use of natural woods thin 1.5 mn vaneers of wood were fixed onto backings of compressed, asbestos-based sheeting called Marinite and in all two million square feet of Marinite, faced with wood or plastic, was used on QE2. The dangers of working with asbestos were just being realised and legislation being introduced had to be accommodated – a bonus for the joiners' unions but a major headache for management was the extra precautions having to be taken when and wherever Marinite was used.

In his annual statement to stockholders, Sir Basil Smallpeice dealt with the question of whether QE2 would make money:

"In the long run, over the next 15 to 20 years, who can tell?

"But in the first years there should be little doubt that, given reasonable economic and political conditions on both sides of the Atlantic, the ship can be made to trade at a profit, although how much no-one in their senses would be rash enough to say at the present time."

The QE2 would, after all, be the newest and finest passenger ship in the world and that would give her great drawing power in the market. She would operate, in alternate weeks with the France, the direct service across the Atlantic in the summer and cruise for the rest of the year. Sir Basil confirmed that she was costing just under £15,000 per bed to build and equip, which was substantially higher than the cost for a hotel ashore, but her operating costs would be at least 20% less than Queen Elizabeth.

In July 1968, as the first wisps of smoke were to be seen emanating from the funnel Cunard announced that the Gross Tonnage of QE2 had increased by 7,000 tons to 65,000 tons. The main reason for the increase was due to the difficulties of the direct calculation the original estimates were made. As QE2's design developed it was possible to increase the volume of the superstructure as a result of the rigid weight-saving policy that was adopted. Because of Cunard's design approach, each passenger on QE2 would have, on average, 60 per cent more space than travellers on the bigger Queen Elizabeth.

Cunard by now were resigned to the fact that the earliest possible date on which QE2 could satisfactorily be completed would be 19 December and the company had agreed to accept a postponement of the ship from 30 November to 19 December.

During the first two / three weeks of the month the builders employees were on holiday but about 1,000 men were retained to continue work on board the ship.

The welders in the yard withdrew their labour on 16 July 1968 following a demand for increased wages (they returned on 22 July) and the next day saw the painters going on strike (they returned on 29 July). On 31 July the deck and machinery engineers, apprentices and brass-finishers withdrew their labour at 12 noon and did not return until 1 August.

On 22 July 1968 Upper Clyde Shipbuilders announced:

"Upper Clyde Shipbuilders Limited announced that the commissioning of 'Queen Elizabeth 2', now under construction in their Clydebank Division, is programmed for the end of October.

"It has been agreed between Upper Clyde Shipbuilders and Cunard Line that she will leave Clydebank mid-November for dry-docking and extensive sea trials prior to delivery to Cunard in Southampton on 19 December 1968.

"Cunard Line will be announcing on 24 July, details of her sailings."

It was announced that *QE2* would sail a special four-day inaugural shakedown cruise in conjunction with a selected charity (the name of which would be given in September but would be the National Society for Cancer Relief) followed by a four-day mini Maiden Cruise departing 10 January 1969 with fares from £98. She would formally enter service on 17 January 1969 with a 13-day 1,500 mile Southampton to New York sailing calling at Le Havre, Las Palmas, Barbados and Kingston. First-class fares: £366 ($920) Tourist-class £190 ($480). The ship would then make Caribbean cruises from New York before returning to Southampton on 26 March after a 15-day voyage from New York calling at Barbados, Las Palmas, Madeira, Lisbon and Le Havre. Her 1969 season would also include 27 Atlantic crossings – 13 eastbound and 14 westbound with first-class fares from £185 and tourist-class from £102 depending on the season (either thrift, intermediate or summer).

The company reported that over 8,000 names had registered with Cunard on both sides of the Atlantic by people who wished to be on the Maiden Voyage had been taken over the previous 10 years.

In August 1968 John Whitworth succeeded Philip Bates as Managing Director and he received this update from Dan Wallace:

"… unless there is a serious dispute we should still meet our completion date of 19 December. The degree to which the ship will be complete then depends on how successful we are in avoiding further labour problems. I feel that we are like a person living in a volcano, which may erupt tomorrow or may never erupt in our lifetime. Mr Rannie and Mr Parker have been extremely successful in resolving minor recent disputes. I am now satisfied that although far from perfect, the general organisation and planning in the shipyard is reasonably efficient and the building is under complete control. As already indicated, the standard and finish in the accommodation will vary, dependent upon the manpower available, but apart from accommodation at the forward and after end of Two Deck and the after end of One Deck, all should be completely habitable by mid-December. The degree to which cabins 2001 – 20033, 2151 – 2152 and 1090 – 1121, will be finished is still problematical and I hope that is possible the passenger departments will not book these until at least the 10 January voyage. From the foregoing you will gather that unless there is a sudden change in the next ten day, you will be able to proceed with details of the Charity Christmas Cruise."

Also in August 1968, UCS received an invitation to tender for the conversion of *Carinthia* and *Sylvania* into cruise liners, following Cunard's disposal of the ships to Fairwind Shipping Corporation (Sitmar Line) of Monrovia. The work on each ship, valued at between £3 and £4 million, had to be turned down because of insufficient labour – *QE2* was consuming every man that UCS had to spare. With a boom in shipbuilding underway, UCS was receiving a large number of enquiries, but lacked the technical capacity to deal with the volume. Similarly, shortages in design and estimating capacity had the effect of reducing steel throughput.

On 5 August 1968 29 stagers withdrew their labour in a stoppage that would result in affecting progress on all parts of the ship. That same day 477 general labourers, helpers and Red Leaders and Drivers also went on strike; both groups returned two days later.

Ten days later the joiners employed by the decorative contractors went on strike for six days, this was followed five days later with the withdrawal of labour by 432 shipyard engineers for 12 days. Before the month of August 1968 had finished 1,100 boilermakers and 233 platers would strike.

On 4 September 1968 Anthony Hepper wrote to Sir Basil:

"I fully understand your concern with regard to QE2. On Monday I spent a couple of hours with John Rannie and at the time of writing we are confident we shall keep our delivery promised." [This promised was for delivery on 19 December 1968].

By September, the workload at Clydebank was building up, with six ships under construction, including *QE2*. Sadly, labour shortages and technical difficulties continued to plague production. One hundred and fifty boilermakers were urgently required, while, in protest at a letter which had been sent out to the men urging greater productivity, the engineers held a one day strike and, crane men, a ten-minute token stoppage. The painters, meanwhile, were considering a complete stoppage.

Traditionally, a ship nearing completion gave the workforce the upper hand, although this was often tempered by lay-offs once the ship left the yard. The level of disruption now being experienced was unprecedented in the Clydebank yard's history which, hitherto, had enjoyed better relations than many other British shipbuilders.

Unfortunately, by the latter 1960s, the Clyde shipyards were no longer in a position to recruit the most talented and motivated of workers. Shipyard jobs often were dangerous, dirty and physically exhausting. Much work took place out of doors in the cold and wet West of Scotland climate and, moreover, there was little security of tenure. The more able of the younger generation suddenly had new and more attractive career possibilities - like going to study at university or technical college, thanks to the post-war expansion of higher education, or seeking employment in the cleaner, safer, more comfortable light industries. In addition, the building of new towns at East Kilbride and Cumbernauld denuded the Glasgow conurbation of population as a whole – meaning that the old shipyards often were left with no option but to supplement time-served 'old hands' with less enthusiastic employees, whose commitment to their trade was less strong than that of previous generations. Productivity suffered as a result and, sadly, theft and vandalism also increased markedly, causing further delays to building contracts - not least the completion of *QE2*.

On 11 September 1968 basin trials were delayed by an

hour when 464 dock and shipyard engineers and apprentices went on strike. In all there would be over 30 work stoppages in 1968.

Eight days later the ship was visited by the press – a visit which backfired as the ship looked most incomplete as was only to be expected some three months before delivery. John Whitworth announced that there would be no press present during any of the trials – an announcement which led to much criticism. The attending press were treated to the sight of smoke emanating from the funnel for the first time as the three boilers were sequentially lit for testing and the start of dock trials which were necessary before QE2 could go to sea. The confidence of John Whitworth and John Rannie that QE2 would be complete and ready to put to sea for the first time on 19 November of John Whitworth and John Rannie could not hide the murmurs from workers spoken to by press that they were less sure. There were now 4,000 men working on the ship and another 500 in the joiners' shops. John Whitworth acknowledged that there was *"plenty to be done"* to commission the ship and make her operational but it was proceeding smoothly.

change that had occurred in the company structure. One aspect covered was the propellers with Tom Kameen stating:

On board *Queen Elizabeth* crew members transferring to *QE2* were given briefings as part of an extensive training programme.

The cover of *QE2*'s first main brochure, issued in October 1968, simply stated 'Ships have been boring long enough' which in one simple statement hinted that the campaign to market and promote the ship would be unlike any other for a new ship.

Other lines were horrified by what they regarded as "knocking copy" at both themselves and the industry and it seemed Cunard was also criticising its former and current ships – could the company really be saying the much-loved *Queen Mary* and *Queen Elizabeth* were boring? Cunard was unrepentant and maintained that it stirred up so much interest that the effect was beneficial to its overall aim of positioning *QE2* as the most exciting ship ever built:

"Whatever your preconceptions about QE2, she's bound to take you by surprise. It's like climbing into the most

The hoisting of the Bridge, still minus its wings, into position, Friday 5 April 1968. *(Author's collection)*

exciting thing to be launched since Apollo 1… With QE2's push-button bedrooms, high up dining rooms, pop groups and cabaret artists, discotheques, acres of open deck, swimming pools, bars and shopping centre, Cunard have introduced a completely new way of thinking about cruise ships… The QE2 concept is a leisure that is not just relaxing but stimulating too!"

In September, the Board of Upper Clyde Shipbuilders noted that John Rannie would reach retirement age at the end of the year and his service with the company would come to an end. However, as finalising the details of QE2's contract was likely to take additional time, he accepted the offer of a further six months service for a retainer of £2,500.

On 1 October 1968 the employees of the ventilation sub-contractors went on strike. A week later the plumbers employed by one of the subcontractors also withdrew their labour.

That same day a three-day Technical Teach-In for ship's officers and Southampton shore staff commenced at a Glasgow airport hotel. Day one covered main and auxiliary machinery and electrical systems. Day two covered hotel, navigational and safety aspects while the final day internal communications systems. Each session included a period for discussion. Such a conference was a departure from normal practice but was considered necessary given the huge

One advert proclaimed:

"For years, ships have been boring their way across the seas. Now, Cunard has launched the ultimate weapon against boredom at sea. The QE2. The new Queen Elizabeth 2. The only thing QE2 has in common with other ships is that she floats. The only thing she has in common with other great Cunarders is a legend called service. Stepping aboard QE2 is like stepping 20 years into the future. Whatever your preconceptions about her, she's bound to take you by surprise."

The campaign was well received by the important traveltrade and portrayed Cunard as starting a new era in shipping with *QE2*. In fact the high-impact campaign received top honours at the American Society of Travel Agents Outstanding Travel Poster Contest at the 1968 convention in San Juan.

The second stage in the build-up was advertisements that said there were only two places left to visit – the moon and the ship. And the moon reappeared in the early advertisements for the sailing schedule when potential customers were told *"Why ask for the moon. Who needs it? QE2 is sailing and if you're interested at all in what 20th Century man has achieved, you can, you must sail in her."*

And sail in her people would if the selling effort to travel agents was anything to go by (to say nothing of the unique status and novelty value that *QE2* would have for some time). This was a key element that Cunard had to establish itself with agencies in a way it had not had not done before, for it used to have its own offices but by the late 1960s it was working almost entirely through the travel men.

Cunard held evening gatherings for travel agents up and down the country – entertaining 3,000 individuals at over 40 meetings in the autumn of 1968 alone – at which a 20-minute film formed part of the sales presentation.

On 4 October the mast was hoisted into place.

The level of work deteriorated during October as the labour problems were increasing. Dan Wallace would later comment:

"I found it almost impossible to make them [the builders] realise the seriousness of this problem… I fear that in

some areas the vessel will not be complete by 19 December, in which case the builders will require working on the vessel until 10 January."

Mountains of tables, chairs, blankets, bed linen, crockery and cutlery was being loaded onto *QE2* at the time. There was so much household paraphernalia to be placed in the ship that Cunard temporarily took over a Glasgow warehouse to store some of it between delivery and loading. Hundreds of men were employed in the organization, transportation and loading the ship and completing one area at a time. At one time the warehouse was crammed with an assortment that included 3,000 chairs, 1,323 different curtains, 1,403 stools, 35 occasional tables, 51 settees, 1,489 separate carpets, 1,596 waste bin, 2,150 trays and 30,000 coat hangers. Linen, blankets and other items not so bulky as furniture went direct to the shipyard. These consignments included more than 23,000 sheets and a similar number of pillow slips, nearly 10,000 blankets, 5,000 table cloths, 24,000 table napkins, some 15,000 pieces of cutlery and about 50,000 towels of assorted sizes.

At a Cunard Board meeting on 22 October, Sir Basil Smallpeice described the condition of the ship as follows:

"…Excluding three blocks of accommodation, in the absence of any major difficulty the ship would be reasonably ready by 10 December, but with a large number of minor fittings to be fitted before 24 December. The main engine had been tested, ship stability was satisfactory and certain trouble with the rudder was under investigation. As had been expected the final stages of completing the ship were

From the quayside on Friday 5 April 1968. *(Author's collection)*

The Mast

James Gardner was responsible for the design of both the funnel and the mast and the latter was the last part of the ship to actually leave the drawing board – in fact the final design was not agreed until three weeks before the launch. Gardner created a mast design was just as equally as remarkable as the funnel – both masterpieces of imaginative and elegant modern design.

Garner's original design for Q3's mast combined the foremast and forward funnel in a tapering white stack. Q4's engine room would be located two thirds aft with the galley forward meaning that an exhaust was required to vent heat and cooking odours. So Gardner reworked the Q3 proposal into a remarkably bold and sculptural mast, which leaned slightly forward to reinforce the dynamic form of the wheelhouse, immediately below.

While the mast was not needed as such, this one structure served so many purposes, each of which was the concern of many different specialists. In all, 15 models were designed before the final choice was made. It was established early on that the mast would not need a Crow's Nest built in.

Poised at the top was a satellite navigation aerial when the ship was first built. Originally there were 8 different aerials; two 11-foot radar scanners; two navigation lights, a 'Christmas tree' of code lamps, in two groups; two whistles, one operated by compressed air and one by electricity; two light detectors which controlled the lighting in the main restaurant; two loud hailers; signal and courtesy flag halyards; and a Bosun's chair and a way up inside for maintenance.

All these were mounted on a mast that was not really a mast, but a duct, designed to carry used air up from the kitchens.

The shape and mass of this structure was important to the ship as a whole for it balanced the rather high funnel, relating to it as a foresail related to the mainsail of a yacht.

Cunard:

"The two white masses – the funnel and the mast – are the key elements which give the ship her scale and dignity."

Next to the funnel the mast was the highest part of the ship, being 169 feet 1 inch above the waterline when the draft was 31 feet 0 inch (200 feet 1 inch above the keel). The height of mast was reduced by five feet when the satellite receiver for the satellite navigation system was removed.

The mast was lifted on board QE2 as a single structure on 4 October 1968.

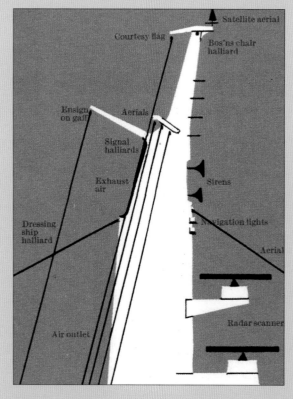

A diagram of the Mast by James Gardner. *(Author's collection)*

The Mast being hoisted on board, Friday 4 October 1968. *(Author's collection)*

attracting a certain amount of labour difficulties. One subcontractor had already offered his labourers a substantial bonus for remaining to complete their work by 19 November and other labour forces including UCS's own men, were looking for similar payments.'

Although such payments were outside the Price Variation Agreement, such was their desperation to get the ship delivered, Cunard agreed to make a contribution towards them.

Dan Wallace still felt at this time that the ship would be reasonably complete for her Maiden Atlantic Voyage on 19 January, except for the three blocks of accommodation. It was also recognised at this time by Cunard that the remaining accommodation would not always be complete in detail but would be of an acceptable standard to embark passengers. It was also expected that there would be some commissioning faults and deficiencies in the ship during the early voyages.

Throughout the summer of 1968, a series of quality inspections, some by Cunard personnel, were carried out on the ship which had been subdivided into a series of work blocks. These inspections were intended to uncover work that still remained to be done. Thus, for example, an inspection dated 17 June 1968 concerning Block 29 Starboard on 3 Deck noted that Cabin 83 required:

- Entrance door to cabin needed adjusting

- Gap at shipside dresser needed to be closed

- The mitre under the shelf support in the hanging space needed to be closed

- Plastic strips to complete the corners in the hanging space needed to be fitted.

- A collar to be fitted to the light in the hanging space.

While this was routine and applied to many cabins, a report dated 25 October, less than three weeks from the ship's departure, noted that the target date of 1 November for completion of joiner work would not be achieved and that it was unlikely that the new target date of 19 November would be met either.

John Rannie searched urgently to find the additional 200 joiners he needed to complete the ship. Delays in the completion programme had been caused when the decorative sub-contractors arrived late, causing ventilation contractors to leave for other work. Nevertheless, Rannie confirmed that the ship would leave Clydebank on 19 November, as originally planned. However, labour difficulties among the work force and sub-contractors meant that the ship would leave Clydebank in an incomplete state, albeit with relatively minor tasks yet to be finished off. At a board meeting held in September 1968, Rannie diplomatically put on record that there had been no requests for last minute alterations or additions to the ship and that Cunard were *'helping us all they can'* to get the project finished on schedule. Significantly, he also reported that he had informed Cunard that three areas within the ship would, in fact, be incomplete on departure from Clydebank.

In October, 150 joiners were lent from Lithgow's Port Glasgow shipyard to work on *QE2*. However, the continuing shortage of boilermakers pushed back delivery times on the

other contracts from between four and eight weeks. The best that could be achieved within UCS was the transfer of 68 men from their Linthouse yard. While these transfers speeded up work on *QE2* to an extent, they also posed problems for shipyard security - especially with so many valuable fixtures and fittings lying around, awaiting installation. Not surprisingly, in the dying weeks of the outfitting process, pilfering became a very serious problem – and this only served to add further delays and on costs.

On 15 and 16 November *QE2* was opened up to staff and workers and their families to visit thus continuing a long-standing tradition at the yard and the visitors were sent on specific routes around the ship to avoid unfinished areas which were described as being a *"shambles."*

At dawn on 19 November 1968 *QE2* was lit from stem to stern as she lay in the fitting out basin. The yard hummed with activity as men reported for work. The only potential issue was winds gusting above 12 mph as that would have stopped the operation but the forecast was for a typical Glasgow weather – a lot of industrial haze but little wind – at the time of year.

By 0800 hours a distinctly chilly-looking Prince Charles was on board after taking the overnight train from London to join the ship and shortly afterwards *QE2* left her birthplace for the first time and headed for the Firth of Clyde Dry Dock at Greenock on her first outing. Originally the presence of the Prince was to have been kept secret until the day before but the secret leaked out – perhaps Cunard had been shrewd enough to realise that a Royal visit would ensure the yard remained focused! Prince Charles was on the Bridge as the new liner gave three blasts of her whistle. Captain Warwick would recall how the Prince's eyes lit up when he was asked if he would like to press the button to sound the whistle.

A special holiday had been declared for the locals and thousands assembled on the fields and shores along the Clyde. Six tugs eased her from the fitting out berth, almost imperceptibly at first, where she had been since 20 September 1967, and she moved ahead, using her own engines for the first time. A total of seven tugs would escort her to Greenock and the Clyde was closed to other shipping for three hours.

As the liner left the fitting out basin she nudged the wooden wharf-side and scraped about 20 feet off her paint causing a plume of smoke because of the friction of the liner's hull against the wharf; the ship was undamaged. John Rannie would later tell reporters that *QE2* was giving a farewell kiss to her birthplace and a welcoming kiss for the sea. The "kiss" would produce a long scar clearly visible 12 feet above the waterline.

There was great cheer from those in the yard as *QE2* finally eased into the river centre where she gathered her first seagull escort.

Thousands of people gathered along the Clyde and *QE2* responded to their cheers with whistle blasts throughout the journey. There was a seven-mile queue of cars on the main Renfrew-Port Glasgow Road. The ship made six knots for the 10-mile journey and navigated the narrow bends of the river as dozens of men watched ashore and on board to make sure her passage was safe.

John Rannie and Sir Basil escorted Prince Charles who lunched on board and spoke with some of the shipyard

Taken in late Spring 1968.

workers during an hour-long tour which also avoided unfinished areas of the ship. He returned to London on a flight from Glasgow.

Internally, the ship looked most incomplete – about 100 cabins remained incomplete and several hundred workmen were on board working continuously to finish them - but Cunard were confident that by 19 December she would be reasonably completed and, by 17 January, she would be in a reasonable condition. John Rannie claimed to the press and on TV that QE2 was ahead of schedule by about 11 days and despite having "*a lot to do*" he claimed the ship would be completely finished when she sailed from the Clyde on 10 December.

Upon arrival in Greenock QE2 lost some more paint as she gave a slight lurch to starboard and a few feet of orange paint was scraped away when her starboard side came into contact with the dock entrance.

The pilot, Captain Peter Thomson, explained the second mishap:

"She leaned on a knuckle – normal maneouvre to bring her round to make her entry."

QE2 entered the Inchgreen Drydock that evening. Cunard would later call the departure from the yard and the drydocking *"a significant achievement"* for the yard.

Until 1964 there was no dry-dock on the Clyde capable of accommodating the large passenger ships built on the river. Cunarders such as *Queen Mary* and *Queen Elizabeth* had to go elsewhere for dry docking before their trials.

Captain Warwick:

"She behaved like a great ship – she came under her own power, ably assisted by the tugs.

"It was her first time on her engine, and she went like a daisy. I was most agreeably surprised. There were no flaps,

and everything went very well."

Until this date the intensity of work in progress had abounded and numerous labour stoppages had occurred and it was evident that a number of these had been engineered by politically motivated men. Cunard expressed its concern at the volume of outstanding work and pressed for improved organization and supervision on the part of the Builders but the situation deteriorated rapidly after the arrival in the drydock. The Builders arbitrarily dismissed 500 tradesmen in the key trades (joiners and electricians) which precipitated a ban on overtime working and meant that the ship was desperately short of labour on her return from technical trails.

At Greenock, John Rannie addressed his men, exhorting them to do their utmost to carry the work on to completion.

Dan Wallace:

"Unfortunately, Mr Rannie continued to carry out the duties if a Personnel Director and had no assistance from Clydebank of from UCS in dealing with the labour problems, with the result that his assistant managers were often left without a leader. His deputy – Mr McLaughlin, tried to organize the ship from a cabin but never attempted to inspect the ship and we all have very vivid memories of his constant assurances that all was well.

"All the managers on the ship were dominated by Mr Rannie and were either unable or unwilling to take action themselves. Only a few of them were efficient and very quickly the Yard's programme of inspections etc became meaningless."

The following information could now be confirmed for QE2:

Official Number	336703
Gross Tonnage	65,862.91 tons
Net Tonnage	38,243.54 tons

While in dry dock the remains of her launch gear was removed, her bottom plates were cleaned and painted and inspections were carried out on her underwater hull. Each day hundreds of workmen were transported from Glasgow and Clydebank to Greenock.

QE2's preliminary sea trials commenced two days later than planned due to severe gales; the delay confusing the onboard situation even more with the labour on board being inadequately organised which would result in little being achieved in terms of finishing during the trials.

Dan Wallace:

"The continual postponing of the departure from 24 to 26 November seriously upset progress but, of course, the builders could not be blamed for this; but even on the morning of 26 November, whilst we were awaiting information from the pilot and Captain Warwick, Mr Rannie, in conversation with Mr Kameen and myself, intimated that he already considered that the weather was unsuitable and the ship would require to be kept in dock for another 2/3 days, since if we missed that day the tides were unsuitable. We were shocked by his attitude, which clearly showed that he was trying to keep the ship in dock to allow work to continue and to this end was prepared to jeopardise the carrying out of the Trials.

"...prior to the ship leaving the drydock, whilst Mr Rannie's managers were agreeing with the decorative contractors that they should pay the joiners who were left on shore until the vessel returned, Mr Rannie was at Clydebank arranging for the sacking of some 500 joiners and 200 electricians. He appears to have done this without consulting any of his colleagues and this was a most crucial action which caused very considerable labour unrest and horrified Mr Rannie's colleagues who were well aware of the fact that there was still much work to be done."

At 1700 hours on Tuesday 26 November 1968 QE2 left the dry-dock in Greenock for preliminary sea trials which would allow a normal working-up procedure of the gearing.

On 27 November, she was off the Isle of Arran for the measured mile where she achieved 164 revolutions per minute with speeds in excess of 29 knots. Tom Kameen reported later that these trials had been successful with a top speed of 29.5 – about 34 miles an hour – being achieved with a maximum speed of 31 knots being expected.

Captain Warwick

"She turned at speed and barely heeled. It was easier than handling a motor car doing 34 miles an hours on a sharp bend."

On the third run over a measured mile QE2 did 28.32 knots as she raced almost silently past watching boats 100 yards away before she turned at speed over a remarkably short distance.

Clyde Captain Willie McCulloach:

"I've never seen a trials ship manoeuvre like that. She turned like a speedboat."

That same day, the Cunard board met and Sir Basil Smallpeice confirmed that, because of the incomplete state of parts of the ship, difficulty was anticipated at the press visit on 10 December. Sir Basil thought this could be addressed by a briefing, explaining that John Brown men would be working throughout the trials period.

The trial had to be abandoned on the morning of 30 November when oil fuel contaminated the feed water system because of a faulty non-return valve. The oil fuel spill occurred in the aft boiler room during a run on the measured mile at 84,000 shp and immediate steps were taken to prevent fire and locate the source of the oil leak, which appeared to come from a drain pipe on the top side of a saturated steam relief valve.

Initially three tugs were despatched from Greenock to provide assistance to QE2 but she returned to port under her own power with the tugs acting as escorts.

Sir Basil advised reporters from his home that he thought there was every chance that the trouble would be cured in time for the ship to continue her shakedown trials on 10 December as scheduled.

At a stroke, delivery was delayed by one week while the trouble was located and put right. This required a lengthy period of cleaning out in dry dock and forced Cunard to cancel the charity cruise. Cunard took these events in its stride and agreed that final acceptance trials would be conducted on a 10-day trip to the west coast of Africa, where the air conditioning plant would also be tested.

On 30 November QE2 was again dry-docked for lengthy cleaning and decontamination of the whole of the ship's main and / or auxiliary steam circulating systems. In all 42 valves were returned to the manufacturer for stripping and re-assembly.

A shipyard statement advised:

"Although the cause of this halt is only minor, the work of decontamination is time-consuming and will occupy up to two weeks, delaying the resumption of the technical trials until about 16 / 18 December. In the light of the otherwise successful trials programme so far, these resumed technical trials should not occupy more than 48 hours."

The main trials to the Canaries, due to sail on 4 December, were postponed and Cunard reluctantly was forced to cancel the fully-booked Christmas charity cruise and made a contribution of £10,000 to the National Society for Cancer Relief.

A meeting between senior Cunard and UCS management took place on board on 1 December to discuss the mechanical problems as well as the unfinished state of the ship. Dan Wallace would report to John Whitworth:

"...I approached Mr Whitworth and expressed to him my fears that Mr Rannie had now lost control of the situation and that Upper Clyde's management should take more positive action."

When John Whitworth raised this concern with Anthony Hepper the latter responded that it would not be politic to change John Rannie's leadership at that time but did agree for John Starks to take on greater responsibility.

John Rannie:

"…extremely happy with the ship, which is showing up to be a real Queen – a success story."

Upper Clyde Shipbuilders:

"The examination has revealed that while there is no damage whatever to the ship, it will be necessary to check and clean the whole of the ship's main and auxiliary steam circulating systems. Although the cause of the fault is only minor the work on decontamination is time-consuming and will occupy up to two weeks, delaying the resumption of the Technical Trials until about 16 – 18 December. In light of the otherwise successful trials programme so far, these resumed Technical Trials should not occupy more than 48 hours."

of minor defects and that certain minor works might need to be carried out during the technical trials but that all these must be fully completed by 22 December.

Cunard was keen to stress that the maiden commercial voyages commencing with the 10 January 'mini Maiden' Preview Cruise followed by the 17 January maiden Westbound Southern Route voyage to New York via Las Palmas, Barbados and Kingston were not affected in any way.

In a statement to staff, John Whitworth advised:

"QE2 is now scheduled to depart on her final acceptance trials on 23 December, and will not be formally handed over to Cunard until her arrival at Southampton on 1 January following successful completion of her trials."

On 9 December John Whitworth, Dan Wallace and Tom Kameen undertook a detailed inspection of the

The *QE2* in drydock at Greenock. *(Author's collection)*

Captain 'Bil' Warwick inspecting the latest progress on his ship during fitting out. *(Author's collection)*

At this stage 1,600 workmen and crew were aboard. The cleaning operation as a result of the feed water contamination added considerably to the difficulties of finishing the accommodation. Lighting supply was very limited and at times there were black-outs and heating was also extremely limited.

The 1 December meeting would conclude that technical trails would be resumed between 16 and 18 December and that Acceptance Trials would begin on 23 December. This meant the postponement of the ship's arrival at Southampton and delivery until 1 January. The Builders were still confident about completion on schedule but John Whitworth would later recall: *"…we expressed grave concern about the prospects if completing the ship by 23 December and pressed again for better organisation and more manpower."* The meeting also agreed that the first target date would be 16 December for the completion of all engineering work both remedial and design and of all hotel work both accommodation and public rooms; that under no circumstances would any labour be carried on in the Acceptance Trials other than for rectification

accommodation as a result of which all three became fearful that, in the absence of a marked acceleration of progress the ship would be in no fit state to undertake her first commercial voyage on 10 January with passenger service and amenities operating to the required standards. The overtime ban imposed by joiners and electricians was still in place and there was only a small night shift working. The incomplete areas were mainly blocks of passenger accommodation on Two and Three Decks and the ancillary public room areas on Boat Deck. Although certain sections of accommodation such as the female ratings' accommodation had been completely ready to receive them, it had in fact suffered some damage due to pilferage of electrical fittings.

The majority of the male ratings' accommodation was inhabitable and again sections had become dirty through use by workmen and pilferage of electrical and plumbing items. Cunard accepted that these blocks would probably still not be complete when the ship entered service but this would not prejudice the commercial programme provided the ship was in a condition to provide an acceptable standard of passenger service and amenities.

The Builders relented and agreed to transfer substantial and specific numbers if joiners and electricians from other divisions of Upper Clyde Shipbuilders and maintained that the ship would substantially complete by 23 December and wholly complete by 1 January. The Builders estimated that there was a shortage of 100 men weeks of joiners and 50 men weeks of electricians (on the return of the ship from Acceptance Trials on 2 January revised figures of 1,500 men for at least three weeks were issued). It was agreed 250 workmen could sail on the Acceptance Trials in order to achieve this. Plans were in hand to clear passengers from unfinished areas if they were still incomplete by 10 January.

Cunard was now in a desperate situation and concluded that it was essential to get the ship away from the Clyde on 23 December in almost any condition provided she had obtained her Passenger Certificate. The company had realised that if it failed to achieve this they faced the prospect of endless delays and deliberate attempts by the labour to prolong the work.

There were four sections, excluding the condition of the public rooms, which required special attention:

- The three blocks of accommodation which were previously accepted for later completion.

- A number of rooms on One, Two and Three decks which need to be completed in detail, particularly connecting up all electrical wiring. The rooms on Four and Five decks were mainly "OK."

- On the public room decks, excluding public rooms, there were lavatories, pantries and lockers which still needed their ceilings and electrics completed and these had to be ready by 23 December.

- The commissioning of kitchen and pantry equipment in general.
It was estimated that the outstanding work would take 100 men weeks for joiners and 50 men weeks for electricians. Cunard impressed on the yard that every possible effort had to be made to have the ship substantially complete by 23 December and fully operational by 10 January but began to plan ahead by having passengers booked in certain blocks of cabins on Two and Three deck on the 10 January cruise relocated elsewhere in the ship.

A passenger certificate was required for the December acceptance trials and to achieve that the ship needed to be registered. It was decided that the ship should be registered in Cunard Line's name in order to avoid the necessity of re-registering the ship on 19 December.

Cleaning completed, she left for a second trial in the Irish Sea on 17 December for three days of trials which has been delayed by two days as high winds had prevented QE2 from leaving the dry dock. John Rannie, John Starks and Graham Strachan were on the bridge as the liner worked up speed over the measured mile off Arran. Contract conditions for speed and power were 32 knots and 110,000 shp. The QE2 lived up to expectations, recording a speed of 32.46 knots at 117,000 shp. It seemed that all was well.

John Whitworth would later recall:

"On 17 December the ship left dry-dock for an anchorage

and it was then discovered by Cunard that although a large number of men had been sent ashore some 1,200 still remained in the ship. The engine rooms were also found to be under only-manual control and the Builders proposed to start the technical trials in these condition. Cunard's Technical Director refused to permit this and the trials finally started on the morning of 18 December."

This trial consisted of stopping, starting, going astern and manoeuvring at full speed and a full technical trial, during which the speed was gradually increased to 177 rpm, at which the full power of 110,000 shp was developed. No vibration or imperfect running was detected with the performance. A full visual inspection of the main gearing was made and everything was found to be in perfect condition.

An internal examination of the turbines was not scheduled until after the acceptance trails which were set for 23 December - 19 days later than scheduled.

On 19 December a programme was agreed with the Builders for the clearing of workmen from the cabin decks, cabins and public rooms to enable the bedroom stewards to start work but this programme was not adhered to and the bedroom stewards did not get into the cabins until 22 December. It was agreed that it would be necessary to carry 450 workmen (mainly consisting of joiners, plumbers and electricians as well as shipyard and engineering workshop staff) on the Acceptance Trials to continue the work of finishing the ship.

On 20 December, the Chairmen of the respective companies agreed that they would join the ship by helicopter while she was coming up the English Channel so that at a meeting on 31 December (instead of 1 January for the Builders' tax purposes), Sir Basil would hand over a cheque for the final amount due and would take delivery of the ship.

One newspaper would later report:

"Three days before her technical trials John Rannie ordered a Christmas bonus, again traditional, of £10 per man, paid in cash half an hour before the pubs opened. Few men turned up for work the next day. Cunard was aghast."

The 'Acceptance Trial' was to be a voyage to tropical waters, during which the air conditioning was to be given a thorough try-out, and the delay meant Cunard had to quickly arrange for over 500 of its employees and their families to act as guinea pigs for the trip. Passengers from the Clyde district would be embarked by tender at 1800 hours that evening while passengers from Liverpool would arrive and proceed to Gourock Pier by coaches for embarkation by tender. 200 men, consisting of joiners, plumbers, electricians and shipyard and engineering staff, from the yard were also to sail so they could hopefully complete the unfinished cabins in the forward section of the ship.

Sir Basil was due to join them but his wife had been taken into hospital so he left his deputy Lord Mancroft in charge and flew back to London from Glasgow. John Rannie embarked with his wide.

While Captain Warwick was in command for the trials the vessel remained the responsibility of Upper Clyde Shipbuilders but was registered in the name of Cunard Line Limited.

Thursday 19 September 1968. *(Author's collection)*

The ship embarked passengers for these trials on the evening of 22 December. John Whitworth would describe how he was *"disturbed"* at the condition of the accommodation. The whole of Five Deck was allocated to UCS workmen and of the 698 cabins on One, Two, Three and Four Decks, 234 were uninhabitable and all the remainder had substantial defects and considerable re-berthing of the guinea pig 'passengers' had to be undertaken.

The Board of Trade Surveyor in charge of the ship advised Cunard that he was unable to issue a Passenger certificate which was essential if the ship were to proceed to sea with passengers unless considerable work had been done to make the ship safe for passengers.

It was common knowledge among the shipping press that the public rooms on board the *QE2* were in a state of chaos. Photographs of these rooms were not available because they were not in a fit condition to be photographed. The guinea pigs would be required to help and tidy and clean the ship.

The Builders arranged for a substantial number of electricians and joiners to work overnight primarily to block off the uncompleted areas and making them safe electrically by isolating electrical circuits and taping up bare wires.

At 0830 hours on 23 December a Passenger Certificate was issued and *QE2* left the Clyde – never to return until 23 July 1990 while undertaking a special Round Britain cruise for Cunard's 150th anniversary.

At 1100 hours *QE2* proceeded slow ahead and dropped off the Pilot at 1554 hours before being worked up to 150 rpm in the normal way.

At 0140 hours on 24 December a distress message from the tug *Francis Hallinan* which had got into difficulty and was disabled by water entering the boiler room. *QE2* and other ships went to her assistance and she was eventually taken in tow by a Dutch ocean-going tug.

The trials were to be sea trials in every sense of the word. On the technical side the main and auxiliary machinery would

be tested included simulated breakdowns and exercising damage conditions. The equipment would be overloaded intentionally. On the hotel side the 570 'passengers' would have to simulate a full ship so they were put into groups and asked to turn up at specific times for particular functions, they had been instructed to order anything from the menus in order to test the kitchens and their next days' activities would be shown in the Daily Programme. Each would complete a form once they had completed a task.

So sensitive were Cunard about the unfinished state of the ship the "strictest secrecy" was to be enforced and all communications between the ship and the UK were to be sent in code for the Chairman's attention. The use of the radio telephone was to be avoided as far as possible.

Sea trials have always been treated sensitively by shipbuilder and shipowner. When *Mauretania* left the Tyne, without fanfare, on 17 September 1907 for the first time on her way to shipyard trials in the North Sea, the trials were so secret that performance reports were sent back to the yard by homing pigeon rather than by more modern but much more generally accessible methods.

It was now apparent to Cunard that it would be unrealistic to maintain the 10 and 17 January voyages. This was not only due to the extent of the uncompleted work but also due to the fact that many items of the ship's equipment had not been properly commissioned by the Builders and when put into operation found to be defective. A press party of 71 was due to join the ship in Las Palmas on 28 December and great difficulty was experienced in finding sufficient cabins in which they could be accommodated regardless of the number of defects these rooms contained.

Technically, all was apparently going well until 1000 hours on Tuesday 24 December when down in the Turbine Room a small-bore pipe on a pressure gauge over the starboard h.p turbine forward bearing fractured and discharged oil over the ahead and astern turbines and the differential expansion indicator, which gave a warning due, apparently, to flooding with oil.

Simultaneously, vibration was noted from this turbine and it was attributed at the time to impingement of cold oil on the hot portion of the rotor external to the glands. Vibration had not been reported before that time.

The only event out of the ordinary during the night had been that the ship had altered course, following a call for help from a vessel in distress in the Atlantic, during which time the machinery had been put in a state of readiness for manoeuvring to render assistance which was not, however, required.

Speed was reduced on the starboard engine was reduced to 75 rpm and investigations were immediately put in hand to try and account for the persisting vibration. It was initially thought that the problem was due to an imbalance in the rotors. Some concern was felt about the apparent lack of expansion of the HP turbine sliding feet and particular attention was paid to determining whether there was any restraint.

By 1535 hours more severe vibration had developed and the turbine was stopped, using astern steam, and the vibration became more sever in the process. The port engine was slowed to 60 rpm to reduce the trailing effect on the starboard shaft and enable the examination of the starboard HP turbine bearings and flexible couplings.

This work was completed at 0645 hours on Christmas Day and at 0830 hours the starboard engine was started again and slowly worked up to 150 rpm on both sets. These revolutions were maintained until 0415 on Boxing Day morning when the starboard turbine once again started to vibrate. Reduce speed was ordered to 90 rpm and superheat temperature to 800° F.

Intensive investigation was proceeding during this time with a view to finding out why the HP turbine was apparently not expanding by the expected amount, the general impression being the cause of the vibration was lack of balance caused by a thermal bend. At 0145 hours on Friday 27 December, the starboard H.P. turbine started to vibrate ad emit a dull throbbing noise and it was decided to stop the engine, engage the turning gear and turn for five hours, allowing the rotor to straighten. The engine was started again at 0725 hours and worked up to about 90 rpm. The vibration was still present but somewhat reduced.

Cunard's Deputy Chairman Lord Mancroft (right) accepts the Britannia figurehead from Lloyds of London. Carved in Quebec yellow pine by Cornish sculptor Charles Moore, the figurehead would adorn the entrance to the Britannia Restaurant on Upper Deck.

The situation worsened when at 1315 hours the port engine, which had been operating at 150 rpm, began to show an increase in vibration level, and its revolutions were reduced to 140 rpm. Two hours later the port engine was reduced to 100 rpm and at 1900 hours, at the request of the Bridge, the speed was reduced to 64 rpm on both sets because of approach to anchorage off the Canary Islands.

On Saturday 28 December QE2 anchored at 0830 hours, with the engines on immediate standby, until 1720 hours when she weighed anchor and proceeded to Las Palmas at about 90 / 95 rpm and anchored there at 2025 hours. At the time of starting up to leave the anchorage, a listener at the starboard HP turbine heard a bumping noise followed by a crunch, whereupon the turbine ran vibration free.

The arrival of the press party added to the catalogue of calamity as they boarded the ship and had to climb five decks as none of the lifts were working and despite it being almost midnight they could hear men labouring with hammers and drills.

Upon their arrival there Sir Basil and Anthony Hepper joined the ship at around 2000 hours and went straight into a meeting in the Card Room that lasted until 0400 hours the next morning with Tom Kameen reporting that John Brown Engineering did not yet know what had caused the damage let alone how to cure it. It was agreed that delivery would not take place upon arrival in Southampton. The Board of Trade Surveyor would withdraw the Passenger Certificate as soon as the ship had berthed in Southampton – the certificate would not be reissued until 17 April 1969.

One of the launches returning some press ashore broke down and had to be towed back to QE2. At 0354 hours on 29 December QE2 left Las Palmas.

A few hours later, at 0930 hours, a joint press conference, which was also broadcast throughout QE2's public address

Cunard's Managing Director John Whitworth discussing **QE2** during a television interview.

system to keep the ship's company informed, was held. Sir Basil confirmed that Cunard would not be taking delivery of QE2 on her return to Southampton and cited two main reasons for this: the degree of uncompleted builders' work in the passenger spaces of the ship including the areas which serviced them being the primary reason and the technical problems which had arisen with both sets of main machinery during the trials.

Sir Basil:

"We will not accept the ship on 1 January, when she finishes acceptance trials…She is not up to Cunard standard.

"…the degree of uncompleted builders' works in the passenger spaces of the ship and the areas servicing them behind the scenes…this would not only prevent the QE2 from carrying its full complement of passengers for some weeks, but it would also make it quite impossible for Cunard to achieve the every high standards of passenger service which we aim to provide in this magnificent ship.

"Under no circumstances are we in Cunard prepared to sail the QE2 on a commercial voyage until we are satisfied that the standards she can offer are what she was designed for, what we have yet to establish and what we know she is capable of achieving. When completed, this ship will be the most wonderful ship in the world.

"I would like to pay a very well deserved tribute to the efforts al all Cunard officers and crew. They are demonstrating their ability — under most difficult circumstances as a result of the volume of this uncompleted work — daily to improve and bring the ship up to the standard of passenger requirements for the new markets that we are seeking. I cannot speak too highly of what our Cunard men and women on board have accomplished.

As well as the fault in the starboard turbine three blocks of cabins were incomplete and a lot of work in the public rooms was still to be done. While not confirmed it was thought delivery would be delayed just three weeks.

Commenting on Sir Basil's statement, Anthony Hepper said he was quite certain that QE2 was going to be a very fine ship, a ship of which Cunard was going to be very proud, and of which they as shipbuilders would be very proud for many years to come. The yard was committed to handing over QE2 in an absolutely first class state. He confirmed that it would not be less than three weeks from the 1 January handing over date before the ship could be handed over but an exact date could not be given until after arrival in Southampton.

Amid a rising tide of complaints and counter charges, including John Whitworth claiming the "intensity of work" had dropped at a crucial stage and "broken assurances", over QE2's continuing troubles Anthony Hepper told 250 workmen during a meeting to get on with the job and urged them to make sure the task of completing the ship would take no longer than three weeks.

One journalist reported:

"At a press conference Smallpeice announced that he would not accept the ship. "Will Mr Rannie be postponing his retirement to finish the ship?" a journalist asked. "Mr Rannie will be retiring as planned", a manager replied. There was a long silence. A scapegoat had been found."

In the last hours of his employment, John Rannie and UCS Chairman Anthony Hepper argued over the condition of the ship, resulting in Rannie's six months' consultancy being withdrawn. John Rannie claimed 86 cabins remained incomplete, half of which were within "striking distance" of being completed while the other half required considerable work. He would not be given the opportunity of continuing the extra work needed for the ship and when QE2 docked at Southampton, he slipped quietly away and into retirement. UCS Technical Director John Starks took over the completion of the ship, for which there was now plenty of time. Nevertheless, this work took until 14 February. The turbines were a different matter, however. Designed by Pametrada, which no longer existed, and constructed at Clydebank by

QE2 was opened up to staff and workers and their families to visit, Friday 15 and Saturday 16 November 1968. *(Author's collection)*

Captain Warwick, HRH Prince Charles and Sir Basil Smallpeice on QE2's port Bridge wing as she sailed down the Clyde to Greenock, Tuesday 19 November 1968. *(Author's collection)*

John Brown Engineering, Upper Clyde Shipbuilders could do little until the extent of the damage was determined and a timetable put in place for repairs.

This would mean Upper Clyde Shipbuilders would have to make other managerial arrangements for the remainder of the period to see the ship handed over to Cunard. Hepper personally assumed control of the operation assisted by John Starks who would now become project manager for the operation.

The 10 January cruise was "cancelled" and 17 January crossing to New York was "postponed" (at an estimated loss to Cunard of ½ million) and the visit for more than 2,000 travel agents on 2 January was cancelled. Those booked on cancelled cruises would be given priority booking on one of the new sailing dates while those who did not wish to sail would be given a full refund. The cruises from New York starting on 1 February were also threatened.

Cunard:

"We would like to express our regrets for the inconvenience caused to you. You will not doubt be aware that the cause of this great disappointment is quite outside our control. However, the delay is only a temporary one, caused by teething troubles, and we are sure this fine new ship will be soon be serving the travelling public in the way you are all expecting."

The expensive advertising and marketing programme was a dead loss. In addition, the crew – trained and ready – had now to be retrained on standby with full pay – that high cost would also have to written off. Cunard had hoped to take £15 million in 1969 and now the QE2 setback would cost at least £1 million.

QE2 had broken down and technical people from both

Cunard and the yard still did not know what had caused the damage let alone how to cure it. The Pametrada turbines which were approved by Cunard for QE2 were a well-known design and had been well proved in many other ships. QE2's previous speed trials demonstrated that these turbines were fully capable of achieving their required performance. The fault was major, could not be rectified at sea and would take some time to repair. To take the ship back to the Clyde was just not practical - Southampton was the nearest port so QE2 headed 'home'. It was decided to proceed home at half speed (14 knots), which gave an acceptable vibration level, and both sets were continuously monitored so that any increase in vibration level could be immediately countered by a reduction in revolutions.

On top of everything else, rumours were running through the ship that a strike was imminent among the 500 workmen on board – rumours that were discounted by shop stewards. On Sunday 29 January there was a mass meeting when workers' complaints were answered by management officials as bad feeling seems to have developed between Upper Clyde employees and Cunard, because of supposedly preferential treatment given to Cunard employees. Morale among UCS workmen on board was reported at a *"low ebb."*

During most of Monday, Tuesday and Wednesday the ship proceeded homeward without further incident. One journalist reported:

"She rides beautifully and handles extremely well. She is extraordinarily quiet and free of vibration…"

Sir Basil also received the news that the Cunard cargo-liner Ivernia had been delayed in Cobh after breaking down twice with engine trouble at the start of her voyage from Liverpool.

121

Watched by thousands who waited patiently QE2 sedately makes her way down the Clyde, Tuesday 19 November 1968. *(Author's collection)*

QE2's Caribbean cruise departing New York on 1 February was also now cancelled but Cunard was praised for its announcement that it would pay £140,000 in commission on voyages cancelled and thus retained the goodwill of the traveltrade which was important. Previously with its own offices in big cities around the world handling the bulk of its business over its own counters Cunard managed quite well without travel agents but the cut back in the fleet and the closure of its offices business over the counter became less and less and its dependence on the travel agent increased.

The Daily Programme for Wednesday 1 January advised the 'passengers':

"The Guinea Pig Exercise is now completed. We should like to thank all passengers for their co-operation in helping us to try out the various public rooms, their constructive suggestions and for completing the various feedback forms. Despite the difficult circumstances a vast amount of information has been obtained from these exercises which will prove of the greatest value to the ship o her commercial voyages."

In his New Year message to Cunard staff, Sir Basil Smallpeice said *QE2* had experienced a disappointing sequence of events but not a calamity:

"I want to convey to you all the certainty I feel that with goodwill, hard work and honest endeavour, the present difficulties will be completely overcome. I feel it is a great privilege to lead this splendid team and I believe that with your loyalty and enthusiasm we can bring our interesting enterprises to a successful outcome in 1969."

On Wednesday evening the revolutions were progressively increased at the rate of one rev/h to a maximum of 92 rpm

until 0810 hours on Thursday 2 January 1969 in the approach to Southampton, when the revolutions were reduced to 60 rpm and then to 45 rpm at the request of the Bridge, finally berthing at Southampton.

Press response to the ship was universally in praise for a "magnificent" vessel. The Times reporter wrote *"I would have no hesitation now in saying to anyone thinking of crossing the Atlantic: 'Go by QE2, she is the finest ship on the run'."*

Sadly a 40-year hotel officer, George Boyle, died after collapsing suddenly meaning a Southampton coroner's officer would be waiting for the ship after her arrival.

Southampton, Thursday 2 January 1969. *(Author's collection)*

CHAPTER SIX

The Reluctant Queen

The planned splendid and triumphant arrival as *QE2* sailed into her homeport of Southampton for the first time on Thursday 2 January 1969, one day later than planned, was cancelled. And there would be no elaborate handing-over ceremony which was perhaps the bitterest pill of all for Cunard.

There should have been Hampshire Police Band to greet her at Southampton Ocean Terminal. It was cancelled. The Mayor and other VIPs should have met *QE2* by launch. The trip was cancelled. Hundreds of balloons should have been released in tribute. There were no balloons, no triumphant whistle blasts or welcoming banners.

Instead only a "few people" (the crowd was estimated at 200) waved and gave muted cheers but most voices were stilled as she edged her way into the Ocean Terminal. The Mayor, Sheriff, Town Clerk and Southampton Recorder, who adjourned the day's Quarter Sessions to attend, were still on hand to welcome her home.

Among the signals flown from *QE2*'s mast was one signalling that she would not be sailing within 24 hours.

QE2 would indeed make her first Southampton arrival embarrassed but she would leave the City for the last time on Thursday 11 November 2008 a much-loved ship in a blaze of glory after the most magnificent and truly record-breaking career.

The engineering difficulties did prove to be a blessing in disguise for the yard as it now gave them extra time to complete the unfinished passenger accommodation. As 175

workers from Clydeside boarded trains for Glasgow some 400 men, including senior managers from John Brown Engineering, were waiting for her on the quayside having been brought to Southampton from Clydebank to join those already on board. Vosper Thorneycroft was engaged by UCS to act as contractors in Southampton. These men would be accommodated on *QE2*, in hotels around the city and on a supply ship, the *Cammell Laird*, which was chartered from Cammell Laird of Birkenhead who used her as a trials accommodation ship.

Four aircraft were organised by Cunard to return 300 guinea pig passengers back to home to Liverpool and Glasgow from Southampton Airport – the largest of the four planes being the four turboprop 132-seater Vanguard of British European Airways which arrived from London Heathrow and became the first Vanguard, the biggest in BEA's fleet, to fly into Southampton. Most of the 110 passengers arriving in Liverpool excitedly told the waiting press that despite the problems *QE2* as "a magnificent ship."

On 3 January, the Daily Sketch reported:

"The £300,000 operation to make the Queen Elizabeth 2 shipshape after her ill-fated ten-day acceptance trials in the Atlantic starts today."

It was agreed that Upper Clyde Shipbuilders would remain responsible for the ship during the "completion period" which was defined as the period between the ship's arrival and the

The first of more than 700 arrivals into her homeport of Southampton, Thursday 2 January 1969. *(Author's collection)*

date of acceptance of the ship by Cunard Line Limited. The latter would act as agents on behalf of UCS and undertake care, maintenance and security of the ship including the operation of the ship's machinery in accordance with the yard's requirements, using the ship's crew and shore personnel for these purposes, all costs and liabilities for these matters being borne by UCS.

Lord Mancroft told reporters that the resultant publicity had the triumphant effect that everyone in America had now heard of his company!

Interestingly most of the press coverage was sympathetic and agreed that while QE2 was then in trouble she would be the success everyone hoped she would be. Michael Baily writing in the Times on 2 January claimed:

"What is so good about her? The moment you step on board you get a feeling this this is something special; that interesting and enjoyable things are going to happen, and that you are going to be very comfortable.

"The result quite simply is a swinging ship and, I expect the food and service, which even in present conditions are the best I have experienced for several years on Cunard, to swing rapidly into line.

"The QE2 is a phoenix rising visibly from the ashes, and knowing she is so good should finally bring the Cunard strands together and send this great old firm steaming full speed ahead again."

And Sir Basil even went as far as to talk about placing further orders on the Clyde:

"Nothing that has happened with the QE2 would influence us in any way against the Clyde."

It had been rumoured on board that during the previous few days discussions had taken place been Sir Basil and Anthony Hepper about a cruise liner of between 25,000 and 30,000 tons after QE2 had operated for at least six months. The new liner would be permanently based in the Mediterranean or the Caribbean with passengers being flown out and back. These discussions had apparently turned a frigid atmosphere between Cunard and UCS into one of warm mutual respect.

Anthony Hepper:

"Sir Basil has been impressed by what a fine ship the QE2 is and we have discussed the order for smaller passenger ships built specially for cruising. This could lead to a series of ships over the years."

Sir Basil:

"We wouldn't do anything until this ship has been in service for about six months but I have no doubt that she will be a great success. This ship will be an absolute winner."

An interesting article appeared in the Sunday Times just a few days later regarding a possible sister for QE2:

"Delighted with their new ship and with her advanced bookings (but not, of course, with her delays), Cunard have ordered a financial and design study for a sister ship to Queen Elizabeth 2.

"The ship would be of similar all-cruise one-class configuration. The success of the weight saving techniques used in QE2 indicate that a slightly larger ship, around 72,000 tons against QE2's 65,000, would be the most economical.

"The financial study indicated that considerable economies of scale would be possible with two ships, and Cunard would have the considerable advantage of having at least one of the sisters continually on cruise service in some warm climate, so that cruises could be sold to "get-away-from-it-all" impulse buyers at any time.

"Cunard are studying the possibility of raising the cost of the new ship on the normal money marker [sic], without asking for a Government loan. This will depend on whether the high hopes the line had for the ship are realised; and this should become clear in her first year or so of operation.

"Who will build her? If Cunard can raise their own finance they can build a new ship anywhere they please, ad relations between the liner and Upper Clyde Shipbuilders, who built QE2, are still very close.

"Top officials of both Cunard and the shipbuilders said last week that they could see no reason why the prospective new ship should not be built at John Brown's shipyard on the Clyde, despite the teething troubles of QE2.

"In Southampton, hundreds of workmen gave up their weekend to continue fitting out the QE2.

"Two hundred more workmen arrive from Glasgow today, giving Upper Clyde Shipbuilders executives more accommodation problems."

In fact both men, Sir Basil and Anthony Hepper, seemed to have struck a working rapport which had been noticeably absent in previous months. Sir Basil expressed confidence in Anthony Hepper who made no bones about his company's management shortfall, which resulted in over-optimistic delivery dates.

After the machinery had cooled, inspection of the turbines was finally carried out. The port and starboard HP casings were opened where it was revealed that blading in both rotors had sustained damage - hundreds of blades had been stripped from the main body of the rotor hub. On the starboard rotor the complete row of blading had been stripped from stage 9, and eight blades were missing from stage 10. Many of the broken blades were piled up against each other near the horizontal joints whilst some were wedged in the nozzle passages. The neighbouring nozzles were extensively bruised and distorted. On further inspection cracking could be seen at the bases, or roots, of other blades. On the port rotor the damage was less extensive with seven blades missing from stage 9 and some cracking in stages 8 and 10.

Some of the fracture faces which had been undamaged by subsequent rubbing showed clear signs of fatigue failure and it was immediately clear that a major repair, requiring entirely new blades, would be needed and that this repair would have to take place in Clydebank. It was equally clear

Southampton had not seen anything quite like **QE2** before when she arrived for the first time but she would become a familiar and enduring sight over the following decades
(Author's collection)

that repair was going to take much longer than a week.

Not long after the casings had been opened a full power failure meant work had to stop around the ship.

The rotors were air freighted to Glasgow the following day. Graham Strachan, Managing Director of JBE, placed Jim Turner, the director of the Marine and General Engineering Division, in charge of co-ordinating the turbine repair. John Brown engineers quickly realised that the cause of the failure was steam excitation. This can develop when the frequency of vibrations set up inside the turbine results in premature metal fatigue of the blades, causing them to snap at the root. The most convenient solution was to redesign and manufacture blades with thicker roots. Sourcing the molybdenum steel, from which the blades were made, began quickly, and manufacturing the redesigned blades was put in hand.

The Clydebank diagnosis was met with scepticism by Cunard's consultants, the Technical Investigation Department at Lloyds. When Cunard discussed the failure with Associated Electrical Industries (AEI), with whom turbine orders for Cunard container ships had recently been placed, both JBE and UCS threatened legal action. After all, AEI was a competitor.

On 7 January a private meeting between Cunard, Upper Clyde Shipbuilders and John Brown Engineering took place. The extent and nature of the turbine failure now disclosed

made it impossible at that time to give a completion date of the ship. UCS rejected JBE's expressed preliminary opinion that the turbines would not be ready for *"not less than five weeks."* There were around 1,500 men working on board and it was clear the rectification of the turbine defects would take longer than the residual work by the finishing trades. UCS indicated to Cunard that the major work would be completed by 31 January but also provided a secondary date of 14 February to allow for cleaning and commissioning and getting men off the ship. It would be down to the efforts of JBE to secure the ultimate delivery of QE2.

In a newspaper article a defiant John Rannie, who received a CBE in the 1968 /1969 New Year Honours, upon his retirement, wrote:

"… the people of Scotland should be proud of QE2 and the men who built her.

"I know I am.

"I've been in charge of building more liners than perhaps any other man.

"The thing that hurts me most is the exaggerated criticisms of the ship, and the Clyde workers.

"I'd like to ask the critics – what did they think we were building? A family car?

"To hear the moaners, you'd think no new ship ever

Above: The Grill Room on Quarter Deck (Dennis Lennon)

Left top: First Class cabin (Jon Bannenberg)

Left bottom: Conference Room on Quarter Deck (Gaby Schreiber)

Below: G Stairway

(All photographs author's collection)

Above: Queens Room on Quarter Deck (Michael Inchbald)

Left: The Double Room on Upper and Boat Decks (Jon Bannenberg)

(All photographs author's collection)

The Boat Deck showing the unusual paint scheme (black davits and khaki deck-house) by James Gardner that helped to reduce the visual impact of the aluminium superstructure which was high in relation to the rest of the ship. *(Author's collection)*

had any trouble.

"What do people expect? We had our share of labour troubles. Sometimes materials went astray. Sometimes sub-contractors were a bit late.

"But don't you get that on any building site? In any car factory?

"The one thing that can't be criticised is the craftsmanship in every corner of the ship from the keel to the tip of her funnel.

"Maybe we're a little late in delivery.

"But there was no skimping or rushing. The men took their time and did things properly as only the men of Clyde can."

The crucial relationship between Dan Wallace and John Rannie would not be looked at favourably in the months and years after *QE2*'s delivery with Dan Wallace writing at different times:

"the minutes [of progress meetings] were written by the builders and very often were biased in their favour. Admittedly these reports were submitted to us for approval but I found it impossible to correct any more than the most glaring errors and you will find occasionally in approval of the Minutes that I have sent the Managing Director comments to this effect."

"…these meetings were always dominated by Mr Rannie and were most difficult as far as I was concerned. Indeed it is well-known that throughout these Progress Meetings I had difficulty with Mr Rannie in trying to obtain from him an accurate assessment of the situation, together with adequate forward planning. In the end this – in my opinion – is what caused the disastrous finish."

"…Mr Rannie was being allowed to manage QE2

entirely by himself and in the end this was the main cause of failure."

Cunard's refusal to accept delivery and the subsequent cancellation of *QE2*'s announced programme of maiden voyages between January and April 1969 resulted in the costs of the expensive ad campaign for the ships introduction and these inaugural voyages having to be written off. The Cunard Report of the Directors dated 15 May 1969 stated:

"The Board has decided not to carry forward the abortive advertising costs and agents' commission incurred in 1968 and the other costs referred to, altogether some £778,000, to be recouped out of subsequent revenue."

A *"big noise fast"* (the bigger the bang the bigger the echoes) became the agreed policy for advertising *QE2* as soon as it became clear in March / April 1969 that the campaign could begin. The bigger the bang the bigger the echoes.

The original starting date, 24 January 1969, had to be suspended but once a Handover Date had been established the programme – costing £150,000 – could go forward. The reasons for the "big noise" included establishing the ship as real and sailing and to show what she was like inside, a job that would have been covered by editorial features in colour magazines.

This meant bringing forward 'The Great One between London and New York' theme and eliminating the initial ads for the Maiden cruise programme. In the build-up to the 2 May sailing colour pages (as well as black and white ads) were used wherever possible with the aim of getting full impact for the pictures of the interior.

The whole aim of the publicity was to market the ship as a place and an experience – certainly not as transport.

Although the new ads were selling sailings now references in them to voyages or distances were relatively few. All the emphasis was on 'QE2 Style' and the ship's value in terms of money, as well as amenities as a hotel or even resort.

Examples of the way in which the company and its advertising agency struck out for a new style occurred in the colour ads. QE2, they stated, has *"Our law of supply and demand. Whatever you demand we supply."* Then, *"There's our Law of Gravity. It's a crime to be grave in QE2."* And again, *"Inhibitions are strictly for dry land, so swing."*

On 9 January Sir Basil instructed Cunard's Chief Accountant that no further payments should be made to UCS. Relations between the two companies became increasingly strained and at one point Cunard withdrew the facility of providing lunch time coffee and sandwiches for all staff.

On 15 January 1969 Cunard issued the following statement:

"Cunard have been told by Upper Clyde Shipbuilders that the statement issued by UCS last night to the effect that the cause of the trouble with the QE2 turbines had not yet been positively identified, is based upon information received from John brown Engineering, the manufactures of the QE2's turbines. Cunard have been given to understand that JBE would be unable to say anything further as to the cause of the turbine blade failure for up to another three weeks.

"With this cause not yet established, coupled with the fact that the only test-bed in this country in which the remedies eventually make can be proved effective is the ship herself, it is clear from the statement issued by UCS last night that the correction of the failure may result in considerable delay.

"This delay is naturally a matter of profound concern to Cunard, not only because of loss of revenue but also because we, Cunard, appreciate the lateness of the ship's delivery and continued uncertainty as to the future are serious matters for our many customers and supporters in the travel trade.

"In these circumstances, Cunard feel an obligation to let those customers and supporters know where they stand. In view of JBE's present inability to determine beyond doubt the cause of their turbine blade failures, and therefore of UCS's inability to guarantee the success of the remedial measures JBE may take, Cunard accept delivery until after the ship's turbines have been thoroughly re-tested and proved in further basin trials, speed trials and a prolonged acceptance trial under maintained pressure, followed by further inspection. It is impossible to say when this programme of correction, testing and proving of the ship's power plant can be completed.

"Cunard deeply regret having to disappoint our friends and prospective passengers. The circumstances are, however, entirely outside Cunard's control. We have accordingly no choice but to say that until further notice, no QE2 advertised sailings can take place.

"It is some satisfaction to have been assure by UCS that the interior finishing of the ship will be completed as promised, by the end of January, except for some work on inspection and commissioning. But it is only when QE2 can be demonstrated by the builders and their turbine subcontractors to be capable of operating fully, and of behaving as the magnificent ship she potentially is, that

In contrast to her first arrival there was a jubilant atmosphere when **QE2** departed for her first Atlantic crossing, Friday 2 May 1969. *(Author's collection)*

Above: Teenage / Juke Box Room on Boat Deck (Elizabeth Beloe and Tony Heaton)

Left top: The Shops on Boat Deck (Dennis Lennon)

Left bottom: Tourist Class cabin (Dennis Lennon)

Below: Double Room upper level (Jon Bannenberg)

(All photographs author's collection)

Enclosed promenade on Upper Deck (starboard side) between Theatre Bar and Britannia Restaurant. *(Author's collection)*

Cunard will be able to announce the revised sailing dates."

The shipyard refused Cunard's request in mid-January for one its own independent consultants to visit the yard and inspect the rotors. The yard stated that it had earlier been agreed at an earlier meeting that it would be their responsibility to report back and make available reports on tests etc when these became available and that as well as appointing their own consultant they had also consulted a well-known American turbine builder as well as placing evidence and conclusions before a panel of experts for their consideration.

This panel would include experts from Rolls Royce, the National Gas Turbines Establishment, the Central Electricity Generating Board and the Department of Engineering at the University of Cambridge.

It was reported that Cunard was considering using the ship for raising revenue while she was alongside in Southampton but no arrangements for this were formalised.

Questions about QE2 were raised in the House of Commons with MPs asking for an enquiry into all the troubles and delays. The Minister of Technology, Anthony Wedgewood Benn, responded that he did not believe a formal enquiry would serve any purpose at all. Reports of widespread pilfering during the building of the liner were raised in the House of Lords and the Government spokesman, Lord Beswick, responded that that was a matter for the management.

John Whitworth would later write:

"Despite the optimism of the Builders, Mr Wallace reported to me on 15 January his concern at the general lack of progress. He had sent the Builders formal letters regarding a number of aspects, notably the lack of detailed work schedules, the draught stops throughout the ship and the poor quality of finish in certain areas. He reported further

Enclosed promenade on Quarter Deck (starboard side) adjacent to the Midships Bar and Queens Room. *(Author's collection)*

on 28 January to the effect that the Builders were becoming increasingly behind schedule; he regarded their estimated completion dates of 31 January /14 February as totally unrealistic."

Despite this UCS was still reducing the numbers of men working on board. On 28 January there were 1,300 UCS men on board; the number was 340 on 27 March.

Cunard appointed Booz Allen & Hamilton to initiate a system of recording individual defects on punched cards which would then be run through Cunard's computer to produce a printout listing each defect individually. This work would continue from mid-January until mid-March and the final printout based on information up to 12 March gave the following figure:

Total recorded defects	19,500
Defects rectified by Builders	11,000
Defects passed by Cunard	5,500

Machinery spaces and a number of general items on the

"QE2 is not a modern version of the former Queens. She is a resort hotel that has the advantage of being able to follow the sun…" – Cunard. *(Author's collection)*

hull side were excluded in the above figures.

John Whitworth:

"Progress meetings were held regularly at weekly intervals during February and March. They followed a consistent pattern. The Builders continued to under-estimate the volume of outstanding work and were continually over-optimistic about completion; their assurances in this respect were constantly proved to be false by Mr Wallace's inspections and Booz-Allen's printouts."

Cunard was concerned over the filthy state of most of the public rooms and stairways as it had become quite obvious that many of the decorative contractors were making little of no attempt to clean up their spaces as per their contract. It was also noted that much unnecessary work was being carried out on carpets and furniture without any protection.

On 5 February, John Brown Engineering held a press conference on their interim report on its findings, confirming they had isolated the factors involved in the turbine failure and announcing that a repair programme had been put in place with the rotors expected to be returned to Southampton by 7 March.

Their findings confirmed their initial diagnosis of steam excitation causing blade failure which they attributed to a design error by the now defunct Pametrada:

"The primary problem is related to a design error and would normally have been accepted for solution by the original design team.

"These turbines were designed for us by Pametrada, an association which is now dissolved. Never-the-less JBE as main machinery contractor is responsible to Upper Clyde Shipbuilders and would not wish in any way to evade this responsibility."

In total 120 blades, mostly in the starboard rotor, had broken.

Sir Basil Smallpeice's reaction was publicly to demand an independent assessor. Newspapers ran headlines quoting the Cunard Chairman *"What Reliance Can We Place on John Brown Engineering?"*

The national importance of the *QE2* and the bitter disagreement between JBE and Cunard required the involvement of the Minister of Technology, Tony Benn.

On 10 February, Tony Benn convened a meeting to appoint an independent assessor, with Sir Basil Smallpeice, Anthony Hepper and Sir George Gardner, JBE's Managing Director, in attendance. Gardner had previously suggested to Benn that Sir Arnold Lindley, President of the Institution of Mechanical Engineers and a former Managing Director of GEC, should be considered. Lindley was eminently suitable and Benn had little difficulty in obtaining approval.

The appointment of Sir Arnold was seen as a major victory for Sir Basil and three main factors emerged from the meeting: Sir Arnold could call on whoever he liked to help him (even GEC-AEI experts to whom JBE had objected in the past); Sir Basil reserved the right to ignore the report and still insist on his own investigation and that UCS was working to a delivery date of 18 April.

The major difference dividing Cunard and JBE was on what basis the final handover would take place. Sir Basil showed no sign of being moved from his declared position if not accepting the ship until he had a guarantee from JBE that the turbines would work effectively for the whole of QE2's operational life which was an undertaking JBE was reluctant to give.

On 11 February, Tony Benn arrived at Clydebank to see the damaged turbines for himself, commenting later at a press conference *"I have come here today to take the steam out of the situation and put it back into the turbines"*, a comment which was greatly appreciated at Clydebank. Meetings between UCS, JBE and Cunard remained difficult, in stark contrast to the friendliness that had existed between John Brown and Cunard in the past. With the exception of formal meetings, communication between parties was discouraged and only took place after thorough vetting by lawyers.

On 12 February Cunard announced:

"You will have learnt, from the various news sources, that the Minister of Technology has called for an independent assessment of the troubles besetting the QE2's power plant.

"It now becomes apparent that the ship cannot be delivered to us by the builders before mid-April and therefore the Easter Cruise due to depart on 3 April cannot take place."

On the same day Cunard's Company Secretary (Frank Leach) wrote to his counterpart at UCS (P Russell):

"We accept that your expenditure certificates should be met, on our part, by the appropriate payment but only in so far as the expenditure has been well spent and has produced an acceptable product. The expenditure so far incurred and paid by us on the turbines and associated machinery has been rendered valueless because of the inability of the turbines to operate, and we are doing no more than withholding amounts against the payments already made to you in respect of work now found to be quite unacceptable.

"You should be aware that we consider that we have a claim against your Company in respect of the losses suffered by us as a consequence of delay in delivery of the vessel...."

On 19 February 1968 Lord Aberconway wrote to Sir Basil to complain about some of things Sir Basil had supposedly been saying to the press about the problems. Lord Aberconway claimed some of the things being said were:

"quite unwarranted by the known facts at this stage, and which are highly damaging to the reputation, and so to the future trading prospects, of John Brown..."

Sir Basil was accused of claiming that John Brown Engineering's attitude *"made one wonder what reliance could be placed on statements made at their press conference"* held in Glasgow on 5 February; the possible need of replacing the turbines with a new set designed and manufactured to Cunard's satisfaction and that Cunard would require a

"QE2 is not so much in competition with the air, which is transportation, as with land-based resort hotels, which are holiday and leisure centres." – Cunard. *(Author's collection)*

guarantee of the turbines for the life of the ship. Lord Aberconway retorted that Cunard were giving the view that the turbines would never work properly and to talk after one failure, caused by a complex of circumstances, of replacing them was quite premature and that a guarantee for the lifetime of the ship would go far beyond the terms of the contract. It was also pointed out that Cunard specified turbines of Pametrada design and approved the actual designs in due course.

Sir Basil responded:

"...I am satisfied that my comments following the press conference on 5 February were, at the time and in the circumstances, justified" and that *"Cunard did not specify the turbines of Pametrada design exclusively, nor did we approve the actual designs. The choice and approval of designs lay with the builders."*

Lord Aberconway finalised his next letter thanking Sir Basil or his response:

"Altogether not the sort of acknowledgment I should have expected to a 'slap-down' letter!"

An investigating team, under the leadership of Sir Arnold

Above: Britannia Restaurant on Upper Deck (Dennis Lennon)

Left top: Tourist Class Library on Upper Deck (Dennis Lennon)

Left bottom: Q4 Room on Quarter Deck (David Hicks)

Below: Double Down Bar on Upper Deck (Jon Bannenberg)

(All photographs author's collection)

The Grill Room Bar on One Deck (Dennis Lennon)

The Look Out on Upper Deck (Theo Crosby / Alan Fletcher and Colin Forbes)

Captain 'Bil' Warwick in command of a reluctant Queen. *(Author's collection)*

Lindley, President of the Institute of Mechanical Engineers, was established to assess the cause of the damage and find a solution to the problem. Subsequently an important paper (by Messrs. Coats and Fleeting) that was read to the Institute of Marine Engineers was produced.

Upper Clyde Shipbuilders would remain responsible for the ship during this completion period while Cunard Line Limited, acting as agents for an on behalf of the builders, would undertake the care, maintenance and security of the ship including the operation of the ship's machinery in accordance with the builder's requirements, use the ship's crew and shore personnel for these purposes with all costs and liabilities being attributable to the builders.

The port and starboard rotors were returned to Clydebank where a detailed examination on the starboard HP rotor revealed that stages one to eight, stage 11 and stage 12 were free from cracks, but in addition to the complete stripping of all blades in stage 9, and the loss of eight blades in stage 10, ether were two cracks at the junction of blade and root in stage 10.

On the port HP rotor, stages 1 – 7 were free of cracks but, in addition to the missing blades from stage 9, there was considerable cracking of blades in stages 8, 9, 10 and 11, all cracks being at the junction of blade and root except blade 63 in stage 8, which was found to be cracked in the aerofoil section approximately half-way up the blade.

It was found that the blade roots, which were square, did not expand as much as could be expected and that the steam supply nozzles, used to deliver steam on to the blades, were of below standard quality. There were also too many of these nozzles.

The resultant vibration and resonances that were induced in the blades proved to be too much and as one cracked and sheared it took away its immediate neighbour until masses of blades had been torn from the rotor.

The remedy was to provide new blades with strengthened roots and to 'tie' them together with a continuous length of one eighth of an inch stainless steel wire welded between all blades of each stage, thus providing stiffness and a resistance to resonance.

All 850 engineers at John Brown Engineering who had worked on correcting the faults received a £10 bonus.

Sir Arnold Lindley's report was made public on 28 February, three days after Cunard had been officially advised, and vindicated the Clydebank engineers. At a press conference, Sir Arnold stated that:

"Steam excitation is a phenomenon well known to steam turbine engineers not only in Britain but also in Europe and America. In the case of marine turbines which operate under variable speed conditions, this excitation is particularly difficult to avoid. It should be made clear that there is no reflection whatsoever on the quality of workmanship or of the material used in any part of the construction of the turbines. The remedial measures proposed [by JBE] were adequate, and when complete, trials could be resumed with every confidence."

Cunard had been advised by their Counsel that a substantial claim could be made against UCS but the company would have to pay the balance of the contract price prior to pursuing the claim. Cunard had no legal right to hold back an amount in respect of claims the company thought it may have had for loss on profits due to the late delivery. Such a claim would have been a *"disagreement"* between the parties which had to be referred to arbitration. Counsel advised Cunard that if the company had tried to do this then it would have placed the company in the wrong light when it came to arbitration and they did not have a legal right to do so.

Sir Basil wrote to Lord Aberconway after the publication of Sir Arnold's report:

"We have all had an opportunity of considering the report of Sir Arnold Lindley to the Minister of Technology dated 28 February 1969 on his independent assessment of the Queen Elizabeth 2 turbines, the contents of which, I understand, have been accepted by John Brown Engineering (Clydebank) Limited, Upper Clyde Shipbuilders and ourselves.

"The Directors of Cunard Line Limited must now consider the steps to be taken to formulate the Company's claim against Upper Clyde Shipbuilders Limited for the delay in delivery of the ship.

"In the absences of any agreement to the contrary, it will be necessary for Cunard Line Limited to resort to arbitration. This would, I have no doubt, be a long drawn out and expensive process.

"In order, however, to limit the matters in dispute between our respective Companies, I shall be glad to know whether, in the light of the Interim Report of John Brown Engineering (Clydebank) Limited dated 27 January 1969 and the report of Sir Arnold Lindley, Upper Clyde Shipbuilders agrees (a) that Queen Elizabeth 2 should have been delivered in full working condition to Cunard Lime Limited not later than 1 January 1969; (b) that liability for the failure lies with Upper Clyde Shipbuilders Limited, as between that Company and Cunard Line Limited; (c) that the amount of damages Upper Clyde Shipbuilders Limited is liable to pay Cunard Line Limited in respect of such failure is the loss of net profits of that Company attributable to the delay in delivery, including costs, charges and expenses incurred by Cunard Line Limited in holding the ship's company in a state of readiness; and (d) that the only issue outstanding between our two companies is the proof of the figures.

The *QE2* makes a majestic first entrance into New York, Wednesday 7 May 1969. She would make a further 709 calls to the City. *(Author's collection)*

"I have only written of the delay attributable to the breakdown of the turbines but I must reserve the rights of Cunard Line Limited in respect of the delay in delivery due to other causes."

Later that year the John Brown and Company's Report and Accounts would state:

"John Brown Engineering (Clydebank) Ltd. Had a difficult year during which they had to contend with the failure of the turbines of the Cunarder, RMS Queen Elizabeth 2. The trouble was found to have arisen from a design fault. The design was not that of JBE but was, even to detail, that of Pametrada, a marine turbine design organization now dissolved. Cunard specified Pametrada design in the tender documents, reserved the right to approve the design, and did so. The workmanship and materials in the turbines that failed were specifically exonerated from blame by Sir Arnold Lindley in his report. This report fully endorsed the early action by JBE which saved much valuable time. The turbines have been from trouble during the several voyages since the ship went into service.

"This unfortunate occurrence was not the responsibility of JBE though much comment, adverse to the company, was made. Also the concentration of effort by all concerned had inevitably an adverse effect upon the progress and completion of other work, and upon the furtherance of the business generally."

The port turbine rotor arrived back in Southampton by road and was inspected at Vospers on the evening of Saturday 1 March with the arrival and inspection of the starboard rotor following shortly afterwards. The port rotor was re-installed on 5 March. By 21 March, both rotors had been returned to the *QE2* and the turbines closed up.

Minister of Technology, Tony Benn, boasted:

"We have given sailing orders for the QE2 and taken the steam out of this controversy."

On 3 March 1969 Cunard announced that *QE2* would make her Maiden Voyage from Southampton to New York on 2 May. In making the announcement Sir Basil said:

"When QE2 sails from Southampton on 2 May she will be as perfect as a ship can be. Her accommodation and public rooms will be 100% complete and there will be no doubt about the reliability of her engines. Sir Arnold Linley's assessment of her turbine troubles sponsored by the British Government and published last Friday means that her technical problems have been positively identified and resolved. There is no foreseeable reason why we should not get delivery of the ship in the last half of April.

"Queen Elizabeth 2 will more than fulfill the promises made to her prospective passengers as to her performance. She will be the most superb example of the shipbuilder's craft the world has yet seen. QE2 is certainly a new place to visit between New York and London or Paris."

During 1969 Cunard had anticipated receiving $16 million gross revenue from *QE2* of which $12 million would come from the US market.

Between 17 and 21 March *QE2* was opened up for visits by VIPs, press and travel agents who would enjoy tours, overnight stays, lunches and dinners on board.

There were problems with crew accommodation with some complaints being made about their location and noise experiences. All kitchen ratings were berthed in 22 cabins on Five deck aft and representations, supported by the National Union of Seamen, were made about the standard of the cabins. It was decided to overcome the problem in two phases. The first phase was to spend £50 on each room and supply a fitted carpet, upholstered chair and curtains and bedspread of the same standard as the petty officers. The second phase involved replacing metal furniture with wood and would be undertaken at a later date.

A team of 26 from Vosper Thornycroft labour would travel on the maiden westbound and eastbound crossings in order to progress the completion of insulation and sound-proofing in the crew accommodation aft on Five deck.

Basin trials were undertaken on 23 March which involved various engine trials while she was tied up alongside the Ocean Terminal. To test the reliability of the main machinery overspeed tests were undertaken which involved the disconnection of the propeller shafts from the engines and running the latter at higher speeds than could be expected in the normal operation of the ship.

QE2 finally left Southampton on Tuesday 24 March for three days of builders' technical trials in the English Channel with the ship at anchor each evening. Tests included full speed trials, a crash stop where she came to a halt in seven minutes, travelling 1½ miles in doing so and compass calibration over a 60 mile stretch between the Isle of Wight and Weymouth. One of QE2's main competitors, the United States, sailed past.

Sir Arnold Lindley was on board proclaimed the three days of testing as *"extremely satisfactory"* and he was able to give the liner a *"maker's guarantee."*

Captain Warwick:

"We put the engines to full astern and the ship pulled up in a mile-and-a-half in seven minutes. This was something completely new to me in efficiency. We kept the engines going and went backwards at 14 knots for 30 minutes passing ships we had previously overtaken."

Upon return to Southampton on 27 March QE2 entered the King George V dry dock and it would be from that flooded dry dock that she would proceed on an eight-day Proving Trial which took her to tropical waters and back to Southampton. The voyage lasted from 30 March to 8 April and called at Cape Verde (3 April) and Tenerife (5 April). Before departure several members of the hotel staff walked off the ship complaining about what they felt was excessive vibration in the crew accommodation area aft on Five deck. The crew re-boarded after Cunard promised to investigate the matter.

Cunard made the welcome gesture of inviting all those who had been working on the ship on the trial trip. During the course of these trials the complete range of revolutions was traversed up to the design maximum of 174 rpm and vibration characteristics were recorded for subsequent analysis. During most of this time, the superheater outlet temperature was the normal 950°, but the three hour trial was done at 100° and 174 rpm. In addition a 24 hour consumption trial held on 3 and 4 April resulted in a speed of 31.10 knots being recorded with the shaft horsepower averaging 95,750 with an average engine speed on 170 rpm.

The trials proved most successful with excellent turbine performance and more satisfactory turbine expansions. Tom Kameen reported to Sir Basil:

"…sufficient preliminary information is available to show that her performance is quite satisfactory and is at least as good as predicted. It should be noted that predicted performance is, for obvious reasons, superior to guaranteed performance."

One 'passenger' later recalled the suggestion about tipping and that *"you might want to tip your steward more if you were sick!"*

However, the life-size figurehead of Britannia, standing at the entrance to the Britannia Restaurant, was found to have been damaged by a souvenir hunter. An attempt had been made to wrench the spear from Britannia's left hand breaking away the fingers.

The continuing problems with crew accommodation, which led to a strike by 150 cooks and members of the catering staff before the ship had sailed, had been dealt with. It had been decided to scrap 10 berths with the occupants being assigned berths in passenger accommodation permanently.

The turbines were opened again and examined by Lloyds, the Board of Trade, John Brown Engineering, Upper Clyde Shipbuilders and Cunard after QE2's return to Southampton and the stages which had previously given trouble were found to be perfectly satisfactory.

Sir Basil, while dealing with an estimated £3 million loss because of her unhappy start, reported to the press:

"I think she is the most wonderful ship in the world. She has exceeded our greatest expectations. Over the whole eight days the ship averaged 29 knots. In the first 36 hours she went rather slowly at 27¾ knots. There was a 24-hours speed trial from 0800 on 2 April to 0800 on 3 April at 94,000 shp, which gave an average of 31.91 knots. There was a six-hour speed trial from 0800 until 1400 on 3 April at 110,000 shp, when she averaged 32.66 knots."

Sir Basil was most keen to obtain a two- to three-year guarantee from the builder from the builders but UCS would not budge on this point claiming that the turbines had been the subject of an independent technical assessment by Sir Arnold.

On 11 April, Sir Basil wrote to the Group Board:

"You will remember that I said that I ought to try and get an extension of the guaranty in respect of any part of the propulsion machinery from the one year period embodied in the contract to two or perhaps three years. They have refused to budge on this point and I am advised that we have no power at all to insist on it. They take their stand from the fact that the turbines have been the subject of an independent technical assessment by the person appointed by the Minister of Technology, Sir Arnold Lindley, who is now satisfied with them. Neither I nor our lawyers can see

The **QE2** has just cleared the Verrazano Narrows Bridge and is escorted by an armada. *(Author's collection)*

any way of persuading them to give a longer guaranty.

On 14 April over 300 VIPs, including the last Captains of the Queens Geoffrey Marr and John Treasure Jones, were entertained on board at a private function hosted by Sir Basil and Captain Warwick. On Friday 18 April 1969 QE2 officially became a Cunard ship when she was finally handed over to her owners by a simple exchange of letters between Sir Basil Smallpeice and Anthony Hepper reserving all rights or claims on both sides. Unusually the handing over took place in London at a private ceremony because Sir Basil was *"flying out of the country immediately afterwards."*

A list of outstanding items and tests in all areas of the ship was agreed by both Cunard and UCS – it came to 216 pages. These items were progressively rectified throughout 1969 and UCS would pay Cunard £20,000 in November that year to be relieved of further responsibility of the work.

The flag raising on board was at first scheduled for 12 noon, the time of the official handing over was to be held in London but because of the delay in the London ceremony the Upper Clyde Shipbuilder's flag remained in place on QE2 for another hour.

Attending the three-minute ceremony on board QE2 was Captain Warwick who had broken his leave to be with Cunard's Managing Director John Whitworth and UCS Technical Director John Starks. With three triumphant blasts on her whistle the Cunard flag was hauled up by coxswain Andrew McGregor at 1315 hours as the Upper Clyde Shipbuilders flag – which had flown over QE2 since her arrival in Southampton on 2 January – was lowered.

The Cunard flag would fly above QE2 for the next 14,468 days or 39 years seven months and nine days.

Cunard made a payment of £2,072,000 to UCS in accordance with the agreement signed by both Chairmen that day and UCS paid Cunard £792,000.

A. Payment by Cunard to Upper Clyde Shipbuilders

1. Cost of construction of ship
Total estimated cost to 18 April 1969
per UCS estimate of 27 March 1969   £24,928,000
Cost of furnishings etc to date   £2,571,000
    <u>£27,499,000</u>
Less: amount paid to 2 January 1969   <u>£25,427,000</u>
    <u>£2,072,000</u>

B. Payment by Upper Clyde Shipbuilders to Cunard
1. Payment in respect of furnishing purchased
by Cunard as agents of UCS   £358,000
2. Payment in respect of oil fuel   £117,000
3. Payment in respect of cost manning,
Victualling and incidentals during the period
19 November 1968 to 1 January 1969   £51,000
4. Payment in respect of costs during period
2 January 1969 to 18 April 1969 incurred by
Cunard as port agents to UCS   £256,000
5. Payment for replacements of furnishings lost
or damaged, the cost of which UCS will with
Cunard's assistance attempt to recover under
Builders Risks Insurance   £10,000
6. Any payment which may be agreed to be due by
UCS to Cunard in Cunard's capacity as agents of UCS

    <u>   </u>
    £792,000

The Handover contract also included an agreement reached between Cunard and UCS for the guarantee for QE2's rudder be extended from the contractual twelve months to five years. Prior to her first sea trials it was discovered that the rudder stock brush had seized during the fitting out and it took prolonged and abortive attempts to remove the brush before the rudder was eventually freed and appeared to be working to the satisfaction of all concerned

The **QE2** and lower Manhattan, Wednesday 7 May 1969. *(Author's collection)*

during trials.

The terms also provided for an extension of the guarantee period in respect of any turbine defects, should the first annual overhaul not take place by 18 April 1970.

On the same day Cunard borrowed from the Board of Trade the remainder of the Government loan (£1.9 million) under the Loan Agreement made in September 1967. This would result in a net inflow of cash to the company of £620,000.

Sir Basil had earlier written to the Cunard Board on 11 April stating:

> *"As to the question of our claim against UCS, the first thing that will happen after acceptance of the ship on the 18 April and after having taken further Counsel's opinion, will be that our solicitors will write to UCS's solicitors setting out the basis of our claim. They will reply saying that they do not accept the claim and in any case have a counter claim (though I don't know what this is). This exchange of correspondence then establishes that a "disagreement" exists under the contract which requires is to submit it for arbitration. The arbitrators are in turn required to submit their report on the matter in dispute within six months."*

QE2 had cost £29,091,000 and everything now depended on her being a success and Cunard was determined to distance itself from all that had gone before in terms of marketing and the ships. themselves. In order to sell the QE2's modernity, a marketing and advertising campaign the like of which had never been seen before was devised that compared cruising on the QE2 to space travel under the provocative slogan *'Ships Have Been Boring Long Enough'*.

Other shipping companies were horrified and thought Cunard was insulting rivals and the industry as a whole, but Cunard was also distancing itself from its own past and the new campaign underlined this radical change of direction.

The designation RMS (Royal Mail Ship) proudly assigned to every Cunarder since the Britannia in 1840 would not be applied to the QE2 as it was seen as too old-fashioned and at odds with the new image being forged by Cunard.

Cunard's Managing Director in 1969, John Whitworth, proclaimed:

> *"This is Queen Elizabeth Two year – the most flexible and sophisticated ship ever to come into service. She represents a complete transformation in Cunard thought. We are not decanting old wines into new bottles, but ruthlessly transforming our image from the 'aspidistra and public bar' image which the dear old ships have carried since 1840. We are getting rid of the images of "dukes and duchesses" on the other hand, and the "knees Up, Mother Brown" type on the other. We want something more sophisticated but still retaining the Cunard tradition with the same high standards. The Queen Elizabeth Two is something new and exciting for the holiday market, not only of today but of tomorrow."*

The fact her fleetmates *Carmania* and the *Franconia* were "old wines into new bottles" did not sit well with the 'new' Cunard, but the QE2 was something new and her 1960s interiors of formica, plastic, vibrant colours and moulded wood appalled some of the Cunard regulars (the "dukes and duchesses") when they first boarded in 1969, but Cunard had changed by then.

QE2 was a hive of activity as preparations continued to

welcome her first paying passengers and one of these preparations was the consecration of her Synagogue by Chief Rabbi Dr Jakobivits.

QE2 officially entered service on 22 April with an eight-day Preview Cruise to Las Palmas (25 and 26 April), Tenerife (26 April) and Lisbon (28 April) – sailing 3,156 miles roundtrip with some 1,350 passengers. The Royal Corps of Transport Band played as the ship left the Ocean Terminal at 1645 hours serenaded by a balloon release and watched by hundreds of spectators. One passenger, Arthur Ward, cycled from his home in Wallasey, Cheshire, to join the ship – a journey of 250 miles that took one day! He would return home by train after the cruise.

All was going well until two young male stowaways were discovered so QE2 turned back to rendezvous with the pilot cutter at 2215 hours two miles south of Nab Tower.

As QE2 sailed between Lisbon and the Canary Islands 11-month old James Clifton claimed a small piece of maritime history by becoming the first baby to be christened on board QE2. The parents had made arrangements to christen James on the ship in January but the various delays meant dates had to be altered several times. His Mother said *"We began to wonder how old he would be before he was finally christened!."*

Sir Basil and Anthony Hepper both flew out to join QE2 in the Canary Islands and the Cunard Chairman claimed that reports from the Proving Voyage had been consistently good:

"The technical people have really put QE2 through her paces. For the past four days the ship has averaged 30 knots."

Despite this Cunard continued to prepare to press a claim of £2 million against UCS for losses and delays in the QE2 contract. Anthony Hepper told Sir Basil Smallpeice that, if he persisted, it would force UCS into liquidation. The threat of a counter claim from UCS for alterations and delays to the contract during earlier construction phases brought the issue to a close. Two days before the Maiden Voyage a special five penny stamp three times the normal size was issued showing the liner of a background of turquoise blue; it was one of six stamps issued as a tribute to British shipbuilders and seamen.

With the Queen visiting Southampton on Thursday 1 May to open the new Ordnance Survey Building it was hoped she would also accept an invitation to visit QE2 which she duly did. This would continue a Cunard tradition set with Cunard's other Queen liners. Queen Mary and other members of the Royal Family visited *Queen Mary* before she entered service and Queen Elizabeth visited *Queen Elizabeth* during her post-war sea trials.

Accompanied by The Duke of Edinburgh The Queen arrived in Southampton by special train at the Ocean Terminal at 1145 hours. She would spend an hour touring the public rooms and told officers *"It really is very lovely."*

The Queen asked the Chief Engineer to explain in non-technical language what was wrong with the ship's engines and received the following response:

"Well, Ma'am, instead of going chug, chug, they went clang, clang…"

In his autobiography 'Of Comets and Queens' Sir Basil would later write:

"The Queen was in splendid form, talking freely to the officers in the Ward Room and to seamen around the ship."

"…we were passing through the Queens Room… Stormont Mancroft pointed out to the Queen the Oscar Nemon bust of herself. 'You are putting it here, are you?' she said. 'How did you manage to finish it so soon?' 'Of it's not finished yet Ma'am, Stormont said. 'This is only a plaster cast, painted over.' The Queen continued: 'He is a great perfectionist, isn't he? I have now sat seven times for this bust, and each time he finds something wrong with it. "that's no good", he says and wrenches my head off' – using her hands as she spoke to demonstrate his wringing her neck."

The Queen arrived in the Midships Bar at 1300 hours to meet with members of the Cunard Board before proceeding to the Grill Room where lunch commenced at 1315 hours and was completed 45 minutes later. The menu consisted of melon ball cocktail, cold fresh Avon salon with mayonnaise boiled potatoes and tossed green salad and fresh strawberries and cream followed by coffee; Batard Montrachet 1962 was served.

Her Majesty sat at table number 3 with Sir Basil, Captain Warwick and the Vice Lieutenant of Hampshire Lord Malmesbury who was standing in for the Lord Lieutenant who was abroad. The Duke of Edinburgh sat at table number 2 with The Mayor of Southampton, and the Deputy Chairmen Lord Mancroft and Ronald Senior.

Sir Basil would later write:

"I had the honour of being placed on the Queen's right, with Captain Warwick on her left and Lord Malmesbury opposite her. The conversation got onto aeroplanes and at one stage the Queen wondered whether the pace of life wasn't getting too hot – 'no wonder people get coronaries'. I confessed that I had just been out to Australia and back in eight days. 'If you don't mind my saying so' she said, 'I think you must be mad'."

Before leaving The Queen remarked on the excellent condition of the ship and expressed her hope for a happy Maiden Voyage and career. After leaving QE2 she opened the £4 million Ordnance Survey headquarters at Maybush in Southampton.

On 2 May 1969 the driving rain which had persisted throughout the morning did not dampen the enthusiasm of the thousands occupying vantage points both within and outside the docks as QE2's departure for New York neared. Baggage delays had made her 15 minutes late in leaving and an earlier bomb scare resulted in a police search but nothing was found. The rain stopped briefly as she pulled away from her berth receiving a warm and grand send off.

1,400 passengers – some 600 of which would be undertaking the complete round voyage – and 906 crew. A Mr Taylor had booked his passage 10 years earlier – he brought with him a newspaper cutting from April 1959 announcing Cunard's intention to build two new superliners and it was then he booked. Cunard also allowed a pet white mouse to cross the Atlantic in First Class for £1. And Royalty would be travelling in the form of Her Highness Princess Pauline of Melikoff who was the Austrian widow of an exiled Russian Duke. The principal entertainment would be provided by Canadian baritone Edmund Hockridge and English pop and beat group The Applejacks.

Despite the low cloud and mist the Royal Navy saluted the ship and there was a fly-past of Buccaneer aircraft of 736 Squadron of the Fleet Air Arm, which streaked over QE2 in anchor formation. This was the same squadron which flew past at the ship's launching ceremony. The Ocean Terminal was packed by more than 3,000 well-wishers who had turned out to cheer her on her way. Bright streamers crisscrossed from ship to shore and a thousand balloons were released from the dockside. The Hampshire Police Band played a specially composed fanfare called 'Cunard Queen'. A flotilla of small boats escorted the ship to the open sea. Among them were fire boats who saluted QE2 in their own fashion, sending jets of water arching high into the sky. Schoolchildren from Fawley and surrounding areas lined the shores at Calshot.

Two passengers from London missed the ship but were able to board off dockhead.

At the ship's first stop in Le Havre QE2 was given probably the biggest welcome the port had extended since the liner France had paid her first visit in 1961. Le Havre had been delighted to have been selected over Cherbourg as Cunard's European port as the latter port had handed the earlier Queens. A huge crowd turned out to greet QE2 and a formal Reception was held for local dignitaries and QE2 was at the port for two hours before sailing at 2130 hours.

As with all maiden voyages there were problems and no matter how prepared the ship or crew is at departure most of the issues only ever arise when the ship is at sea. Key complaints on QE2 included poor food and service, slow food service, too much vibration in certain areas and crew complaints of excessive hours and 17 or 18 hours working days. Both passengers and crew thought that the 1,000-strong crew was not sufficient for the number of passengers. Captain Warwick reported a *"definite depression"* in the spirits of the more senior and reliable bedroom stewards and stewardesses because of their workload and thought it time to reconsider the re-introduction of Bell Boys or Junior Ratings for general purpose use as *"embarrassment"* was being caused because of the lack of messenger facilities. Sadly a 61-year old steward, Jack Sharp, died and his remains were committed to the sea when QE2 made a temporary stop mid-Atlantic.

Sheila Black of the Financial Times would later write in Vogue:

"I honestly hadn't liked QE2 very much when I spent a night aboard as she lay moored in Southampton's Ocean Terminal. There were jazzy rooms and somber rooms and huge rooms and small rooms. It all looked so lacking in cohesive design. I did, in fairness, recognise that she was on target commercially. She was after the American trade and she was, as I have bored people by saying, a sea-going Hilton.

"Once aboard, I fell in love with her. Of course, the maiden voyage is rather special, though Cunard did nothing to make it so in the way of galas, so that judgement could well have been the same way after any trip. But those mixed up rooms made sense in action. I discovered that there is something for everybody…

"…All of this sounds rather mundane and not at all indicative of my emotional reaction to the ship, which culminated in tears during that triumphal, magnificent entry into wildly enthusiastic New York. I fell in love with QE2 before we docked in New York to the strains of Hello Dolly."

For weeks before her American debut New York was ready to welcome QE2 – "Welcome the Queen" signs were in many Fifth Avenue shop windows alongside photographs of the ship. And on the morning just before her arrival American newspaper front pages were filled with aerial images of QE2 taken hundreds of miles out in the Atlantic and broadcasters proclaimed her arrival would be *"fit for a Queen."*

Four days, 16 hours and 35 minutes after leaving Le Havre QE2 arrived at Ambrose Light and thousands turned out to welcome the new Queen in New York on 7 May. Mayor John Lindsay boarded the ship from a coastguard cutter outside the Verrazano Bridge along with other civic dignitaries and press for the last leg of her journey and he honoured Cunard by officially proclaiming it 'QE2 Day' in New York. It certainly was a tremendous welcome.

Hundreds of small craft including a Chinese junk escorted her to her berth at Pier 92 and helicopters jockeying for space with light aircraft buzzed around her. Ship whistles made a chorus and geysers of water cascaded up from a flotilla of tugs and fire boats. Two RAF Harrier jump jets raised a cheer from British passengers as they screamed in at high speed and then hovered on either side to escort QE2 towards the Statue of Liberty. QE2 made a leisurely entrance two miles up the Hudson north of her pier at west 52nd Street before turning round in mid-river and berthing alongside just after 1500 hours.

During a short ceremony in the Queens Room Mayor Lindsay was presented with a gold medallion by Sir Basil to commemorate the ship's first arrival in the city.

The gold medal, inscribed on one side with an outline of QE2, had caused a little bother, both with the Bank of England and the United States Treasury Department. The first difficulty had been in getting permission from the Bank of England to take gold out of the country. Then Washington had to give permission for the medal to be imported into the United States without being put into Fort Knox along with America's gold reserves. The letter authorizing the importation was not issued until Mayor Lindsay promised to sign a declaration that he would not melt the medal down for its gold content!

Mayor Lindsay, who claimed "the new Queen is a pride of New York as it is of Britain", presented Sir Basil with a glass seahorse.

Of the arrival welcome, Captain Warwick would later write:

"It was a sight and experience which I am sure many more than myself will never forget."

QE2 remained in New York for two days where various

receptions took place on board and many arrival celebration dinners were held all over New York. 1,000 supper dance guests included the Admiral of the Fleet Earl Mountbatten, who was to return with *QE2* to Southampton; Mary Soames, the wife of the British Ambassador to Paris and daughter of Sir Winston Churchill; John Freeman, Britain's Ambassador to America; Lord Caradon, the British Ambassador to the United Nations and John A Roosevelt, son of the late President of the United States. Other ambassadors included those from France, Sweden, the Soviet Union, Ghana and Morocco. *QE2* was the biggest happening in New York.

Her first eastbound crossing, with Earl Mountbatten on board, left on 9 May and arrived back into Southampton on 14 May.

The Earl informed Captain Warwick that he would be writing a report to Sir Basil Smallpeice which would include adverse comment on the sound reproduction equipment. He thought that the news broadcasts both off air and off tape were rendered inaudible by distortion. He also thought the taped music channels lacked variety – but then there were only two tapes available for each channel – and he pointed out that there were no inscriptions or plaques to indicate one Royal Standard from the other.

On the westbound passage *QE2* had averaged 28.02 knots while eastbound the average was 28.74 knots. Captain Warwick reported very little criticism from the passengers and a high number of compliments about the ship, the cuisine and service. The performance of the main engines and auxiliary machinery was generally satisfactory with the exception of the cranes on the foredeck and the car lifts – all of which failed at crucial times and caused embarrassment. The port crane failed in New York resulting in some 800 bags of mail not being unloaded and the car lift failed and delayed work as well as holding captive the New York Pier Manager for 60 minutes. And at Le Havre on the return voyage the aft car lift failed which delayed sailing.

At the annual shareholders meeting in London in June of that year Sir Basil reported that *QE2* was right on target making the profits Cunard expected from her. Sir Basil had

confirmed the day before the meeting that passenger numbers were increasing and that *QE2* had brought 1,868 passengers from America to France and the UK, earning a total gross revenue on this single one-way voyage of over $700,000.

But Cunard was clearly still insecure about its future: on 7 August Lord Mancroft, Cunard's Chairman, while speaking on board at a ceremony attended by the officers and chief petty officers of the 736 Squadron of the Fleet Air Arm gave an assurance that *QE2* would stay under the Cunard flag for the duration of her anticipated 30-year career:

"People who say she will be transferred to P&O or go to the Americans will have to think again.

The final cost of *QE2*, as calculated by UCS in an internal memo of 27 March 1970, was £28,062,467. A memo circulated within Cunard in December 1971 revealed that the final cost of *QE2* had been £28,825,185 and that the gross book value of the ship was £20 million. Other costs revealed were £54,980 agreed with John Brown Engineering for the repairs to the turbines and £21,317 for items stolen or damaged while the ship was at the shipyard.

UCS survived the construction of *QE2* only to lurch from one crisis to another, finally succumbing to insolvency in July 1971. The last ship to be built at Clydebank left in 1972. The yard never built another ship, but continued as an offshore yard until the end of the 1990s, when it finally closed. From 2002 onwards, the works was dismantled and the site redeveloped. Today Clydebank Campus (formerly Clydebank College and West College Scotland) now stands at the site of the former John Brown and Company Shipyard and Engineering Works – the birthplace of *QE2* and some of the most famous ships in history.

And, despite the odds, the combined efforts of Cunard and John Brown / Upper Clyde Shipbuilders produced a masterpiece with *Queen Elizabeth 2*.

The Bank and Bureau on the Forward Lobby on Two Deck (Dennis Lennon).

CHAPTER SEVEN

The most exciting thing since Apollo 1

Many guests and the first passengers were astonished by the modern leather and chrome vibrancy of the *QE2* and how different she was from the muted art deco of the earlier Queens with their traditional brass and various wood vaneers. *QE2* made extensive use of modern durable materials that were as hard wearing and easily cared for as they were elegant and functional. Rather than having to be constantly groomed and polished, they only needed to be wiped clean and some 186,000 square metres (two million square feet) of Formica laminate went into *QE2*. One Cunard advert proclaimed she was *"The most exciting thing since Apollo 1."*

Most passengers boarded *QE2* on Two Deck and immediately met the full impact of the designers' ingenuity in the dazzlingly modern Midships Lobby.

The Lobby was circular with a sunken seating area, navy carpets, walls lined with navy hide and sofas covered in green leather. The ceiling was silvered fibre glass which flowed to the outer walls in concentric circles like the pattern made by a stone dropped in a pool. A central column was covered in white fibre glass and white painted ribs that emanated from the mirror finish of the ceiling.

Ascending to the highest deck, Signal, passengers found an observation platform giving spectacular views in all directions, while on Sports Deck below, apart from the usual shipboard games, could be found the Children's Room including a crèche and a cinema.

One deck down on the Boat Deck and decorated in Indian laurel vaneer was the 736 Club, after the shipyard number by which *QE2* was known, and the venue for the evening discotheque. Next was the 24-hour Coffee Shop and The Juke Box which was orientated towards the young and had an area set aside of pin tables, a juke box and other teenage playthings. To the port side could be found the London Gallery which featured showcases for the display of small objects as well as display pictures. Midships on Boat Deck was the balcony of the Theatre and the Shops with several showcase windows.

Beyond the shopping arcade doors was the top level of the Double Room, the main tourist-class lounge and the largest and most dramatic room on the ship. Of 20,000 square feet and with seating for about 800 the room glowed in shades of red from scarlet through to plum. From the upper gallery a great stainless steel, curved staircase, with treads five feet wide, swept down into the lower room.

Upper Deck below was the home for the principal tourist-class public rooms. Forward was The Lookout, a two-level room where passengers could enjoy views overlooking the bow of the ship. Aft was the red, white and blue Britannia Restaurant with seating for 815 passengers. The 500-seat

The *QE2* officially entered service on in April 1969 with an eight-day Preview Cruise and she is shown here leaving Southampton, Tuesday 22 April 1969. *(Author's collection)*

The *QE2* on cruise service in the Caribbean in 1970. *(Author's collection)*

Theatre was a room with four principal functions: a theatre, a cinema, a conference room and, on Sundays, a church. The Theatre Bar adjacent was featured a wall of bright red fibreglass moulded in an egg-crate patter and a red piano. A more restrained atmosphere was to be found in the Upper Deck Library opposite – a cool, quiet room with a thick beige carpet, blue leather lined cases for the books and big leather sofas and a great circular rosewood table with a top partly lined in leather. Aft of the Double Room was Double Down Bar.

The principal first-class public rooms were to be found on the Quarter Deck. Forward, and discreetly accessible by a circular staircase up from its own private bar on One Deck was The Grill Room. This exclusive and exquisitely decorated extra-tariff room had a capacity of 100 and was decorated in Bordeaux red leather and velvet with shiny metal trim. The Columbia Restaurant, decorated in ochre leather, extended the full width of the ship and was divided into smaller areas with the use of bronze tinted glass screens between the webs. The ceiling was in specially designed *Q4* gold aluminium and the chairs, like in the Britannia Restaurant,

were specially designed by Robert Heritage.

Aft of the Columbia Restaurant, on the starboard side, was the Midships Bar with sumptuous curved sofas in rich green leather and mohair velvet, and walls lined with the same material. On the port side was The Quarter Deck Library where Michael Inchbald used traditional ship finishes of wood and brass to achieve his peaceful effect.

The white and silver Queen's Room was a brilliantly successful space-age yet elegant main lounge with a sunny garden room atmosphere by day. A slotted white ceiling gave an airy trellised effect and the structural columns were encased in great inadverted trumpets of white fibreglass complemented by the white fibre-glass space-age chairs which had bases of this trumpet shape in reverse and upholstered in natural hide. Rounding off the main public areas was the *Q4* Room aft, a nightclub which had the added appeal of opening up to the swimming pool.

There were, in fact, four swimming pools on *QE2* – on the Quarter Deck, One Deck, Six Deck and on Seven Deck. Elsewhere could be found passengers' launderettes, the Beauty Shop, a Synagogue, Pursers Office, a well-equipped hospital and Turkish Baths.

Passenger cabins could be found on One to Five Decks and there was immense variety, from suites which consisted of one, two or three main rooms as required through to family cabins where two are adjoining and sharing a bathroom, to smaller single berth rooms. There were innumerable permutations of colour and room arrangements.

Crew accommodation and facilities on *QE2* were among the finest afloat and colours were chosen to make the rooms cheerful and attractive. There were four messes and five recreation rooms for the various ranks.

The whole ship was as strikingly redolent of the sixties as her predecessors had been of the thirties; obviously so, maybe – but almost everyone was surprised.

The *QE2* and *United States* arriving in Southampton, Wednesday 20 August 1969. *(Author's collection)*

The triumph

For most of her almost 40 years in service *QE2* was the most famous ship in the world being rarely far from the news, for good reason or bad. She became a strikingly potent symbol, recognised around the world, not just of all that is best in Britain, but of the enduring excellence of Scottish engineering. She sailed over five million nautical miles, more than any other ship ever, completed 25 full world cruises, and crossed the Atlantic, surely the world's cruelest sea, over 800 times; yet her hull was as sound in 2008 as the day she first slipped into the waters of the Clyde four decades earlier.

QE2 was a magnet for well-wishers wherever she went; thousands turned out to greet her, not just out of passing curiosity but because they loved her. It is impossible to say just why this was so, but it was so.

QE2 was celebrated, acclaimed, revered and respected.

Yet it was a miracle she ever came into being at all. In the early sixties, in a miasma of muddled management and indecision, Cunard began planning replacement tonnage for the ageing *Queen Mary* and *Queen Elizabeth*. With alarming consistency the company made the wrong decisions, and only as late as the last minute was it pushed by external forces into avoiding disaster. But what this relatively conservative company eventually embarked on was a revolutionary replacement, at least 25 years ahead of her time: *QE2*.

Even when she took to sea and could be seen by all to be one of the most beautiful ships ever built, truly the pride of the Clyde, she was dismissed by City analysts rather unoriginally as 'a white elephant' that, in another inappropriate metaphor, would be 'mothballed' within six months. The age of the transatlantic liner, they said, was dead.

Well, how wrong they were.

QE2 spent her service life in the limelight, and her career at sea was even more eventful than her birth. It was not all exotic voyages and ecstatic welcomes. It included sailing 6,000 nautical miles south, partly through an icefield in the dark, without radar, to make her singular contribution to the Falklands Campaign; it involved various threats, from extortionists, from the IRA and from the Libyan government; it included rescuing all the passengers from a liner in distress, and having all hers similarly rescued after she hit rocks; it featured visits from every senior member of the Royal Family, from prime ministers and presidents, rock stars and film stars, and from Nelson Mandela. Not a year passed without something happening that would have been once-in-a-lifetime for any other ship – and usually hitting the headlines in the process.

QE2 was a phenomenon and there is no doubt she will continue to be one for many more years in Dubai where she retired in 2008. She was just one of a long line of noble Cunard transatlantic liners, but she served longer than most and she travelled further than any other.

In 39½ years of service, *QE2*...

- completed 1,419 voyages
- sailed 5,875,493.22 million nautical miles –more than any other ship ever
- carried almost 2.5 million passengers
- completed 812 Atlantic crossings
- called at New York 710 times
- called at Southampton 726 times
- completed 25 full World Cruises
- completed ten 'extended' voyages
- been commanded by 25 Captains

FASTEST CROSSINGS

Westbound (Southampton to New York)
    June 1970
    3 days 20 hours and 42 minutes
    Average speed: 30.36 knots
    Steamship

Eastbound (New York to Southampton)
    17 – 22 July 1990
    4 days 6 hours and 57 minutes
    Average speed: 30.16 knots
    Motorship

Leaving the Clyde for an uncertain yet ultimately magnificent future

Career highlights

1969

29 May	HRH The Duke of Edinburgh visits in Southampton.

1970

23 March	Welcomes her 75,000th passenger less than one year after entering service.
June	Crosses Atlantic westbound in a record time of 3 days, 20 hours and 42 minutes, an average speed of 30.36 knots.
October	Departs on her first long cruise: 37 days to North America, Africa and South America.

1971

9 January	Rescues 501 passengers and crew from the burning French Line cruise ship Antilles in the Grenadines and lands them in Barbados.
5 March	Suffers power failure for four hours off Trinidad as a result of jelly-fish being sucked into intakes.

30 June	Trafalgar House purchases Cunard and QE2 for £27.3 million.

1972

23 April	Arrives 36 hours late in Southampton following one of the worst North Atlantic storms.
17 May	Extortionist informs Cunard in New York that there are six bombs on board, as QE2 sails to Southampton. RAF Nimrods parachute a bomb disposal team of four into the Atlantic, who are picked up by the ship. No bombs found. Extortionist arrested and sentenced to 20 years.
October	First major refit changes external appearance with the addition of ten penthouse suites.

The **QE2** in her short-lived (August 1982 – June 1983) post-Falklands livery of light pebble-grey hull which proved problematic to maintain so was replaced by its original colouring after nine months. The introduction of this livery also involved finally applying the Cunard red and black to the funnel – a welcome addition and one that would remain with the ship for the rest of her career, probably to the disdain of James Gardner! *(FotoFlite)*

No ship underwent as many significant transformations as *QE2* during her career. During her service more than ten times the amount it cost to build QE2 was spent on refitting her. In this view can the seen the installation of the Queen Mary and Queen Elizabeth suites in 1977 The former is shown here. *(Author's collection)*

1973

14 April — Leaves Southampton on first of two chartered cruises to Israel to commemorate 25th anniversary of the state's founding. Intense security for the ship through the Mediterranean following Arab terrorist threats. On 16 July 1974, President Anwar Sadat of Egypt reveals in a 'Panorama' interview on BBC Television that he personally had countermanded an order given to an Egyptian submarine commander by President Gaddaffi of Libya to torpedo the vessel during the cruise to Israel.

1974

1 April — Loses power after a boiler oil leak. Passengers transfer at sea to Sea Venture.

25 September — Rescues six passengers from sinking French yacht Stephanie in the Mediterranean.

28 October — Breaks loose from moorings during gale in Cherbourg and strikes pier, suffering 30' gash and 48 hours delay.

1975

4 January — Sails from Southampton on first World Cruise – a journey of 38,000 miles and a total of 3,965 passengers.

25 March — First transit of Panama Canal; QE2 breaks two records – she is the first Cunard Queen to transit and becomes the largest ship to travel through the Canal and pays the highest toll for the transit.

4 December — Completes first million miles, between Antigua and Boston.

31 December — Bulbous bow holed when ship strikes incorrectly charted reef at Nassau.

1976

23 July — A huge engine room fire travels up the funnel uptake, severely distorting the funnel plating which is evident for the rest of her career.

26 November — IRA plot to blow up the ship in drydock in Southampton foiled; three men arrested and sentenced to 20 years.

1977

27 June — Takes part in the rehearsals for the Jubilee Review of the fleet by HM The Queen.

December — Queen Mary and Queen Elizabeth Suites added.

1978

January — Visits Australia and New Zealand for the first time.

1979

May — Celebrates her tenth year of service, having carried half-a-million passengers to 63 countries.

1980

January — First transit of the Suez Canal from the Mediterranean to the Red Sea.

1981

July — Special screening of the Royal Wedding

Nearing the completion of her massive £110 million re-engining – a conversion that still remains the biggest and most complex of its kind in history (October 1986 – April 1987). *(Author's collection)*

between the Prince and The Princess of Wales takes place while *QE2* crosses the Atlantic.

1982

25 April	Maiden arrival in Philadelphia as part of the city's tricentennial celebration.
3 May	Requisitioned for use by the British Government as a troopship in the Falkland Islands Campaign.
5 May	Arrives in Southampton and immediately undergoes conversion to a troopship, including the installation of three helicopter pads.
12 May	Leaves Southampton for war with 3,000 troops and 650 crew volunteers.
26 May	Arrives in war zone.
11 June	Welcomed home with 604 survivors from Royal Navy ships Ardent, Coventry and Antelope in Southampton by HM Queen Elizabeth The Queen Mother on board Royal Yacht Britannia.
7 August	Hull repainted light charcoal grey and the funnel in Cunard's traditional red and black, (in place of her previous non-traditional white).
2 December	HM Queen Elizabeth The Queen Mother visits in Southampton.

1983

June	Hull repainted black but the Cunard funnel colours retained.
November	The Magrodome, a sliding glass roof, installed

over Quarter Deck outdoor swimming pool.

1984

1 April	When leaving Piraeus blown onto the south breakwater head and suffered a large dent in the area of the mechanics accommodation.
April	By the completion of her World Cruise, *QE2* had visited 145 different ports worldwide. New York was the most visited port with 325 calls while Southampton was second with 240.

Her Majesty Queen Elizabeth The Queen Mother with Captain Peter Jackson on board on Thursday 2 December 1982 to attend a Reception and Lunch to honour *QE2*'s Falklands service.

Queen Elizabeth 2 – the most famous ship in the world. *(FotoFlite)*

The *QE2* in her second homeport, New York – a City she would call at 710 times. *(Author's collection)*

June First sea-going branch of Harrods opens.

1985

13 February Cunard charters Concorde to take passengers out to Sydney, to join *QE2* and *Sagafjord* – both in port together. The Concorde trip breaks the records: 17 hours, 3 minutes and 45 seconds.

18 May *QE2*, the Red Arrows and Concorde photographed at the same time in the English Channel.

1986

3 May HM Queen Elizabeth The Queen Mother visits the ship in Southampton to mark the 50th anniversary of the Queen Mary's maiden voyage in 1936.

4 July Participates in centennial celebration of the Statute of Liberty.

20 October Leaves New York for the last time as a steamship and undertakes Cunard's last crossing of the Atlantic under steam, ending a 146-year tradition.

QE2's steam turbines had taken her a total of 2,622,858 miles – the equivalent of 120 times around the world.

October–April 1987 Re-engined with nine diesel electric engines and totally refurbished at a total coast of £110 million. Appearance altered with bulkier funnel and additional penthouse suites.

1987

29 April HRH The Princess of Wales attends a children's party on board, and Concorde makes a special flypast, to mark the ship's successful re-engining. First crossing under diesel electric power to New York commences.

1988

14 December HM Queen Elizabeth The Queen Mother lunches on board to celebrate the 50th anniversary of her launching the Queen Elizabeth in 1938.

Nelson Mandela being interviewed for a live BBC broadcast in the Captain's Cabin by Sir David Frost when he was travelling on board in 1998.

Her Royal Highness The Princess of Wales attended a children's party and watched a fly-past from Concorde as *QE2* sailed up the Solent on 29 April 1987 as part of the festivities to welcome *QE2* back into service after her re-engining. *(Author's collection)*

Former Prime Minister Margaret Thatcher attended a Reception and Lunch in Southampton on 10 May 1992 to commemorate the tenth anniversary of *QE2*'s Falklands service. *(Author's collection)*

1989

27 March Chartered by a consortium of Japanese companies for 72 days to celebrate the 130th anniversary of the city of Yokohama.

1990

January–June Again chartered by the Japanese.

22 July Arrives in Southampton after completing her fastest diesel crossing in 4 days, 6 hours and 57 minutes at an average speed of 30.16 knots. Sets out on a Round Britain cruise to celebrate 150 years of Cunard.

23 July Greeted by 60,000 people on her maiden arrival at Cobh, Ireland. Mr Charles Haughey, the Taoiseach, boards for lunch to mark the event.

24 July An estimated 1,000,000 spectators greet her maiden arrival in Liverpool.

25 July Goes home to the Clyde for the first time.

27 July Royal review of Cunard and Royal Navy ships at Spithead by HM The Queen and HRH The Duke of Edinburgh on board Royal Yacht Britannia. The Queen and Duke of Edinburgh transfer to *QE2* by Royal Barge. The Queen then becomes the first reigning monarch to sail on a commercial liner with passengers.

Tuesday 24 July 1990 saw *QE2* become the first Cunard Queen to arrive in Liverpool. One million people – the largest crowd ever attracted by a single vessel – lined the River Mersey to welcome the liner which was making a special Round Britain cruise to commemorate the 150th anniversary of the departure of Cunard's Britannia from the City in July 1840. *(Author's collection)*

After reviewing QE2 from the Royal Yacht **Britannia** Her Majesty The Queen became the first reigning Monarch to sail on a commercial ship with other passengers as she joined **QE2** with His Royal Highness The Duke of Edinburgh, for lunch, 28 July 1990. It was the first time The Queen had been onboard since 1 May 1969 and she would visit again on 2 June 2008 to say farewell. *(Author's collection)*

| | Captain Ronald Warwick temporarily assumes command. This was the first time that a Cunard Master had captained the same ship as his father (Commodore W E Warwick was QE2's first Captain). |
| 9 August | Completes 500th scheduled crossing of the Atlantic. |

1991

| 15 June | HRH Prince Edward and HRH The Duke of Edinburgh attend a Royal Ball on board in Southampton. |

1992

10 May	The Rt Hon Margaret Thatcher lunches on board in Southampton to mark the 10th anniversary of the Falkland Islands Campaign.
11 June	One of the nine diesel engines (Engine Echo) experiences a catastrophic failure.
7 August	Strikes uncharted rock off the coast of North America, all passengers transferred ashore and QE2 goes to Boston for temporary repairs. Full repairs subsequently made in Hamburg. Returns to service on 4 October.

1993

12 June	HRH Prince Edward lunches on board on 40th anniversary of the Queen's accession.
	BBC's 'Keeping Up Appearances' filmed on board.
13 June	First call at Edinburgh.

1994

| 8 – 13 May | Special Silver Anniversary crossing to New York. |
| 22 May | Albert Reynolds, Irish Taoiseach, visits in Cobh. |

4–8 June	Leads flotilla of ships commemorating 'D' Day, reviewed by HM The Queen and HRH The Duke of Edinburgh (as well as other world leaders) on board Royal Yacht Britannia. Sails past the Normandy beaches. Dame Vera Lynn and Bob Hope on board.
20 November	Arrives in Hamburg for extensive refurbishment costing £45 million, which includes removal of the Magrodome.
17 December	HRH Prince Andrew guest of honour at lunch on board in Southampton to mark return to service. Controversially, the ship sets sail for New York with workmen still on board.

1995

3 – 10 May	First call at Plymouth as part of the VE Day commemoration.
14 June	Leaves New York for Southampton on her 1,000th voyage, having sailed 3.8 million miles and carried 1.7 million passengers.
17 July	HRH Princess Anne lunches on board in Edinburgh. Leads the Tall Ships out of the Firth of Forth.
10 September	Encounters Hurricane Luis on a voyage to New York experiencing 130 mph winds and a 90-foot wave.
13–25 October	Special episode of UK's 'Coronation Street' filmed on board.

1996

January	Begins 20th World Cruise from New York, a voyage covering 53,000 miles and 38 ports on 4 continents.
2 January	QE2 clocks up he four millionth mile at 2100 GMT, the equivalent of sailing around the world 185 times.
4 April	Trafalgar House, including Cunard Line, is sold to the Norwegian Kvaerner Group.
28 September	HRH Prince Edward attends a Royal Ball on board in Southampton.
22 November	Goes into the A&P Yard in Southampton for a £12 million refit.

1997

| 4 January | Marks the 75th anniversary of the first World Cruise (Cunard's Laconia in 1922) with her own World Cruise departure from New York. |
| 20 September | 30th anniversary of QE2's launch by HM The Queen. |

1998

| 29–31 March | South African President Nelson Mandela (accompanied by future wife Graca Machel) sails from Durban to Cape Town. A Gala Dinner for the Nelson Mandela Children's Fund held on board in Cape Town. Mandela writes in QE2's visitor's book: "Travelling on QE2 was an unforgettable honour and pleasure". |

3 April	A consortium led by the Carnival Corporation purchases Cunard Line from Kvaerner for $500 million.
1 August	Visits the Orkney Islands for the first time.
30 October	Visits Malta for the first time.

1999

14 April	Celebrates the 30th anniversary of her first transatlantic crossing with a special birthday party in Southampton.
	In 30 years QE2 has made 1,159 voyages, sailed 4,648,050 nautical miles and carried over 2 million passengers.
13 June	QE2 marks another milestone in her 30-year career: at 15.00 hours, while enroute from Madeira to Southampton, she exceeds 175,296 hours steaming time. This equates to exactly 20 years (including four leap years).
12 November–10 December	QE2 undergoes a £19.5 million refit at the Lloyd Werft Shipyard in Bremerhaven, Germany.
31 December	QE2 is positioned off Barbados to welcome the third Millennium. A special rendezvous with Cunard's 'new' Caronia (on her inaugural cruise) takes place.

2000

January	Proclaimed a 'British Icon of the 20th Century' in one of the exhibitions at the Millennium Dome.
	Embarks on her first World Cruise of the Millennium: 124 nights (Southampton – Southampton).
	John Brown, principal naval architect of all three Queen liners, knighted in the Queen's New Year's Honours List.
July	Two pigeons stow away on QE2 and make headline news when handed back over to their owners in Southampton.
	Chartered to a travel company for a week for use as a hotel for golfers taking part in the Open Golf Championship in St Andrews.
18 August	Deputy Prime Minister and Secretary of State for Environment, Transport and the Regions, the Rt Hon John Prescott, visits in Southampton.
November	Line Voyages to Cape Town introduced.

2001

(General)	Both QE2 and Caronia recall the 1940s and 1950s when their 2001 schedules are linked to allow passengers to cross the Atlantic on a Queen and then transfer to a Caronia for a cruise to the Baltic, Mediterranean or Canada prior to re-joining QE2 for the trip home.
March	QE2 officiates at the opening of the new cruise terminal in Dubai.
May and June	Two transatlantic crossings (3 May and 6 June) commemorate the 65th Anniversary of the 1936 Maiden Voyage of Queen Mary. The

QE2 in 1995 sporting another new livery – dark blue and red, blue and gold 'speedstripe' the length of her superstructure. Even after 29 years in service **QE2** would occasionally make 32 knots – one gallon of fuel would move the ship 49.5 feet; with the previous steam turbine engines, one gallon of fuel moved the ship 36 feet. *(FotoFlite)*

The *QE2* arrived in Sydney for her penultimate call on Tuesday 20 February 2007 to be met by *Queen Mary 2* and an armada of small boats – once again bringing Sydney to a complete standstill! *(Author's collection)*

Fireboats saluted **QE2** when she departed New York on Wednesday 14 June 1995 on her 1000th Voyage. A special Dinner with commemorative menu was held during the voyage and each passenger and crew member was given a certificate and a special lapel badge. For QE2's arrival on 19 June it was arranged for all the ships in port to sound their whistles to mark the completion of the voyage. *(Author's collection)*

	May crossing includes a performance by Larry Adler who entertained on the Queen Mary voyage.
Autumn	The 11 September World Trade Centre attack results in *QE2* being diverted to Boston as the American terminus for the remainder of her 2000 Atlantic programme.
4 October	Captain Warwick conducts the wedding service for his daughter on board *QE2* in Boston; the first wedding to take place on board.
November/December	Undergoes further refitting and refurbishment at the Lloyd Werft Shipyard in Bremerhaven.

2002

8 January	*QE2* becomes the first passenger ship to call again at New York following the 11 September attacks. Wreath is laid as a mark of respect. The visit is *QE2*'s 668th call at the port.
World Cruise	Opera singer Russell Watson sails between Honolulu and Auckland. Open air concert given in Auckland with *QE2* as the backdrop.
14 June	Baroness Thatcher lunches on board in Southampton to mark the 20th anniversary of the Falkland Islands Campaign.
29 August	At approximately 2150 hours ship's time *QE2* completes five million miles – a world record and a world first. It's the equivalent of sailing to the moon and back nine times, sailing around the world 230 times or sailing 1570 consecutive transatlantic crossings.

2003

24 October	As Concorde passes over *QE2* on the Atlantic for the last time the Master of *QE2*, Captain Ray Heath, sends the following message to the Captain of Concorde: "From one British icon to another: *QE2* and Concorde have been an improbable, unique and successful transatlantic partnership for the past 20 years. We are sorry to see you go."

2004

25 April	*QE2* meets Queen Mary 2 for the first time in New York after completing her last westbound transatlantic crossing as Cunard flagship.
25 April–1 May	Both ships cross the Atlantic in tandem and are greeted by a Nimrod and a Harrier Hawk off the Cornish Coast on 30 April.
1 May	*QE2* completes her last scheduled eastbound crossing of the Atlantic upon her arrival with Queen Mary 2 in Southampton.

Hours after relinquishing the role of Cunard flagship to **Queen Mary 2** on 1 May 2004 **QE2** is seen here leaving Southampton for refitting in Germany and passing the new Queen as Stevie Wonder's 'Isn't She Lovely' is played to honour the former flagship. *(Author's collection)*

At a ceremony that day the flagship status of QE2 passes to Queen Mary 2 when the Boston Cup is transferred to Commodore Warwick, Queen Mary 2.

1–22 May	QE2 in drydock at Lloyd Werft (Bremerhaven); work includes preparations for her new role as ex-UK cruise ship.
November	Having completed 35 years, six months and three days in service QE2 reaches a notable milestone in her life becoming the longest serving Cunard express liner in the company's history. QE2 took the record from the company's Aquitania which served Cunard

Line, in peace and war, from May 1914 to December 1949. During her service QE2 has carried almost three million passengers, completed 797 Atlantic crossings.

2005

2 May	Celebrates the 36th Anniversary of her maiden Voyage departure with a special birthday party while in Southampton.
25–29 June	Undertakes a special four-night cruise to commemorate the 200th Anniversary of the battle of Trafalgar and takes part in the Trafalgar 200 Fleet Review.

The **QE2** in her homeport of Southampton. She arrived there for the first time embarrassed but she would leave for the last time a much-loved ship in a blaze of glory after the most magnificent and truly record-breaking career. *(Miles Cowsill)*

| 4 September | Having completed 36 years four months and two days record in service *QE2* becomes the longest serving Cunard Atlantic liner ever taking the record from the Scythia which served from 1921 to 1957. |
| December | For the first time since her Acceptance Trials in 1969 *QE2* spends Christmas in European waters. |

2007

2 January	Departs Southampton on her 25th World Cruise.
20 February	Meets Queen Mary 2, undertaking her Maiden World Cruise, in Sydney Harbour.
18 June	Sale of *QE2* to the Government of Dubai announced.
15–23 September	Undertakes a 'lap-of-honour' around the UK to mark the fortieth anniversary of her 1967 launch. The voyage includes a maiden call to the Tyne, a visit to the Clyde exactly forty years to the day and a return visit to Liverpool.

2008

6 January	Departs Southampton with Queen Victoria and both ships undertake a tandem crossing to New York.
24 February	Arrives in Sydney for the final time.
18 March	Achieves 32.8 knots on a voyage.
30 September	Embarks on her Farewell to Britain cruise.
10 October	Departs on her final westbound crossing to New York.
16 October	Arrives in New York for the final time. Departs on her final eastbound crossing.
11 November	Commences her Final Voyage with an emotional departure to Southampton.
26 November	Arrives at Port Rashid, Dubai, exactly 40 years to the day she first took to open water in 1968.
27 November	*QE2* is officially handed over by Cunard to her new owners Nakheel.

2009–2017

| Dubai - | |

QE2 salutes Douglas, Isle of Man, as she sailed past for the first time in 2008. *(Miles Cowsill)*

Two Elizabeths Meet: Three years into her Dubai retirement *QE2* and he namesake *Queen Elizabeth* met on Thursday 31 March. The contrast in ship design could not be more obvious! *(Author's collection)*

Bibliography

Author	Publication	Publisher & date
Arnott, Captain Robert	Captain of the Queen	Quadrant Books 1984
Hutchings, David	QE2 – a ship for all seasons	Waterfront 2002
Johnson, Howard	The Cunard Story	Whittet Books 1987
Newall, Peter	Cunard Line: a Fleet History	Ships in Focus Publications 2012
Potter, Neil & Frost, Jack	The Queen Elizabeth 2 – the authorised story	George Harrap & Co 1969
Smallpeice, Basil	Of Comets and Queens	Airlife 1981
Thatcher, Carol	QE2: Forty Year Famous	Simon and Schuster 2007
Thatcher, Carol	A Voyage of Discovery	Lancaster Publishing 1999
Warwick, Commodore Ronald	QE2	W.W. Norton & Co. 1999
Warwick, Sam and Roussel, Mike	Shipwrecks of the Cunard Line	The History Press 2012

Other

The Cunard Archive, Liverpool University
Unreleased files of Dan Wallace, John Whitworth, Tom Kameen, Sir Basil Smallpeice, Sir Percy Bates and Lord Mancroft.

The **Queen Elizabeth 2** alongside the Queen Elizabeth II Terminal in Southampton. The 2 and II did not mean the same Elizabeth! *(Miles Cowsill)*